Fresh From France

DINNER INSPIRATIONS

ALSO BY FAYE LEVY

Fresh from France: Vegetable Creations
Faye Levy's Chocolate Sensations
Classic Cooking Techniques
Sensational Pasta
La Cuisine du Poisson (in French, with Fernand Chambrette)
French Cooking Without Meat (in Hebrew)
French Desserts (in Hebrew)
French Cakes, Pastries and Cookies (in Hebrew)
The La Varenne Tour Book

FRESH FROM FRANCE
DINNER INSPIRATIONS

FAYE LEVY

ILLUSTRATIONS BY MAUREEN JENSEN
PHOTOGRAMS BY BILL WESTHEIMER

E. P. DUTTON   NEW YORK

Published in the United States by E. P. Dutton,
a division of Penguin Books USA Inc.,
2 Park Avenue, New York, N.Y. 10016.

Published simultaneously in Canada by
Fitzhenry and Whiteside,
Limited, Toronto.

Library of Congress Cataloging-in-Publication Data
Levy, Faye.
Dinner inspirations/Faye Levy. — 1st ed.
p. cm. — (Fresh from France)
Includes index.
ISBN 0-525-24814-5
1. Cookery, French.   2. Dinners and dining.   I. Title.
II. Series: Levy, Faye.   Fresh from France.
TX719.L485 1989
641.5944–dc20   89-7786
                                          CIP

DESIGNED BY EARL TIDWELL

1 3 5 7 9 10 8 6 4 2

First Edition

*To the memory of Henri Flammarion,
the publisher of France's greatest chefs—
Escoffier, Montagné, Pellaprat, Point, Bocuse, and Le Nôtre—
for having added a young American cook
to his distinguished list.*

Contents

ROAST AND BRAISED TURKEY   71

Roast Turkey with Calvados Sauce • Apple, Calvados, and Turkey Stuffing • Roast Turkey Breast with Fresh Cranberries • Braised Turkey Breast with Madeira, Mushrooms, and Olives • Languedoc Turkey Wing Stew with Rice and Colorful Vegetables

DUCK AND GOOSE   80

French Roast Duck • Roast Duck with Madeira and Dried Fruit • Roast Duck with Chestnuts • Home-Style Roast Duck with Orange Sauce • Deviled Duck with Brussels Sprouts • Duck with Pears and Port • Cassoulet with Roast Duck • Duck Breast with Mango Sauce • Duck Ragoût with Tomatoes, White Wine, and Peas • Roast Goose Stuffed with Figs, Pine Nuts, and Rice • Goose with Grapes, Oranges, and Kiwis

GAME BIRDS   101

Quail with Wild Mushrooms • Quail with Raspberry Vinegar and Onion Compote • Squab en Cocotte with Rosemary and Zucchini • Braised Squab in Tomato-Saffron Sauce on a Bed of Pasta • Pheasant with Cognac, Braised Shallots, and Grapes • Pheasant with Armagnac and Vegetable Julienne • Cornish Hens with Potatoes, Leeks, and Dill • Cornish Hens with Garbanzo Beans and Raisins • Cornish Hens with Brandy-Port Sauce and Peas

•

MEAT   116

VEAL SCALLOPS AND CHOPS   118

Veal Paillardes with Light Tarragon Cream • Veal Scallops with Mediterranean Vegetables • Veal Chops with Cider and Pearl Onions • Herbed Veal Chops with Cognac • Marinated Grilled Veal Chops with Walnut Butter • Veal Scallops with Chanterelles and Glazed Onions • Veal Scallops with Watercress Sauce • Sautéed Calf's Liver with Cèpes

Eight pages of color plates follow page 172.

Acknowledgments

I am sincerely grateful to my editor, Carole DeSanti, for making the Fresh from France series possible. Because of her belief in my work, I was encouraged to commit several years to writing the books.

Fernand Chambrette, French chef par excellence, influences and inspires my cooking more than any other person, and I appreciate the years of lessons he gave me. The day our cookbook, *La Cuisine du Poisson,* was published was one of the high points of my life. Co-authoring the book with my teacher was my greatest achievement, and I am forever grateful to him for his partnership.

I owe a million thanks to Anne Willan, founder of La Varenne Cooking School in Paris, for teaching me how to write clear recipes and well-organized cookbooks during the years I worked with her in directing the school's extensive publishing program. Thanks also to the other excellent chefs at La Varenne with whom I had the privilege of studying and working closely in developing recipes, particularly Claude Vauguet and Albert Jorant.

I would like to express my gratitude to the many other chefs in France from whom I took classes in the art of fine cooking, including chefs Denis Ruffel, Gilbert Le Coze, Alain Dutournier, Antoine Bouterin, Michel Marolleau, Michel Comby, Jacques Cagna, Guy Legay, Marc Alix, Michel Pasquet, Michel Rostang, Pierre Vedel, Georgette Descat, Gérard Besson, Jean-Pierre Morot-Gaudry, Pierre Ferranti, Claude Perraudin, Jean-Jacques Jouteux, Daniel Météry, Gérard Pangaud, John Desmond, three-star chefs Claude Deligne and Michel Lorain, Robert Noah of Paris en Cuisine, and Gregory Usher of École de Gastronomie Française Ritz-Escoffier; and to the people in food shops, markets, and restaurants who kindly took the time to answer my numerous questions.

I feel that testing the recipes is the most important aspect of producing a cookbook, and I would like to thank Annie Horenn, Leona Fitzgerald, and Patsy Allen for working side by side with me to thoroughly test and perfect the recipes.

Some of the recipes in this book appeared, in different form, in national magazines and in newspapers, and I truly appreciate the suggestions of the editors who published my articles, especially Zanne Zakroff and Kemp Miles Minifie of *Gourmet* magazine; Marilou Vaughan, Barbara Fairchild, and Jan Weimer of *Bon Appétit* magazine; Jane Freiman and Judith Hill of *Cook's* magazine; Russ Parsons of the *Los Angeles Times* Syndicate; Jim Burns and Kit Snedaker of the *Los Angeles Herald Examiner*; Maureen Clancy of the *San Diego Union*; Evelyn Kramer and Patti Doten of the *Boston Globe*; Jane Ellis and Elizabeth Sutherland of the *New York Post*; Bob Kelleter and Phyllis Richman of *The Washington Post*; Ken Bookman of the *Philadelphia Inquirer*; Carol Haddix of the *Chicago Tribune*; Iris Bailin of the *Cleveland Plain Dealer*; Michael Bauer and Jane Benet of the *San Francisco Chronicle*; Ginger Johnston of the *Portland Oregonian*; Susan Puckett of the *Fort Lauderdale News* and *Sun-Sentinel*; Taffy Jacaway of the *Miami News*; Candy Sagon of the *Dallas Times Herald*; Tom Sietsema of the *Milwaukee Sentinel*; and Helen Dollaghan of the *Denver Post*.

Thanks also to Joyce Engelson, Judy Courtade, Mary Wagstaff, and Maureen and Eric Lasher for their support.

Finally, heartfelt thanks to my husband and associate, Yakir Levy, for helping me write this book.

FRESH FROM FRANCE
DINNER INSPIRATIONS

Introduction

In recent years distinctions between the cuisines of the western world have become blurred. French nouvelle cuisine of the seventies and its principles were the inspiration and the model for fine food in many countries. We experienced new American cooking, the Italians had *nuova cucina,* and chefs and writers in Spain, Germany, Austria, Morocco, Israel, and other countries all proclaimed their own new culinary styles.

"Nouvelle cuisine" as a label lost its charm not only because it was no longer new, but because of the inexperienced or untalented cooks all over the globe who committed sins in its name by presenting weird, unappetizing combinations, portions that were absurdly small, and contrived garnishes. Many people, including food professionals, never knew what the nouvelle style really was. Others confused it with its offshoot, *cuisine minceur,* currently known here as "spa cuisine." While nouvelle cuisine promoted lighter entrées, these were not meant to be diet dishes at all. Culinary writers went on to call today's French style "modern" or "contemporary cuisine." Some describe it as a combination of the classic and the nouvelle. When top chefs are asked to define their cooking style, they often portray it as "personal" or "spontaneous," but their work clearly reflects the French spirit, tastes, and traditions.

Whatever the terms being used to define current culinary trends, the essence of nouvelle cuisine—creativity within the bounds of good taste, harmony of color, strong emphasis on fresh ingredients and natural flavors, abundant use of herbs and vegetables, and sauces that are light in consistency—continues to guide fine cooks everywhere. So do the classic specialties and the basic techniques of French cooking.

The message from France for the last twenty years has been that inventive cooks frequently make use of flavorings from other parts of the world. Thus we see French chefs using such ingredients as star anise, ginger, cumin, filo dough, and couscous. As a result, it has become harder than ever to distinguish between the style of cooking in the fine restaurants of major cities like Paris, New York, Los Angeles, Rome, or even Jerusalem. Although there are some regional differences in ingredients, special dishes, and prejudices (for example, we don't have calf's head on menus, and the French don't have chili), many features are common to all fine restaurants. If a chef prepares a fish with a cilantro-flavored beurre blanc, for example, his style may be labeled modern French, new Moroccan, nouvelle Mexican, Californian, or new American! Part of the reason for this is that many of the chefs responsible for "new American" and other "new" cuisines have been trained in France. We all look to France for culinary inspiration and fresh ideas. In fact, in order to really understand modern cooking in America, it is essential to follow the food fashions of France.

So, what is true French cooking today? Some say it is the work of professional chefs in the best French restaurants and insist that it must be innovative. Others feel that only the products of home and country kitchens are "real," because authentic cuisine must have its roots in the land; they extol the virtues of traditional recipes and time-honored flavor combinations, claiming that the new creations will disappear.

The truth, in my opinion, is that all of these are "real" and influence each other. There is not one dominant French culinary style.

Elegant, classic entrées are wonderful, and so are rustic dishes, and so are inventive and modern ones. The French repertoire covers all of these. We all enjoy the comforting taste of a simple roast chicken with a creamy potato gratin; at other times we love to treat ourselves to a glamorous dinner of sautéed venison with wild mushrooms and a rich sauce, or quail with raspberry vinegar and onion compote.

The Fresh from France series presents fine dishes and new ideas from all the styles of French cooking. Freshness is probably the single most important characteristic of today's cuisine, and these recipes reflect that quality. Most include generous amounts of fresh vegetables and herbs. I have developed the recipes based on what I learned in France, keeping American tastes in mind and making use of common American ingredients. Some of the recipes are not new inventions; rather, they represent my own adaptation and simplification of classic dishes for easy preparation in home kitchens.

Since all cookbooks are personal to a certain extent, this book reflects my view of cuisine and my own background. My six-year experience as the culinary-technique columnist at *Bon Appétit* proved invaluable for a thorough understanding of American taste. But most important were the years I spent living in France.

Before I went to France to study cooking, I knew that French food was reputed to be the finest in the western world, but I was not prepared for what I found when I arrived. I was astounded by how delicious the food was! Of course, I was tasting fabulous dishes every day at the famous Parisian school, École de Cuisine La Varenne, something not every visitor to France, nor even the average Frenchman, gets to do.

Like any enthusiastic student of French cuisine, I saved every *centime* to buy the best cookbooks in France and to taste the creations of the most illustrious chefs. I spent time in the various provinces and sampled the regional specialties at the markets, in small restaurants, and in charcuteries.

I learned that French entrées are not necessarily long or complicated, and French cuisine is not only sophisticated restaurant food. Home cooks in France are just like us—they don't have a staff of chefs, but they use fresh ingredients in season, give their cooking a little attention, and take time to enjoy their meals.

I have presented recipes for entrées that I find as delicious as those served in great restaurants, but I made sure they are practical for preparing at home, and in keeping with today's tastes. Although this is a book for the home cook, restaurant chefs will also find new useful ideas.

I have included here numerous tips learned during my professional training, but the recipes are straightforward and easy to follow. They do not require expertise in boning, cutting, rolling, or other intricate techniques that demand practice or need to be taught. You will not find foods that are larded with larding needles, or wrapped in barding fat, or meats enclosed in pastry. Accompaniments are simple and natural—mainly vegetables and fruits, rather than pastries or elaborate garnishes.

I have avoided time-consuming restaurant preparations, such as dishes in aspic, old-fashioned espagnole sauce, and modern demiglace, which requires lengthy reduction of homemade stock. Sauces are most often made from the natural juices of meats and quick reduction. I have utilized a variety of cooking techniques, but I have concentrated on those that are preferred today. I stayed away from procedures such as deep frying, which most people would rather not do at home. And because I love cookbooks that teach the art of cooking, I have organized the books in this series around cooking methods, so that once you have prepared, for example, one chicken *en cocotte,* you will recognize other recipes that follow this pattern and find them easier to prepare.

Many of the dishes are complete main courses and contain a generous amount of fresh vegetables. With the busy cook in mind, I have added plenty of hints on preparing dishes ahead. I have emphasized the cuts of meat that are relatively quick-cooking, favoring small cuts over large roasts, for example.

Mainly, I used ingredients that can be found easily at our markets, and concentrated on types of meat, poultry, and seafood that are popular both in France and America. I have tried to avoid expensive ingredients, except for a few recipes with wild mushrooms and game that are fun to cook for special occasions. In some cases I have given a range of butter quantities, so you can adjust the richness to your preference. I like the finer flavor of unsalted butter, but you may use salted in the recipes if you wish.

You will not need special equipment or gadgets in order to use this book. With a few good saucepans and skillets, a whisk and a wooden spoon, you can prepare most of the recipes.

My own introduction to cooking was from cookbooks. When I was first learning to cook, I was often impressed by the results I could obtain by following a clear, concise recipe. This brought me great pleasure, and I hope that this book will bring you a similar joy in cooking.

Bon appétit—et vive la cuisine française!

Poultry

CHICKEN
TURKEY
DUCK
GOOSE
GAME BIRDS

Chicken is the most widely used poultry in France, appearing in the most simple country homes as well as on the most lavish of tables. Each region has its own chicken creations. I have savored delicious chicken with Riesling wine sauce and fresh noodles in little restaurants in Alsace, herb-accented chicken with tomatoes and olives in southern France, and hearty chicken with cabbage in Auvergne in central France. A large number of French poultry dishes—from coq au vin to creamy chicken sautés with mushrooms to roast turkey with chestnuts to duck with orange sauce—have become famous worldwide.

Many of the French poultry specialties are simple, because each bird's meat and cooking juices give its characteristic flavor to the dish. One memorable entrée that perfectly illustrates this is the braised chicken with tarragon I feasted on at l'Auberge du Père Bise restaurant on the beautiful Lake of Annecy near the Alps. The natural cooking juices of the chicken were enriched with cream, and the chicken was served on a bed of rice. The meltingly tender chicken and its delectable sauce, enhanced by the freshness of the tarragon, made a heavenly entrée.

At the market, fine poultry has a label designating high quality and often the area of France where it was raised; free-range blue-footed chickens from Bresse, near Lyon, are especially prized for their tasty meat. At our markets, quality varies. It's best to try several brands of chicken to see which is most tasty, and to buy from a reputable butcher.

Like meat, poultry is categorized, for the purpose of cooking, into birds with white meat, such as chicken and turkey, and those with dark meat, which include duck, goose, and squab. In general, white-meat poultry can be paired with more delicate ingredients and sauces.

Chicken is the most versatile of poultry. Because of its size, it lends itself to the greatest number of cooking techniques. I have therefore described these cooking methods in the most detail in the sections devoted to chicken.

Stuffings

"Stuffing" generally conjures up an image of a mixture of chopped or ground ingredients. In this country they would generally be held together by bread, and in France, by ground meat. Indeed, the stuffing of the two most famous French holiday main courses, *dinde aux truffes* (turkey with truffles) and *dinde aux marrons* (turkey with chestnuts) consists in large part of ground pork. This type of stuffing is discussed in "Roast and Braised Turkey."

Yet there is another type of French stuffing for poultry, a composite stuffing made of larger, more distinct pieces of food that keep their character. This type of stuffing does not need to be bound. Lightly sautéed vegetables, especially mushrooms and root vegetables, are favorite ingredients, as in Roast Chicken with Vegetable Stuffing, and so are rice and pasta. Sometimes a small amount of diced meat might be included, but as a flavoring rather than as the main body of the stuffing. These light stuffings provide a welcome change from the heavier bread and ground-meat stuffings and are good complements for chicken, turkey, and goose.

There are few rules to follow in preparing these stuffings. The mixture should not be packed too tightly in the bird, so the ingredients will not be crushed. Root vegetables are better than most green vegetables, which would overcook in the bird and might lose their color.

A convenient feature of composite stuffings is that they can be easily made in larger quantities and served around the bird as well as inside. Because the ingredients are precooked, these mixtures need only be briefly reheated in a lightly buttered skillet just before serving time. They can even be used to stuff vegetables, such as tomatoes or zucchini, for an especially festive accompaniment to chicken, turkey, or other poultry.

By following these simple guidelines cooks devise endless combinations to suit their families' and friends' tastes. Nuts add a wonderful crispness and flavor, olives add piquancy, and dried fruits or even lightly sautéed fresh fruits such as apples add a pleasant sweetness.

Chicken Sautés

Chicken sautés are one of the most versatile of entrées. Manuals of classic French cuisine list numerous variations, and cooks from diverse areas of France add the ingredients characteristic of their region to create their own versions. Chicken sautés are as good with modern flourless sauces as with the traditional veloutés and brown sauces, a quality that helped them hold their own and survive the revolution of nouvelle cuisine.

A chicken sauté is basically a dish of chicken pieces cooked briefly in a small amount of fat and served with a concentrated sauce. Unlike a braised or stewed chicken, it does not cook in its sauce. In its simplest version, it can be chicken sauté à la minute, for which the chicken is sautéed in butter, set on a platter, and sprinkled with a little lemon juice, its cooking butter, and chopped parsley. And the quickest form of chicken sauté of all is one that uses only chicken breasts, which cook faster than the other cuts. All sorts of garnishes can be added, from a few chopped tomatoes to elaborate mixtures of vegetables, but the dish is generally uncomplicated and quickly prepared.

The chicken pieces are first browned in fat, which can be oil, clarified butter, or a mixture of oil and fresh butter. Next they are covered and cooked gently just until they are tender, without the addition of liquid. Sometimes flavoring ingredients such as chopped onions or sliced mushrooms are cooked with the chicken. The breast pieces, since they are done first, are removed from the skillet first. If boneless chicken is used, the step of cooking in a covered pan is omitted entirely.

Next the pan is deglazed: a liquid is added to the pan juices in order to form the basis for the sauce. The favorite deglazing liquid is white or red wine, but stock, vegetable juice, fruit juice, heavy cream, or a fortified wine such as Madeira can serve as well. Usually the liquid is boiled so it thickens slightly and its flavor becomes more intense. Then the sauce is thickened more, either by continuing the process of reduction or by the addition of a small amount of velouté sauce, brown sauce, tomato sauce, beurre manié (butter creamed with flour), or arrowroot.

Coming up with new chicken sauté combinations is easy and fun. If the cream is omitted from Chicken Sauté with Paprika Sauce, and diced red bell peppers, fennel, and minced garlic are added, the result is a classic dish called Bohemian Chicken. Chicken Sauté with Snow Peas, Carrots, and Vermouth becomes Chicken Vichy if the cream and vermouth are replaced by stock, and the snow peas are omitted; it becomes Chicken à la Bretonne if the vermouth and snow peas are omitted, and leeks and mushrooms cook in the sauce along with the carrots. Fresh herbs in season are a welcome addition to most chicken sautés. Or you can serve the chicken, as I enjoyed it at the Parisian restaurant Le Trou Gascon, with peppers, tiny broccoli florets, glazed pearl onions, carrot strips, and peas. It's a game that can go on and on. The only limits are those of imagination and good taste.

Hints

• Chicken sautés can be prepared with only breast pieces or leg pieces, if desired.

• Try to keep the breast pieces together after cutting the chicken, for easy recognition when it's time to remove them from the skillet.

• Use a large, deep, heavy skillet or sauté pan with a tight cover.

- A frying screen or splatter screen is useful for covering the pan while the chicken is being browned.

- It is easier to remove the skillet from the heat just before removing browned chicken pieces from the skillet, so the hot fat won't splatter during the process.

- The cooking time of the breast pieces depends partly on the size of the skillet. If the skillet being used is large enough so that all chicken pieces touch the bottom, the cooking time will be relatively short. If the pan is smaller, put the breast pieces on top of the others; they will cook by steam, so their cooking time will be slightly longer than usual, but still shorter than that of the other pieces.

- Most vegetables are best cooked separately, then added to the sauce or arranged around the chicken, so they will not be overcooked or crushed. Mushrooms, chopped or sliced onions, and other vegetables that do not overcook easily can be cooked with the chicken.

- A considerable amount of fat is rendered from a chicken during cooking. Thoroughly skim the fat from the surface of the pan juices before deglazing.

- Although sautés are meant to be served immediately, leftover chicken sautés with brown sauces or tomato sauces, such as Burgundy Chicken Sauté and Chicken Sauté with Herbed Mushroom-Tomato Sauce, can be reheated in their sauces.

CHICKEN SAUTÉ WITH SNOW PEAS, CARROTS, AND VERMOUTH
Poulet sauté aux pois gourmandes, aux carottes, et au vermouth

A generous amount of vegetables are part of this colorful chicken sauté. When sugar snap peas or sweet peas with edible pods are available, they are a wonderful partner for the chicken instead of the snow peas.   MAKES 4 SERVINGS

1 chicken (3 to 3 1/2 pounds), cut
   in pieces, or 2 1/2 to 3 pounds
   chicken pieces
Salt and freshly ground pepper
1 tablespoon vegetable oil

1 tablespoon butter
4 medium-size carrots (about 3/4
   pound), peeled, cut in 2-inch
   lengths

2 cups Chicken Stock (see recipe) or
    packaged broth
4 to 5 ounces snow peas, ends and
    strings removed

1/3 cup dry or extra-dry vermouth
2/3 cup heavy cream

Pat chicken pieces dry. Season lightly on all sides with salt and pepper. Heat oil and butter in large heavy skillet or sauté pan over medium heat. Add chicken leg and thigh pieces and brown lightly on all sides. Set them on a plate, using tongs. Add breast, wing, and back pieces to skillet and brown lightly.

Return leg and thigh pieces to skillet. If chicken pieces do not fit in one layer, arrange breast and wing pieces on top. Add chicken juices from plate. Cover and cook over low heat about 15 minutes, or until breast pieces are tender.

While chicken is cooking, cut thin carrot pieces in half lengthwise and thick pieces in quarters lengthwise. In a medium saucepan, combine carrots and chicken stock and bring to a boil. Reduce heat, cover, and simmer about 15 minutes, or until barely tender. Remove carrots with a slotted spoon. Reserve cooking liquid.

Transfer breast pieces to a platter, cover, and keep warm. Cook remaining chicken pieces another 10 minutes, or until tender. Add leg and thigh pieces to warm platter. Discard back pieces, neck, and wing tips. Reserve chicken juices in skillet.

Cook snow peas in a medium saucepan of boiling salted water uncovered over high heat 1 minute, or until crisp-tender. Drain, rinse with cold water, and drain well.

Skim as much fat as possible from chicken juices in skillet. Reheat juices; add reserved carrot cooking liquid and boil, stirring, until reduced to about 1/2 cup. Add vermouth and bring to a boil. Add cream and simmer over medium heat, stirring often, until thick enough to coat a spoon. Add carrots and snow peas and heat 1 or 2 minutes. Taste and adjust seasoning.

Using paper towels, remove any fat or liquid from platter of chicken. Spoon vegetables over or around chicken in platter, spoon sauce over chicken, and serve immediately.

CHICKEN SAUTÉ WITH SUGAR SNAP PEAS AND CARROTS
Substitute 1/2 pound sugar snap peas for the snow peas. Pull off ends. Cook them in the boiling salted water 3 minutes, or until just tender, before rinsing and draining.

❧ CHICKEN SAUTÉ WITH CITRUS FRUIT
Poulet sauté aux agrumes

The light sauce for this chicken is made simply from the sautéing juices with a little orange juice, lime juice, and Grand Marnier. I like to serve the chicken with buttered rice or, for a more exotic presentation, with couscous or orzo. Seedless grapes can be used for garnish instead of the diced lime.   MAKES 4 SERVINGS

1 chicken (3 to 3 1/2 pounds), cut
   in pieces, or 2 1/2 to 3 pounds
   chicken pieces
Salt and freshly ground pepper
1 tablespoon vegetable oil
1 tablespoon butter
2 oranges, room temperature
1 lime, room temperature
1/2 cup Chicken Stock (see recipe)
   or packaged broth

1/2 cup dry white wine
2 tablespoons strained fresh orange
   juice
1 teaspoon strained fresh lime juice
1 tablespoon orange liqueur, such
   as Grand Marnier or Curaçao
3 tablespoons cold butter, cut in 6
   pieces

Pat chicken pieces dry. Season lightly with salt and pepper on all sides. Heat oil and butter in large heavy skillet over medium-high heat. Add chicken leg and thigh pieces and brown on all sides. Using slotted spoon, remove to a plate. Add neck, breast, wing, and back pieces to skillet and brown lightly.

Return leg and thigh pieces to skillet. If chicken pieces do not fit in one layer, arrange breast and wing pieces on top. Add chicken juices from plate, reduce heat, cover, and cook over low heat about 15 minutes, or until breast pieces are tender.

Cut peel from oranges and lime, cutting away any white pith. Section each orange by cutting to center of fruit on each side of the membranes that divide sections; hold orange over bowl to catch juice. (This juice can be used as part of 2 tablespoons orange juice needed for recipe.) Discard membranes. Section lime in same manner. Cut lime sections in half.

Meanwhile, boil chicken stock in a small heavy saucepan over medium heat until reduced to ¼ cup. Reduce heat to low and simmer until reduced to 2 tablespoons.

When chicken breast pieces are tender, transfer to a platter with a slotted spoon. Cover and keep warm. Continue cooking remaining chicken pieces about 10 minutes more, or until all are tender. Add leg and thigh pieces to the platter. Discard back pieces, neck, and wing tips.

Skim as much fat as possible from juices in skillet, tilting skillet to make skimming easier. Reheat juices until boiling, pour in wine, and return to a boil. Boil, stirring and skimming often, until reduced to ¼ cup. Add reduced stock, orange juice, and lime juice and bring to a boil. Add liqueur and bring barely to a simmer. Remove from heat. Add butter, 2 pieces at a time, shaking skillet to incorporate butter into sauce after each addition. Taste and adjust seasoning. Add orange and lime pieces and shake to mix.

Discard any fat from platter of chicken and blot with paper towels. Using a slotted spoon, garnish chicken with fruit. Spoon a little sauce over chicken and serve remaining sauce separately. (This sauce should not be reheated.)

CHICKEN SAUTÉ WITH CURRY-COCONUT SAUCE
Poulet sauté au curry

For this sautéed chicken, rich coconut milk is used to deglaze the pan and make the sauce. It is nothing like an Indian curry; rather, it is a delicate entrée in which curry powder seasons the chicken pieces before they are sautéed and also flavors the creamy sauce. As curry powders vary both in the selection of spices included and in their proportions, experiment with different brands until you find the one you like best. Serve the chicken with rice, preferably Basmati, either the white or brown variety, and with crisp-tender broccoli or cauliflower florets or green beans.   MAKES 4 SERVINGS

RICH COCONUT MILK
1 cup milk

1 cup dried unsweetened coconut

1 chicken (3 to 3½ pounds), cut
*   in pieces, or 2½ to 3 pounds*
*   chicken pieces*
Salt and freshly ground pepper

2 teaspoons curry powder
2 tablespoons vegetable oil
1 onion, cut in thin slices

QUICK CURRY SAUCE
1 tablespoon butter
½ teaspoon curry powder
1 tablespoon all-purpose flour

⅔ cup Chicken Stock (see recipe)
*   or packaged broth*

RICH COCONUT MILK

Heat milk until warm. Combine milk and coconut in food processor or blender. Process for 30 seconds. Strain, pressing hard to extract as much liquid as possible; discard coconut.

Pat chicken pieces dry. Season lightly on all sides with salt, pepper, and 1½ teaspoons curry powder. Rub seasonings into chicken pieces. Heat oil in large heavy skillet over medium heat. Add chicken leg and thigh pieces and brown lightly on all sides. Using slotted spoon, remove to a plate. Add neck, breast, wing, and back pieces to skillet and brown lightly. Transfer them to plate.

Add onion to skillet and cook over low heat, stirring, until tender. Sprinkle ½ teaspoon curry powder over onion and cook 30 seconds, stirring. Return chicken pieces to skillet. If they do not fit in one layer, arrange breast and wing pieces on top. Add chicken juices from plate. Cover and simmer about 15 minutes, or until breast pieces are tender when pierced with a knife. Using slotted spoon, transfer breast pieces to a platter. Cover and keep warm. Cook remaining chicken pieces about 10 minutes more, or until tender. Add leg and thigh pieces to platter. Discard back pieces, neck, and wing tips. Reserve chicken cooking liquid.

QUICK CURRY SAUCE

While chicken is cooking, prepare sauce: Melt butter in a small heavy saucepan over low heat. Add curry powder and flour and heat, whisking, until bubbling. Remove from heat and whisk in chicken stock. Bring to a boil, still whisking. Remove from heat.

Skim excess fat from chicken cooking liquid. Add coconut milk and bring to a boil, stirring constantly. Add curry sauce and return to a boil, stirring. Taste and adjust seasoning. Return chicken pieces to sauce and heat gently, stirring. Transfer to platter and serve.

BURGUNDY CHICKEN SAUTÉ
Poulet sauté à la bourguignonne

This chicken is enhanced by the favorite ingredients of Burgundian cuisine: red wine, bacon, baby onions, and mushrooms. All it needs as an accompaniment is good crusty French bread.

MAKES 4 SERVINGS

12 pearl onions
1/4 pound thick-sliced bacon, cut
    crosswise in 1/4-inch strips
3 tablespoons butter
1/4 pound mushrooms, quartered
Salt and freshly ground pepper
1 chicken (3 to 3 1/2 pounds), cut
    in pieces, or 2 1/2 to 3 pounds
    chicken pieces

2 teaspoons all-purpose flour
1 garlic clove, minced
1 cup dry red wine
2/3 cup Chicken Stock (see recipe)
    or prepared broth
Pinch of sugar (optional)

Put pearl onions in a small saucepan, cover with water, and bring to a boil. Boil 1 minute. Drain, rinse under cold water, and drain well. Peel with a paring knife.

Heat bacon in large heavy skillet over medium-low heat until the fat runs. Add onions and sauté with bacon over medium-high heat, shaking pan often. When bacon browns, use tongs to transfer it to paper towels. Continue to sauté onions, turning them over carefully, until browned on all sides. Transfer to paper towels. Discard all but 1 tablespoon fat from skillet. Add 1 tablespoon butter. Heat over medium heat. Add mushrooms and salt and pepper to taste and brown lightly. Transfer to paper towels.

Pat chicken pieces dry. Season lightly with salt and pepper on all sides. Add 1 tablespoon butter to skillet and heat over medium-high heat. Add chicken leg and thigh pieces and brown on all sides. Using slotted spoon, remove to a plate. Add neck, breast, wing, and back pieces to skillet and brown them. Return leg and thigh pieces and pearl onions to bottom of skillet. Scatter mushrooms over them and arrange breast and wing pieces on top. Add chicken juices from plate. Cover and cook over low heat about 15 minutes, or until breast pieces are tender when pierced with a knife.

While chicken cooks, mash remaining tablespoon butter with a fork in a small bowl until softened. Mix in flour until mixture becomes a uniform paste.

Using slotted spoon, transfer chicken breast pieces to a platter. Cover and keep warm. Continue cooking remaining chicken pieces and vegetables about 10 minutes, or until all are tender. Add leg and thigh pieces to platter. Discard back pieces, neck, and wing tips. Spoon mushrooms and pearl onions into a bowl and add bacon.

Skim as much fat as possible from chicken juices in skillet. Reheat juices until very hot. Add garlic and stir over low heat 30 seconds. Add wine and bring to a boil. Add stock, return to a boil, and cook, stirring and skimming fat often, until mixture is reduced to about ¾ cup. Pour mixture into small heavy saucepan and keep at a simmer. Gradually whisk butter-flour paste into simmering sauce, a small piece at a time, whisking constantly. Bring to a boil, whisking.

Return vegetable-bacon mixture to sauce and heat 2 minutes over low heat to blend flavors. Taste sauce and adjust seasoning; if flavor is too acid, add a pinch of sugar. Spoon sauce and vegetable-bacon mixture over chicken and serve.

CHICKEN SAUTÉ WITH PAPRIKA SAUCE
Poulet sauté à la hongroise

Classic names for many French specialties are based on the association of a certain ingredient with a specific cuisine. Because it contains paprika, this French dish is known as Chicken, Hungarian Style. The traditional way to present the chicken is in a ring of rice pilaf. Lightly steamed or sautéed zucchini sticks complement this dish well.

MAKES 4 SERVINGS

*1 chicken (3 to 3 1/2 pounds), cut
    in pieces, or 2 1/2 to 3 pounds
    chicken pieces*
Salt and freshly ground pepper
5 teaspoons paprika
1 tablespoon vegetable oil
1 tablespoon butter

1 onion, chopped
*1 pound ripe tomatoes, peeled,
    seeded, coarsely chopped, or one
    28-ounce can whole plum
    tomatoes, drained and chopped*
2/3 cup heavy cream

Pat chicken pieces dry. Season lightly on all sides with salt, pepper, and a total of 2 teaspoons paprika. Rub seasonings into chicken. Heat oil and butter in large heavy skillet over medium heat. Add chicken leg and thigh pieces and brown lightly on all sides. Using slotted spoon, remove to a plate. Add breast pieces to skillet and brown lightly. Transfer them to plate.

Add onion, chicken wing tips, neck, and back pieces to skillet. Cook over low heat, stirring, until onion is tender. Add tomatoes and 1 teaspoon paprika and stir over high heat for 1 minute.

Return chicken pieces to skillet. If they do not fit in one layer, arrange breast and wing pieces on top. Pour chicken juices remaining on plate over chicken. Cover and simmer over low heat about 15 minutes, or until breast pieces are tender when pierced with a knife. Using slotted spoon, transfer breast pieces to a platter. Cover and keep warm. Continue cooking remaining chicken pieces about 10 minutes more, or until all are tender. Add leg and thigh pieces to platter. Discard back pieces, neck, and wing tips.

Skim as much fat as possible from mixture in skillet. Add 1/3 cup cream and remaining 2 teaspoons paprika to skillet and bring to a boil, stirring. Simmer over medium-high heat, stirring, until sauce is reduced to 1 1/2 cups. Purée sauce in a food processor or blender until smooth. Strain into a medium saucepan, pressing hard so as much mixture as possible goes through. Stir in remaining 1/3 cup cream and bring to a simmer. Taste and adjust seasoning. Pour sauce over chicken and serve.

❧ CHICKEN PAILLARDES WITH TRICOLORED PEPPERS AND BASIL
Paillardes de poulet aux trois poivrons et au basilic

Chicken breasts flattened into thin *paillardes* make a very quick main course. They can either be grilled or sautéed, as in this entrée, where they are topped with sautéed red, green, and yellow peppers. For a light summer meal all you need to add is a salad of mixed lettuces topped with toasted pine nuts, if you like, and some fine French or Italian bread.   MAKES 4 SERVINGS

4 boneless chicken breast halves (6 to 7 ounces each), skinned and trimmed
1 medium-size red bell pepper (about 5 ounces)
1 medium-size green bell pepper (about 5 ounces)
1 medium-size yellow bell pepper (about 8 ounces), or 1 additional red bell pepper

7 tablespoons olive oil
1 fresh jalapeño pepper, seeds and ribs discarded, minced, or a pinch of cayenne pepper
Salt
¼ cup all-purpose flour
Freshly ground pepper
1 tablespoon minced fresh basil
4 small sprigs basil for garnish (optional)

Using a flat meat pounder or rolling pin, pound each chicken breast between 2 pieces of plastic wrap or wax paper to thickness of ¼ inch. Cut bell peppers in half and discard seeds and ribs; cut into 1 ½-by-¼-inch strips.

Heat 3 tablespoons oil in large skillet over low heat. Add jalapeño pepper (but not cayenne) and cook until soft but not brown, about 4 minutes. Add bell peppers and a pinch of salt and cook, stirring often, until tender but not brown, about 15 minutes. Add cayenne if using; taste and adjust seasoning. (Peppers can be cooked up to 1 hour ahead and kept at room temperature.)

Preheat oven to 275°F. Spread flour in plate. Sprinkle chicken with salt and pepper on both sides. Heat remaining 4 tablespoons oil in large heavy skillet over medium-high heat. Lightly coat 2 chicken breasts with flour on both sides; tap and shake to remove excess. Add chicken to skillet and sauté until brown and just tender when pierced

with sharp knife, about 2 minutes per side. Arrange in a single layer
on an ovenproof platter and keep warm in oven. Repeat flouring and
sauté remaining chicken. Reheat peppers over low heat if necessary,
stirring.

Blot fat from chicken platter with paper towels. Spoon peppers
around chicken. Sprinkle chicken with basil. Garnish with basil sprigs.

CHICKEN SUPRÊMES WITH CHIVE CREAM
Suprêmes de volaille à la crème de ciboulette

Suprême is a term for breasts of chicken and sometimes of game
birds, and is used on menus to emphasize their delicacy. Here their
subtle taste and light texture are complemented by a luscious chive
sauce, which is also good with sautéed veal or turkey slices. Baked or
steamed potatoes and sautéed yellow squash or zucchini are excellent
accompaniments.   MAKES 4 SERVINGS

1 small carrot, peeled and cut in quarters lengthwise	2 tablespoons vegetable oil
1 small zucchini, cut in eighths lengthwise	3 tablespoons butter
	2 medium-size shallots, minced
Salt	1/2 cup dry white wine
4 boneless chicken breast halves (1 to 1 1/4 pounds), skinned, trimmed, and patted dry	1/2 cup Chicken Stock (see recipe) or packaged broth
	1 cup heavy cream
Freshly ground pepper	2 tablespoons finely snipped fresh chives

Cut carrot quarters and zucchini pieces in 1/8-inch slices to make small
dice. Put carrots in small saucepan and cover with water. Add a pinch
of salt and bring to a boil. Reduce heat, cover, and simmer until
tender, about 4 minutes. Add zucchini dice, cover, and cook until
nearly tender, about 1 minute. Drain vegetables, rinse with cold
water, and drain thoroughly. (Vegetables can be cooked 1 hour ahead
and kept at room temperature.)

Preheat oven to 275°F. Season chicken with salt and pepper on
both sides. Heat oil and 1 tablespoon butter in a large heavy skillet
over medium-high heat. Add chicken and sauté, pressing on chicken

occasionally with slotted spatula, about 3 minutes per side, or until just tender and no longer pink inside; cut to check. Transfer to a platter, cover, and keep warm in preheated oven.

Discard fat from skillet. Add 1 tablespoon butter and melt over low heat. Add shallots and cook until softened, about 1 minute. Pour in wine and bring to boil, stirring and scraping browned bits from base of pan. Boil, stirring, until wine is reduced to about 1/4 cup. Add chicken stock and boil until mixture is again reduced to about 1/4 cup. Stir in cream and a pinch of salt and pepper. Simmer over medium heat, stirring, until sauce is thick enough to coat a spoon, about 7 minutes.

While sauce is simmering, melt remaining tablespoon butter in small skillet over low heat. Add diced zucchini and carrots and cook just until heated through. Season to taste with salt and pepper.

Stir chives into sauce and taste to adjust seasoning. Transfer chicken to plates, discarding any liquid that has escaped from chicken. Spoon sauce over chicken, spoon vegetables onto plate on both sides of chicken, and serve immediately.

CHICKEN SAUTÉ WITH HERBED MUSHROOM-TOMATO SAUCE
Poulet sauté chasseur

In this simplified version of the classic, the sauce is enriched with a quicker yet tasty version of the traditional brown sauce. Fine-quality noodles are a natural ally for the chicken, while fresh herbs lend zip to the sauce.   MAKES 4 SERVINGS

1 chicken (3 to 3 1/2 pounds), cut in pieces, or 2 1/2 to 3 pounds chicken pieces
Salt and freshly ground pepper
1 tablespoon vegetable oil
1 tablespoon butter
1/4 pound mushrooms, sliced
2 medium-size shallots, finely minced (about 4 teaspoons)

1/2 cup dry white wine
2/3 cup Tomato-Flavored Brown Sauce (page 310), made with chicken stock
4 teaspoons Cognac or brandy
2 teaspoons chopped fresh tarragon, or 3/4 teaspoon dried leaf tarragon, crumbled
2 teaspoons chopped fresh parsley

Pat chicken pieces dry. Season lightly with salt and pepper on all sides. Heat oil and butter in large heavy skillet over medium-high heat. Add chicken leg and thigh pieces and brown thoroughly on all sides. Using slotted spoon, remove to a plate. Add breast pieces to skillet and brown thoroughly, then transfer to a plate. Add wing and back pieces and mushrooms to skillet and brown them.

Return leg and thigh pieces to skillet. If chicken pieces do not fit in one layer, arrange breast and wing pieces on top. Add chicken juices from plate. Cover and simmer over low heat about 15 minutes, or until breast pieces are tender when pierced with a knife.

Using slotted spoon, transfer breast pieces only to a platter. Cover and keep warm. Add shallots to skillet. Continue cooking remaining chicken pieces about 10 minutes more, or until all are tender. Add leg and thigh pieces to platter. Discard back pieces, neck, and wing tips. Leave mushrooms and shallots in skillet.

Skim as much fat as possible from mixture in skillet. Reheat until very hot. Add wine and bring to a boil. Boil, stirring and skimming often, until mixture is reduced by about half. Add brown sauce and 3 teaspoons Cognac and simmer over medium heat, stirring often, until sauce is thick enough to coat a spoon. Add tarragon and remaining teaspoon Cognac. Taste and adjust seasoning. Spoon sauce over the chicken and sprinkle with chopped parsley. Serve immediately.

Roast Chicken

"My favorite dinner is a roast chicken with some green beans," the chef of a two-star Parisian restaurant once told me. His comment demonstrated to me that fine food is not necessarily elaborate, and a perfectly roasted chicken, accompanied by a well-cooked vegetable, makes an ideal entrée.

The French like to roast chickens and other poultry at relatively high temperatures so the meat cooks quickly and remains succulent and the skin becomes brown and slightly crisp. Although French cooks prefer fresh free-range chickens, this roasting method produces good results with the common supermarket chicken as well.

Roast chicken is moist enough to be served without sauce, but it can also be served with a simple deglazing sauce made with the pan juices. It is delicious when stuffed, either with the vegetable, rice, or pasta stuffings used in this section, or with meat stuffing, as in Roast Turkey with Calvados Sauce.

For a complete main course, all sorts of vegetables can be matched with roast chicken. Fresh asparagus, green beans, peas, and artichoke bottoms are great choices in spring and summer, while sautéed mushrooms, chestnuts, turnips, and Brussels sprouts add interest in fall and winter. Potatoes, pearl onions, or carrots, alone or paired with other vegetables, are tasty companions for the chicken all year round. For a festive dinner you may wish to present the chicken with more elaborate mixtures of seasonal vegetables, as in Roast Chicken with Spring Vegetables.

Hints

- Choose chicken with its skin intact. The skin protects the meat and prevents it from drying.
- Skim excess fat from the pan juices by tipping the roasting pan before adding liquid to make a sauce. Some fat can be left in if desired, because it adds flavor.
- Poultry shears facilitate carving chicken.
- If some chicken is left over, do not try to reheat it whole; the heat will take too long to reach the chicken's interior and the meat will dry out. The best way is to remove the meat from the bones and heat it briefly in any remaining pan juices or sauce, or in a little butter or oil, in a skillet.
- Although roasting chickens are slightly more flavorful, frying chickens can also be roasted.

ROAST CHICKEN WITH VEGETABLE STUFFING
Poulet farci Matignon

The aromatic, light stuffing for this chicken contains no bread or ground meat, but rather consists of a colorful mixture of diced vegetables, a little ham, and Madeira.   MAKES 4 SERVINGS

2 tablespoons butter

2 medium-size carrots, scraped and
    finely diced

1 large onion, finely diced

2 celery stalks, peeled and diced

1/4 teaspoon dried leaf thyme,
    crumbled

1 bay leaf

1/3 cup Madeira

2 ounces ham, diced

Salt and freshly ground pepper

1 chicken (3 to 3 1/2 pounds)

Preheat oven to 400°F. Melt butter in a skillet or sauté pan and add carrots, onion, celery, thyme, and bay leaf. Cook over low heat, stirring often, about 10 minutes, or until softened. Cover and cook, stirring occasionally, about 20 minutes, or until tender. (Stuffing can be prepared ahead to this point and kept, covered, in refrigerator. Reheat before continuing.) Add 1 tablespoon Madeira and bring just to a boil. Remove from heat and stir in ham. Discard bay leaf. Taste mixture and adjust seasoning.

Remove neck and giblets from chicken. Pull out fat from inside chicken on both sides near tail. Cut off tail and wing tips and pat chicken dry. Spoon half the vegetable mixture into chicken. Truss chicken, if desired, and season with salt and pepper.

Set chicken on its side on a rack in a roasting pan. Roast 15 minutes. Turn it on its other side and roast 15 minutes longer. Set chicken on its back and roast 20 to 30 minutes more, basting occasionally, or until juices run clear when thickest part of leg is pierced with thin knife or skewer; if juices are still pink, roast a few more minutes and test again. Transfer chicken to a platter. Discard any trussing strings.

Discard excess fat from roasting pan. Heat pan until juices are very hot. Add remaining Madeira and stir to dissolve pan juices. Pour into remaining vegetable mixture and heat gently. Taste and adjust seasoning. Spoon mixture onto platter around chicken and serve.

ROAST CHICKEN WITH ROSEMARY, SAGE, AND NEW POTATOES
Poulet rôti au romarin et aux pommes de terre nouvelles

In this aromatic and somewhat unusual recipe for roasting chicken from southern France, the partially cooked bird is carved and finishes roasting with the potatoes. The advantages are clear: the chicken flavors the potatoes with its juices and it is easy to serve. An ideal accompaniment, in keeping with the Provençal character of the dish, would be grilled peppers or a simple tomato salad with black olives or fresh basil.   MAKES 4 SERVINGS

1 roasting chicken (4 1/2 to 5 1/2 pounds), room temperature
10 sprigs rosemary, each about 5 inches long
15 large sage leaves
6 tablespoons dry white wine
6 tablespoons extra-virgin olive oil

Salt and freshly ground pepper
2 pounds small red-skinned potatoes (about 1 1/2 inches in diameter), scrubbed
Rosemary sprigs and sage leaves, for garnish

Preheat oven to 425°F. Remove neck and giblets from chicken. Pull out fat from inside chicken on both sides near tail. Cut off tail and wing tips. Set chicken in a small roasting pan and put 7 rosemary sprigs and 10 sage leaves into cavity. Pour wine and 3 tablespoons olive oil over chicken, season with salt and pepper, and rub seasonings into chicken. Tuck remaining rosemary and sage, except those for garnish, under chicken.

Add remaining 3 tablespoons oil to a shallow baking dish that will hold potatoes in one layer. Peel potatoes completely or, if desired, peel a strip around the center of each. Put potatoes in dish and sprinkle with salt and pepper. Roll potatoes in oil to coat.

Put chicken and potatoes in oven. Roast 20 minutes, basting chicken twice. Turn potatoes over. Continue roasting both chicken and potatoes 25 minutes more, basting each occasionally with its juice. Turn potatoes again.

Transfer chicken to carving board and cut in 5 pieces (2 legs, 2 lengthwise breast pieces with wings attached, back piece), catching juices on board. Set chicken pieces on top of potatoes. Pour chicken juices with herbs over chicken and potatoes. Bake 10 to 15 more minutes, or until potatoes are very tender and chicken juices run clear when thickest part of leg is pierced with a thin knife. (If chicken is done before potatoes, remove it and keep warm.) If desired, cut breast meat from bone for serving, and split leg piece in two. Taste juices and adjust seasoning. To serve, spoon pan juices and sage leaves over chicken and potatoes. Garnish with fresh rosemary and sage.

ROAST CHICKEN WITH CHAMPAGNE HERB SAUCE
Poulet rôti au champagne

Champagne, called by the French *"le roi du vin,"* the king of wine, is France's best-known product. In fact, more people have heard of the wine than of the region in which it originated, even though the wine is named for its birthplace. (In French they are distinguished from one another, the drink being the masculine *le champagne* and the region the feminine *La Champagne.*) This unique wine is what gives the cuisine of the province of Champagne and of northern France refinement and vitality. Cooks happily splash a great variety of foods with it, from sauces to onion soup to baked fish to sauerkraut.

A common misconception regarding cooking with champagne should be clarified. It is not the bubbles that make champagne good for use in the kitchen, as they disappear rapidly once the wine is heated, but rather the superior quality of the wine. An opened bottle of champagne loses its effervescence but remains fine for cooking.

Great accompaniments for this entrée with its creamy champagne sauce are potato-leek crêpes or potato cakes.   MAKES 4 SERVINGS

1 chicken (3 1/2 pounds)
Salt and freshly ground pepper

2 tablespoons butter, softened
2 teaspoons thinly sliced chives

CHAMPAGNE HERB SAUCE
1 1/2 tablespoons butter
4 ounces mushrooms, cut in half
*   and sliced thin*
Salt and freshly ground pepper
1 1/2 cups brut champagne
3/4 cup Chicken Stock (see recipe)
*   or packaged broth*

1 medium-size shallot, minced
3/4 cup heavy cream
6 tablespoons cold butter, cut in 6
*   pieces*
1 1/2 tablespoons thinly sliced chives
1 1/2 tablespoons minced fresh
*   parsley*

Preheat oven to 400°F. Remove neck and giblets from chicken; reserve neck. Pull out fat from inside chicken on both sides near tail.

Cut off tail and wing tips. Pat chicken dry and season evenly outside and inside with salt and pepper. Rub chicken all over with 1 tablespoon softened butter. Mix remaining tablespoon softened butter with chives, put mixture inside chicken cavity, and rub it well. Skewer skin underneath legs to body to keep chicken in a neat shape. Set chicken on a rack in a roasting pan and add chicken neck to pan.

Roast chicken about 1 hour, basting occasionally, or until juices run clear when thickest part of leg is pierced with thin knife or skewer; if juices are still pink, roast a few more minutes and test again.

CHAMPAGNE HERB SAUCE

While chicken is roasting, begin sauce: Melt 1½ tablespoons butter in a medium skillet. Add mushrooms and salt and pepper. Sauté over medium-high heat, tossing often, about 3 minutes, or until tender and lightly browned.

When chicken is done, transfer it to a carving board or platter and keep warm. Pour off excess fat from roasting pan. Reheat juices in pan. Add ¾ cup champagne and boil, scraping to dissolve juices in pan, until reduced to about ¼ cup. Strain into a sauté pan or wide saucepan and add stock, shallot, and remaining ¾ cup champagne. Boil mixture, stirring often, until it is well-flavored and reduced to about ¾ cup. Add cream and boil until sauce is thick enough to coat a spoon. Stir in sautéed mushrooms.

Carve chicken, cover pieces, and keep warm.

To finish sauce, bring to a boil. Reduce heat to low and stir in cold butter, 1 piece at a time. Stir in chives and parsley, and taste and adjust seasoning. Serve sauce separately.

ROAST CHICKEN WITH ALMOND AND BROWN RICE PILAF
Poulet rôti, pilaf de riz complet aux amandes

A pilaf of brown rice, enhanced with raisins and toasted almonds, is the stuffing for this chicken. The hearty rice mixture acquires a marvelous taste from the roasting juices. I like to serve the chicken with grilled or sautéed eggplant and peppers.   MAKES 4 SERVINGS

2 tablespoons butter
1 onion, finely chopped
1 cup long-grain brown rice
2 cups hot Chicken Stock (see
    recipe) or packaged broth, or
    water

1/2 cup dark raisins
Salt and freshly ground pepper
3/4 cup whole blanched almonds
2 tablespoons chopped fresh parsley
1 chicken (3 to 3 1/2 pounds)

Preheat oven to 400°F. Melt butter in a heavy saucepan, add onion and cook over low heat, stirring often, until soft but not brown. Add rice and cook, stirring, 2 minutes. Add stock or water, raisins, and salt and pepper and bring to a boil. Reduce heat to low, cover, and simmer 35 minutes. Let cool for 10 minutes. (Stuffing can be kept, covered, 1 day in refrigerator. Bring to room temperature before continuing.)

Meanwhile, toast almonds in oven for about 5 minutes, or until golden brown. Cool slightly. Using a fork, fluff rice and gently stir in almonds and parsley. Taste and adjust seasoning.

Remove neck and giblets from chicken. Pull out fat from inside chicken on both sides near tail. Cut off tail and wing tips and pat chicken dry. Spoon about two-thirds of pilaf into chicken or enough to fill it loosely. Truss chicken, if desired, and season with salt and pepper.

Set chicken on its side in a roasting pan and roast 15 minutes. Turn it on its other side and roast 15 minutes longer. Set chicken on its back and roast 20 to 30 minutes more, or until juices run clear when thickest part of leg is pierced with thin knife or skewer; if juices are still pink, roast a few more minutes and test again. Stuffing should be hot. Transfer chicken to a carving board if carving in kitchen, or to a platter if serving it whole. Discard any trussing strings.

Reheat remaining pilaf in a buttered skillet over low heat or in a buttered baking dish in oven. Serve it around chicken or in a separate dish.

ROAST CHICKEN WITH SPRING VEGETABLES
Poulet rôti à la printanière

This classic dish is very popular today because it combines everything we love in a fine entrée—the natural tastes of a perfectly roasted chicken and a variety of fresh herb-scented vegetables.

"Spring" appears frequently on French menus. It evokes pleasant images of freshness, new life, and abundance. Many restaurants feature meats *à la printanière* (from *printemps*, or spring). These dishes include a selection of spring vegetables spooned around or alongside the main course. Traditionally, these are tender green peas, asparagus tips, new carrots, new turnips, and pearl onions. However, the word has been extended to mean an assortment of vegetables, some of which should be at the height of their season in spring.

MAKES 4 SERVINGS

1 roasting chicken (3½ to 4 pounds)

Salt and freshly ground pepper

16 pearl onions (about 4 ounces)

8 medium-size asparagus spears (about ½ pound), peeled

12 baby carrots (about 3 ounces), scrubbed, large ones cut in half crosswise

¾ pound fresh peas (about ¾ cup shelled), or ¾ cup frozen

2 or 3 tablespoons butter

1 tablespoon thinly sliced chives (optional)

1 tablespoon minced fresh parsley (optional)

A few drops fresh lemon juice (optional)

Preheat oven to 400°F. Remove neck and giblets from chicken; reserve neck. Pull out fat from inside chicken on both sides near tail. Cut off tail and wing tips. Pat chicken dry and season evenly outside and inside with salt and pepper. Truss chicken, if desired.

Set chicken on a rack in a roasting pan. Roast chicken 50 minutes to 1 hour, or until juices run clear when thickest part of leg is pierced with thin knife or skewer; if juices are still pink, roast a few more minutes and test again.

Meanwhile, prepare vegetables. In a small saucepan, cover pearl onions with water and bring to a boil. Boil 1 minute. Drain, rinse under cold water, and drain well. Peel with a paring knife.

Cut off asparagus tips and cut stalks in 1-inch pieces, discarding about 1½ inches of bases. Boil asparagus in a saucepan of boiling salted water for 2 minutes. Drain, rinse under cold water, and drain thoroughly.

Put carrots in a medium saucepan and cover with water. Bring to a simmer, cover, and cook over medium heat until they are just tender, about 12 minutes. Remove with a slotted spoon. Add pearl onions, cover, and simmer over medium heat until just tender, about

10 minutes. Remove with slotted spoon. Add peas and boil uncovered until just tender, about 4 minutes for fresh, 2 minutes for frozen. Remove with slotted spoon. Drain all vegetables in a strainer.

When chicken is done, transfer to a platter or carving board. Let stand 5 to 10 minutes before serving.

Melt butter in a sauté pan or skillet. Add vegetables, sprinkle with salt and pepper, and cook over low heat until heated through. Add chives, parsley, and lemon juice, if desired, tossing gently. Taste and adjust seasoning.

Serve chicken and vegetables on a platter; or carve chicken and serve on individual plates.

CHICKEN STUFFED WITH PASTA AND PARMESAN
Poulet farci à l'italienne

When preparing pasta stuffings for poultry, French chefs like to mix in a small quantity of diced foie gras and truffles. Even without these expensive delicacies, macaroni or noodles and cheese can taste wonderful in a roast chicken. The noodle stuffing is easier to prepare than most versions of macaroni and cheese, because no white sauce is necessary.   MAKES 4 SERVINGS

1 pound short, medium-width egg
   noodles or macaroni
Salt
½ cup heavy cream
6 tablespoons freshly grated
   Parmesan cheese
Freshly ground pepper
Freshly grated nutmeg
1 truffle, diced (optional)
3 ounces foie gras, either fresh or
   canned "bloc," chilled and
   diced (optional)
1 chicken (3 to 3½ pounds)

Cook noodles in a large saucepan or pot of boiling salted water about 8 minutes, or until nearly tender. Drain thoroughly and return to saucepan. Add cream and simmer over low heat, stirring gently, until cream is absorbed. Remove from heat. Stir in 4 tablespoons cheese, and add a little pepper and nutmeg. Taste and adjust seasoning. Gently stir in truffle and foie gras, if using.

Remove neck and giblets from chicken. Pull out fat from inside chicken on both sides near tail. Cut off tail and wing tips and pat chicken dry. Spoon enough stuffing into chicken to fill it loosely. Spoon remaining stuffing into a buttered baking dish and sprinkle it with remaining cheese.

Truss chicken, if desired. Season chicken with salt and pepper and set it on its side in a roasting pan. Roast 15 minutes, then turn it on its other side and roast 15 minutes longer. Put baking dish of extra stuffing in oven to reheat. Set chicken on its back and roast 20 to 30 minutes more, basting occasionally, or until juices run clear when thickest part of leg is pierced with thin knife or skewer; if juices are still pink, roast a few more minutes and test again. Stuffing in bird and in baking dish should be hot. Transfer chicken to a carving board if carving in kitchen, or to a platter if serving it whole. Discard any trussing strings.

To serve, either arrange stuffing from inside chicken on a platter, set chicken pieces on top, and serve baking dish of noodles separately; or set whole stuffed chicken on dish of baked noodles and carve at table.

Chicken en Cocotte

For those who adore roast chicken, the rich buttery flavor and golden brown skin of chicken *en cocotte* will come as a pleasant surprise. The two have much in common in the way of taste and appearance, but chicken *en cocotte* is somewhat simpler in that it does not require any basting as it bakes. This technique deserves to be better known to American cooks; it has long been a favorite in France.

Chicken *en cocotte* is sometimes referred to as "casserole-roasted chicken" or "casseroled chicken." First the bird is browned in a small amount of fat. The pan is then covered and transferred to the oven, where the chicken cooks in its own juices. The steam created by the juices keeps the bird moist. The tender meat is served with the cooking essences, which make a delectable sauce.

This cooking procedure is perfect for other medium-size to small poultry and game birds, such as Cornish hens, pheasant, squab, and quail. Lean birds remain moister when cooked *en cocotte* than they would be if they were roasted.

The cooking technique is named for the *cocotte* or casserole that is used. A *cocotte* is a heavy oval or round deep casserole, with thick walls, two handles, and a heavy cover. It is usually made of enameled cast iron, which is durable enough to withstand the relatively high heat necessary for browning, is ovenproof, and does not rust. Also, foods tend not to stick to enameled cast iron. These casseroles come in a variety of attractive colors and are designed for serving, too. Oval ones are best suited to the shape of a chicken.

The juices that develop during cooking make wonderful sauces. In the simplest version of the dish, the cooking essences are degreased and served as a sauce without further embellishment. To give the juices a delicate aroma, a few fresh herb sprigs or a little garlic butter can be placed inside the chicken before cooking, or a bouquet garni of fresh thyme sprigs, a bay leaf, and parsley stems tied together can be added to the casserole after the chicken is nicely browned.

The juices can also be used as the basis for a quick, light sauce. Once the juices are degreased, a small amount of liquid can be added to them and brought to a boil. White wine is the most common deglazing liquid, but Madeira and Cognac are also popular. The trick here is not to dilute the taste of the juices with too much of the wine. Once the liquid is stirred in, the sauce is boiled until it thickens; flour is not generally used. The sauce can be enriched with cream or butter or flavored with fresh herbs.

For a complete main course, seasonal vegetables are often added. Bacon is also a frequent garnish and is combined with potatoes and baby onions for the classic *poulet bonne femme,* "good woman's chicken." Fresh fruit, especially apples and grapes, or dried fruit can be used also.

In the past, the vegetables were cooked in the casserole with the chicken, but timing it all to be done simultaneously proved tricky. A foolproof approach, and one much more common today, is to blanch or sauté the vegetables first, then to finish cooking them in the chicken juices for extra flavor. The exceptions to this rule are mushrooms, onions, and carrots, which can be baked along with the chicken because they do not overcook easily.

Although the traditional way to serve chicken *en cocotte* is right from the casserole, the bird is easier to carve and more festive-looking if presented on a platter, surrounded by its accompanying vegetables. For even simpler serving, cut the chicken in pieces in the kitchen, return it to the casserole and offer the dish "country-style."

Round out a chicken *en cocotte* dinner with French bread, rice, or pasta for soaking up the delicious juices. Couscous, as in Cornish Hens with Garbanzo Beans and Raisins, also makes a nice addition to the meal.

Hints

• Your favorite stuffings for roast chicken can also be used for chicken *en cocotte.*

• It is important to use a heavy casserole, preferably enameled cast iron, and cover it tightly to prevent the juices from evaporating and burning. If one is not available, brown the chicken in a sauté pan or skillet, then bake it in any casserole with a tight-fitting lid.

• Using the oven for cooking chicken *en cocotte* is easier, quicker, and ensures that the chicken will cook evenly. You can cook it on top of the stove, as long as you turn the chicken often.

• It is important to skim the fat from the chicken juices thoroughly if the sauce will be finished with butter or cream.

• To degrease the cooking juices, tilt the casserole and remove the fat from the surface of the juices with a large spoon. To make skimming easier, an ice cube can be added to the juices to coagulate the fat quickly. Traces of remaining fat can be removed from the sauce by very quickly running a paper towel across its surface.

CHICKEN EN COCOTTE WITH FRESH HERBS
Poulet en cocotte aux fines herbes

This is chicken *en cocotte* in its simplest form—a casserole-roasted chicken served with its natural juices. The traditional French mixture of fresh *fines herbes*—tarragon, chives, and chervil or parsley—adds a delicate flavor, but you can add 2 or 3 tablespoons of a single herb instead, or you can use other herbs such as basil, dill, or thyme, when these are particularly fragrant at the market. Cauliflower gratin with light cheese sauce, or pumpkin gratin with fresh tomato sauce make delightful accompaniments. MAKES 4 SERVINGS

1 chicken (3 1/2 pounds), room
temperature
Salt and freshly ground pepper
3 sprigs fresh tarragon
2 tablespoons vegetable oil
1 tablespoon butter
1 tablespoon snipped or thinly sliced
chives

1 tablespoon minced fresh tarragon
1 tablespoon minced fresh chervil or
parsley
2 teaspoons strained fresh lemon
juice

Preheat oven to 400°F. Remove neck and giblets from chicken. Pull out fat from inside chicken on both sides near tail. Cut off tail and wing tips. Pat chicken dry and season evenly outside and inside with salt and pepper. Put tarragon sprigs inside cavity and truss chicken, if desired.

Heat oil and butter in heavy 4- to 5-quart oval enamel-lined cast-iron casserole over medium-high heat. Set chicken on its side in casserole. Cover pan with a large splatter screen, if desired, and brown about 3 minutes. (If fat begins to turn dark brown at any time, reduce heat to medium.) Using 2 wooden spoons to prevent chicken skin from tearing (and standing back to avoid splatters), gently turn chicken onto its breast and brown about 3 minutes. Turn chicken onto other side and brown 3 minutes more. Turn chicken on its back and brown 2 minutes.

Baste chicken with pan juices. Cover casserole and bake chicken in oven until juices run clear when thickest part of leg is pierced with thin knife or skewer, about 35 minutes; if juices are still pink, bake a few more minutes and test again. (Chicken can be kept warm in casserole, covered, for 15 minutes.) Lift chicken, draining its juices into casserole, and transfer to a platter. Discard trussing strings, if used.

Skim some of fat from pan juices and bring to a boil. Pour juices into a small bowl. Add herbs and lemon juice, and taste and adjust seasoning. Carve chicken in kitchen, discarding tarragon sprigs from inside; or serve chicken whole and carve it at table. Pour herb-flavored juices over each portion.

CHICKEN EN COCOTTE WITH RATATOUILLE RICE
Poulet en cocotte, riz à la ratatouille

Often the best-loved new recipes are old favorites in a different guise. Here a quick version of ratatouille is made with diced vegetables, which is then heated with rice so that the rich taste of the ratatouille permeates it. The chicken is presented on a bed of the colorful ratatouille rice. You might want to follow the custom of cooks in Provence and prepare a large quantity of ratatouille, since it keeps well, and serve it again the next day, either hot with eggs or fish, or cold as a refreshing side dish.   MAKES 4 SERVINGS

RATATOUILLE

5 tablespoons olive oil

1 pound ripe tomatoes, peeled,
    seeded, and chopped, or one
    28-ounce can whole plum
    tomatoes, drained and chopped

Salt and freshly ground pepper

1 small eggplant (¾ pound),
    peeled, cut in ½-inch dice

1 onion, chopped

1 small green bell pepper, seeds and
    ribs removed, diced

1 small red bell pepper, seeds and
    ribs removed, diced

½ pound zucchini, cut in ½-inch
    dice

4 large garlic cloves, minced

1 tablespoon chopped fresh thyme,
    or 1 teaspoon dried leaf thyme,
    crumbled

1 chicken (3½ pounds), room
    temperature

Salt and freshly ground pepper

2 or 3 tablespoons olive oil

1½ cups long-grain rice

3 to 4 tablespoons coarsely chopped
    fresh basil

Basil sprigs for garnish (optional)

RATATOUILLE

Heat 1 tablespoon oil in a medium, heavy saucepan over medium-high heat. Add tomatoes and salt and pepper and cook, stirring often, 10 minutes.

Heat 2 tablespoons oil in a large sauté pan over medium-high heat. Add eggplant and salt and pepper and sauté, tossing often, about

3 minutes, or until most of the pieces are moistened. Transfer to a bowl. Add 2 tablespoons oil to pan and heat over medium heat. Add onion and peppers and cook, stirring often, about 8 minutes, or until onion is tender but not brown. Add zucchini and cook, stirring, about 2 minutes.

Return eggplant to pan. Add tomato mixture, garlic, and thyme and heat until sizzling. Reduce heat to low, cover, and simmer, stirring occasionally, about 15 minutes, or until vegetables are just tender. Mixture should be thick. If necessary, cook uncovered over medium-high heat 2 or 3 minutes to evaporate excess liquid. Taste and adjust seasoning. (Ratatouille can be kept, covered, 2 days in refrigerator.)

Preheat oven to 400°F. Remove neck and giblets from chicken. Pull out fat from inside chicken on both sides near tail. Cut off tail and wing tips and pat chicken dry. Season evenly outside and inside with salt and pepper, and truss, if desired.

Heat oil in heavy 4- to 5-quart oval enamel-lined cast-iron casserole over medium-high heat. Set chicken on its side in casserole. Cover pan with a large splatter screen, if desired, and brown about 3 minutes. (If fat begins to turn dark brown at any time, reduce heat to medium.) Using 2 wooden spoons to prevent chicken skin from tearing (and standing back to avoid splatters), gently turn chicken onto its breast and brown about 3 minutes. Turn chicken onto other side and brown 3 minutes more. Turn chicken on its back and brown 2 minutes.

Baste chicken with pan juices. Cover casserole and bake chicken in oven until juices run clear when thickest part of leg is pierced with thin knife or skewer, about 35 minutes; if juices are still pink, bake a few minutes more and test again. (Chicken can be kept warm in casserole, covered, for 15 minutes.)

While chicken cooks, add rice to a fairly large saucepan of 2 quarts boiling salted water and boil, uncovered, over high heat about 12 minutes, or until just tender but still slightly firm. Drain, rinse with cold water until cold, and drain well. Reheat ratatouille.

Remove chicken from casserole, draining its juices back into casserole, and transfer to platter. Discard trussing strings, if used. Pour juices from casserole into a dish. Return 3 tablespoons chicken juices to casserole and heat over medium heat. Add rice and heat, stirring with a fork or slotted spatula, until hot. Add hot ratatouille and heat 2 or 3 minutes, tossing gently so vegetables do not break up too much.

Gently add basil to rice mixture. Add an additional tablespoon chicken juices, if desired. Taste and adjust seasoning. Serve chicken whole and carve it at table. Serve ratatouille rice next to or under each serving of chicken. Garnish with basil sprigs.

CHICKEN EN COCOTTE WITH SHRIMP, CÈPES, AND ASPARAGUS
Poulet en cocotte aux crevettes, aux cèpes, et aux asperges

Chicken with shrimp might seem like a surprising "nouvelle" combination, but this festive new dish is inspired by two classics in which chicken is paired with crayfish—chicken Nantua and chicken Marengo. Try to find dried cèpes or porcini mushrooms that are aromatic and in relatively large pieces.   MAKES 4 SERVINGS

1 chicken (3 1/2 pounds), room temperature
Salt and freshly ground pepper

2 tablespoons vegetable oil
1 tablespoon butter

CÈPE CREAM
1 ounce dried cèpes or porcini, soaked 30 minutes in hot water to cover

2/3 cup Chicken Stock (see recipe) or prepared broth
1 cup heavy cream

12 asparagus spears, peeled if thick, cut in 2- or 3-inch lengths
1/3 cup dry white wine

1/4 pound medium-size shrimp, shelled and deveined
1 tablespoon minced fresh parsley

Preheat oven to 400°F. Remove neck and giblets from chicken. Pull out fat from inside chicken on both sides near tail. Cut off tail and wing tips and pat chicken dry. Season evenly outside and inside with salt and pepper, and truss, if desired.

Heat oil and butter in heavy 4- to 5-quart oval enamel-lined cast-iron casserole over medium-high heat. Set chicken on its side in casserole. Cover pan with a large splatter screen, if desired, and brown about 3 minutes. (If fat begins to turn dark brown at any time, reduce heat to medium.) Using 2 wooden spoons to prevent chicken skin from tearing (and standing back to avoid splatters), gently turn chicken onto its breast and brown about 3 minutes. Turn chicken onto other side and brown 3 minutes more. Turn chicken on its back and brown 2 minutes.

Baste chicken with pan juices. Cover casserole and bake in oven until juices run clear when thickest part of leg is pierced with thin knife or skewer, about 35 minutes; if juices are still pink, bake a few minutes more and test again. (Chicken can be kept warm in casserole, covered, for 15 minutes.)

While chicken cooks, prepare sauce and asparagus.

CÈPE CREAM

Remove cèpes from water, rinse with cold water, and drain well. Cut in 1-inch pieces. In a medium saucepan, bring cèpes and stock to a boil. Cook, uncovered, over medium heat 7 minutes. Add cream and return to a boil. Simmer over medium heat, stirring occasionally, until thick enough to lightly coat a spoon, about 5 minutes.

Cook asparagus in a medium saucepan of boiling salted water until barely tender, about 2 minutes. Drain, rinse with cold water, and drain well.

When chicken is cooked, transfer it to platter, reserving juices in casserole. Discard trussing strings, if used. Carve in 4 pieces (2 breast pieces with wings attached and 2 leg pieces with thighs attached). Cover chicken with foil and keep warm.

Skim as much fat as possible from juices in casserole. Bring juices to a boil, add wine, and return to a boil, skimming fat frequently. Boil until reduced by about half, about 2 minutes. Reduce heat to low, add cèpe sauce, and bring to a simmer. Add shrimp and asparagus and cook, stirring, about 2 minutes, or until shrimp are pink. Taste and adjust seasoning.

Spoon some sauce, with shrimp and asparagus, over chicken pieces, and sprinkle with fresh parsley. Serve remaining sauce separately.

CHICKEN EN COCOTTE WITH BELGIAN ENDIVE
Poulet à la flamande

In northern France, where Belgian endive is grown and used in a variety of ways, cooks often prepare this entrée with either chicken or pheasant. The bird and the endive finish cooking together so that the poultry juices lend their aroma and flavor to the endive. Diced onion and carrot bake in the casserole with the chicken to enhance the sauce, which is a simple essence of the juices deglazed with wine and stock. The ideal partner for this regional specialty is a sweet vegetable, such as glazed carrots or steamed or baked beets, to balance the endive's natural bitterness. For a special dinner, accompany the chicken with a timbale of carrots or beets, for which you can find recipes in *Vegetable Creations*, the first volume of the Fresh from France series.   MAKES 4 SERVINGS

3 tablespoons butter	1 onion, finely diced
1 pound Belgian endives	1 small carrot, finely diced
Salt and freshly ground pepper	1/4 cup dry white wine
1 roasting chicken (4 1/2 to 5 pounds), room temperature	1/4 cup chicken stock or packaged broth
2 tablespoons vegetable oil	1 tablespoon minced fresh parsley

Preheat oven to 400°F. Soften 2 tablespoons butter and spread in a heavy ovenproof saucepan just large enough to hold endives in one layer. Trim any brown spots from endive leaves and from bases. Set endives in saucepan and season with salt and pepper.

Remove neck and giblets from chicken. Pull out fat from inside chicken on both sides near tail. Cut off tail and wing tips and pat chicken dry. Season evenly outside and inside with salt and pepper, and truss, if desired.

Heat oil and remaining tablespoon butter in large, heavy oval enamel-lined cast-iron casserole over medium-high heat. Set chicken on its side in casserole. Cover pan with a large splatter screen, if desired, and brown about 3 minutes. (If fat begins to turn dark brown at any time, reduce heat to medium.) Using 2 wooden spoons to prevent chicken skin from tearing (and standing back to avoid splatters), gently turn chicken onto its breast and brown about 3 minutes. Turn chicken onto other side and brown 3 minutes more. Turn chicken on its back and brown 2 minutes.

Baste chicken with pan juices. Add onion and carrot, placing them around chicken in pan, and stir into juices. Cover casserole and transfer to oven.

Cover endives very tightly and heat over medium heat until butter begins to sizzle. Transfer to oven and bake both endives and chicken 30 minutes.

Remove chicken and endives from their respective pans. Skim as much fat as possible from chicken juices. Bring juices to a boil. Add wine and stock and return to a boil. Boil, stirring and scraping any browned bits from sides and bottom of casserole, until slightly thickened, about 2 minutes. Strain sauce into a small saucepan, pressing on vegetables, and reserve sauce.

Transfer endives and their juices to casserole, turning them over and pushing them to side of pan. Set chicken in center. Cover, return to oven, and bake about 10 minutes, or until juices run clear when thickest part of leg is pierced with thin knife and endives are very tender when pierced near base. If chicken juices are still pink, bake a few minutes more and test again. If chicken is tender but endives are not, remove chicken, keep warm, and bake endives a few minutes more. Discard juices remaining in casserole. Carve chicken, cover, and keep warm.

Skim fat from reserved sauce, bring to a boil, and taste and adjust seasoning. Serve chicken pieces over or next to endives, and spoon juices over chicken. Sprinkle with parsley.

CHICKEN EN COCOTTE WITH PEPPERS, PERNOD, AND PEAS
Poulet en cocotte aux poivrons et aux petits pois

Both the colorful vegetable mélange and the Pernod-accented sauce are enriched by the chicken's cooking juices. Steamed rice, especially fragrant Basmati, which is now becoming better known in France, is a delicious accompaniment. MAKES 4 SERVINGS

2 medium-size red bell peppers,
    cored, cut in half crosswise,
    ribs and seeds removed
1 chicken (3 1/2 pounds), room
    temperature
Salt and freshly ground pepper
5 tablespoons olive oil

1 pound fresh peas (about 1 cup
    shelled), or 1 cup frozen
2 onions, cut in half and sliced
    thin
2 celery stalks, peeled and sliced
    thin

PERNOD SAUCE
1/2 cup dry white wine
1 teaspoon tomato paste
1/4 teaspoon dried leaf thyme,
    crumbled

2 tablespoons Pernod, plus 1
    teaspoon more, if desired
1 tablespoon butter (optional)

Preheat oven to 400°F. Cut each red pepper half in lengthwise strips about 1/4 inch wide. Remove neck and giblets from chicken. Pull out fat from inside chicken on both sides near tail. Cut off tail and wing tips and pat chicken dry. Season evenly outside and inside with salt and pepper, and truss, if desired.

Heat 3 tablespoons olive oil in heavy 4- to 5-quart oval enamel-lined cast-iron casserole over medium-high heat. Set chicken on its side in casserole. Cover pan with a large splatter screen, if desired, and brown about 3 minutes. (If fat begins to turn dark brown at any time, reduce heat to medium.) Using 2 wooden spoons to prevent chicken skin from tearing (and standing back to avoid splatters), gently turn chicken onto its breast and brown about 3 minutes. Turn chicken onto other side and brown 3 minutes more. Turn chicken on its back and brown 2 minutes.

Baste chicken with pan juices. Cover casserole and bake in oven until juices run clear when thickest part of leg is pierced with thin knife or skewer, about 35 minutes; if juices are still pink, bake a few minutes more and test again.

Prepare vegetables while chicken bakes.

If using fresh peas, cook them in a medium saucepan of boiling salted water about 3 minutes, or until just tender, rinse with cold water, and drain.

Heat remaining 2 tablespoons oil in large skillet over low heat. Add onion and salt and pepper and stir well. Cover and cook, stirring occasionally, 15 minutes. Add peppers and celery, cover, and continue cooking until vegetables are tender, about 20 minutes. If using frozen peas, add them and cook, covered, until just tender, about 2 minutes; if using fresh peas, stir them in. Uncover and remove from heat.

When chicken is tender, transfer it to platter, reserving juices in casserole. Discard trussing strings, if used. Cover chicken with foil and keep warm.

Reheat vegetables, if necessary. Stir in 1 tablespoon pan juices. Taste and adjust seasoning. Cover and keep warm.

PERNOD SAUCE

Skim most of fat from juices and bring to a boil. Add wine and return to a boil, skimming fat frequently. Whisk in tomato paste and thyme. Boil, stirring and scraping any browned bits from sides and bottom of casserole, until sauce is slightly thickened, about 1 minute. Stir in Pernod and bring to a boil. Taste and adjust seasoning. Pour juices from platter of chicken into sauce. Stir in butter, if desired. Taste and add an additional teaspoon Pernod, if desired.

Carve chicken and serve on bed of vegetables, pouring sauce over each chicken piece.

Braised Chicken

Perhaps the best-known French chicken entrée is coq au vin. In my library I have a book on coq au vin that contains sixty-one recipes for the dish, from the various regions of France. Yet coq au vin is only a particular preparation in the general category of braised or stewed chicken, for which the pieces are browned, then simmered gently in a sauce or other liquid. Throughout France cooks use white or red wine as the cooking liquid, but good cooks usually add some chicken stock as well to balance the acidity of the wine. In northern France, the butter-sautéed chicken may cook in beer, while in Provence it is typically sautéed in olive oil, then moistened with a zesty tomato sauce and embellished with black olives. The cooking juices become the sauce for the chicken.

Many of these simple stews have inspired elegant restaurant specialties as well. Braised chicken with fresh tarragon has been featured on the menus of some fine restaurants. For special occasions some cooks finish a braised chicken sauce with foie gras, as in our Chicken with Foie Gras Sauce and Mushroom Purée.

In these easy-to-prepare dishes, the chicken is very moist and tender. Like any stew, braised chicken can be prepared ahead and reheated. Although the traditional way is to use a chicken cut in pieces, you can, of course, buy only those pieces you prefer, such as legs and thighs, and use them instead.

Often vegetables cook alongside the chicken to make a complete main course, as in Beer-Braised Chicken and in Country Chicken with Carrots and Cabbage. Crusty bread is always on the table, and steamed potatoes, rice, or pasta are customary accompaniments.

NIÇOISE CHICKEN WITH TOMATOES AND BLACK OLIVES
Poulet à la niçoise

Black olives, olive oil, and fresh tomato sauce are the hallmarks of many dishes called *à la niçoise*. Niçoise and other French olives are quite strong-flavored and are simmered in water for 2 or 3 minutes before they are added to the sauce, but this is not necessary with American olives. This chicken recipe is also popular with rabbit and is delicious hot, with its traditional accompaniment of fettuccine or ravioli, or cold with a green salad.   MAKES 4 SERVINGS

12 pearl onions
4 tablespoons olive oil
1 teaspoon chopped fresh thyme, or
    1/4 teaspoon dried leaf thyme,
    crumbled
1 chicken (3 to 3 1/2 pounds), cut
    in 8 serving pieces, or 2 1/2 to
    3 pounds chicken pieces

Salt and freshly ground pepper
1 medium-size shallot, minced
2 garlic cloves, minced
2 pounds ripe tomatoes, peeled,
    seeded, and chopped, or two
    28-ounce cans whole plum
    tomatoes, drained and chopped
2/3 cup dry white wine

6 parsley stems, tied with string or
   in cheesecloth

2/3 cup pitted black olives
A few drops of lemon juice

Put pearl onions in a small saucepan, cover with water, and bring to a boil. Boil 1 minute, drain, rinse under cold water, and drain well. Peel with a paring knife.

In a stainless-steel or enameled skillet large enough to hold chicken in one layer, heat 2 tablespoons oil over medium heat. Add onions and thyme and sauté 5 minutes, or until onions are lightly browned. With a slotted spoon, transfer them to a plate.

Pat chicken dry. Add remaining 2 tablespoons oil to skillet and heat over medium-high heat. Season chicken with salt and pepper on both sides and brown it in batches in oil, transferring it with tongs to a plate as it is browned. Discard all but 2 tablespoons fat from skillet.

Add shallot and garlic to skillet and cook over medium heat, stirring, for 30 seconds. Stir in tomatoes and white wine, and add parsley stems. Return chicken pieces to skillet with any juices from plate and bring liquids to a boil. Partially cover and simmer 15 minutes. Add onions, cover, and simmer about 20 minutes, or until chicken breast pieces are tender when pierced with a sharp knife. Using a slotted spoon, transfer them to a plate. Uncover and cook about 15 minutes more, or until onions and remaining chicken pieces are tender; transfer them to plate.

Simmer sauce over medium-high heat for 15 minutes, stirring often, or until it is thick. Discard parsley stems. Taste sauce and adjust seasoning; do not oversalt because olives will be added.

Return chicken and onions to skillet and add olives and lemon juice. Cover and warm over very low heat for 3 minutes. (Chicken can be kept, covered, 1 day in refrigerator. Reheat chicken in sauce in covered skillet over low heat.) Transfer to a platter or plates and serve.

CHICKEN WITH FOIE GRAS SAUCE AND MUSHROOM PURÉE
Poulet au fois gras et à la purée de champignons

This is one of the most marvelous chicken creations I have ever tasted—the secret is its superb sauce. Finishing sauces with foie gras is a special technique that was popular in haute cuisine, lived through the nouvelle revolution, and is still well-loved today. The sauce is very rich and is only for those days when you want to pamper yourself and your guests! The dish is based on a recipe I learned from Michel Comby, the former chef of the celebrated Lucas Carton restaurant in Paris and now the chef of Chez Comby.   MAKES 6 SERVINGS

3 sprigs fresh thyme, or 3/4
    teaspoon dried leaf thyme,
    crumbled
1 bay leaf
5 sprigs parsley
1 1/2 large chickens, cut in 12
    pieces, or 4 pounds chicken
    pieces

Salt and freshly ground pepper
1/4 cup butter
1/2 cup port

MUSHROOM PURÉE

1 1/2 pounds mushrooms
1/4 cup heavy cream

Salt and freshly ground pepper
2 tablespoons bread crumbs

FOIE GRAS SAUCE

6 tablespoons butter, slightly
    softened
6 tablespoons canned foie gras
    "bloc," not mousse or purée
    (one 3 1/2-ounce can)

3/4 cup heavy cream
1 tablespoon chopped fresh parsley

Tie thyme, bay leaf, and parsley sprigs together in cheesecloth to make a bouquet garni. Season chicken on both sides with salt and pepper. Melt butter in a very large sauté pan, or divide between 2 large sauté pans, over medium-high heat. Add chicken pieces in batches and brown lightly. Return all chicken to pan or pans. Add port and bouquet garni. Cover and cook over low heat, turning pieces once or twice, until tender, about 20 minutes for breast pieces, about 5 minutes more for remaining pieces.

MUSHROOM PURÉE

Cut mushrooms in half or quarters, depending on size. Chop mushrooms in 2 batches in food processor or with a knife until fairly fine, but with some distinct pieces remaining. Heat cream in a large sauté pan or skillet until bubbling, and add mushrooms and salt and pepper. Cook, uncovered, over medium-high heat about 7 minutes. Add bread crumbs and heat briefly over low heat. Mixture should be a thick purée. If it is thin, cook it over low heat until it thickens. Taste and adjust seasoning. Cover and set aside.

When chicken is tender, put pieces on a platter, cover and keep warm in a 250°F. oven. Discard bouquet garni. Reheat mushroom purée, if necessary, and keep warm over very low heat.

FOIE GRAS SAUCE

Mash softened butter slightly in a small bowl. Add foie gras and mash together until very smooth.

Pour chicken juices into a measuring cup and skim off most of fat. Pour into a medium saucepan and boil, stirring, until reduced to about ⅓ cup. Add cream, bring to a boil, and simmer until thick enough to lightly coat a spoon.

Remove from heat. Add foie gras–butter mixture by spoonfuls and whisk into sauce. Taste and adjust seasoning. Do not reheat.

To serve, spoon mushroom purée onto plates, top with chicken pieces, spoon sauce over them, and sprinkle with parsley.

BEER-BRAISED CHICKEN
Poulet à la bière

Beer, like wine, becomes mellow after simmering and is often poured into the poultry and meat casseroles of northern and eastern France. In this dish, the sweetness of carrots and turnips balances the beer's slight bitterness.　　　　　MAKES 4 SERVINGS

4 large thin carrots of uniform size
    and shape (about 1 pound)
5 small turnips of uniform size and
    shape (about 12 ounces)
2 sprigs fresh thyme, or 1/2
    teaspoon dried leaf thyme
1 bay leaf
5 sprigs parsley
2 pounds chicken legs and thighs
    (4 legs and 4 thighs), patted
    dry

Salt and freshly ground pepper
1 tablespoon vegetable oil
1 tablespoon butter
1 onion, chopped
1 tablespoon all-purpose flour
One 12-ounce bottle or can of beer
    (1 1/2 cups)
Pinch of cayenne pepper
1 garlic clove, crushed
1 tablespoon minced fresh parsley

Dice enough carrot to make 1/2 cup and reserve. Cut remaining carrots in 1 1/2-inch lengths and cut them in half lengthwise. Cut turnips in quarters from top to bottom. Tie thyme, bay leaf, and parsley sprigs together with string or in cheesecloth to make a bouquet garni.

Season chicken lightly with salt and pepper. Heat oil and butter in a large deep skillet or sauté pan over medium-high heat. Add chicken in several batches and brown lightly on all sides. Transfer to a plate. Pour off fat into small bowl and return 2 tablespoons to pan.

Add onion and diced carrot and cook over medium heat until onion is soft and beginning to brown. Sprinkle with flour and stir over low heat 2 minutes. Stir in beer. Return chicken to pan and add juices from plate. Add cayenne pepper, bouquet garni, and garlic, and bring to a simmer. Cover and cook over low heat, stirring occasionally, about 20 minutes, or until chicken is tender.

Meanwhile, cook vegetables. Put remaining carrots in a saucepan, add water to cover and a pinch of salt. Bring to a boil. Reduce heat to medium-low, cover, and simmer until carrots are tender, about 15 minutes. Drain well. Cook turnips same way as carrots, but only until barely tender, about 7 minutes. Drain well.

When chicken is done, remove pieces to a plate. Cook sauce, uncovered, until thick enough to lightly coat a spoon. Strain sauce, pressing on vegetables. Return to sauté pan. (Chicken and vegetables can be kept in sauce, covered, 1 day in refrigerator.)

Reheat chicken and vegetables gently in sauce. Taste and adjust seasoning. Sprinkle with parsley and serve.

CHICKEN IN FRESH TARRAGON SAUCE
Poulet à l'estragon

Tarragon is a favorite herb in the French kitchen, especially with chicken, and many versions of this classic are prepared by home cooks and restaurant chefs. Here the tarragon combines with the chicken juices, along with tomatoes and cream, to make a luscious sauce. Steamed potatoes or rice would make a perfect complement, as would green or wax beans. Or, follow the example of Maxim's in Paris, and add glazed pearl onions and sautéed mushrooms to the sauce at the last moment.   MAKES 4 SERVINGS

1 bunch fresh tarragon	8 to 10 ounces ripe tomatoes,
1 chicken (3 1/2 pounds), cut in 8	peeled, seeded, and chopped, or
serving pieces, or 3 pounds	3/4 cup chopped canned
chicken pieces	tomatoes
Salt and freshly ground pepper	1/2 cup Chicken Stock (see recipe)
1 tablespoon vegetable oil	or packaged broth
1 tablespoon butter	1 cup heavy cream

Remove tarragon leaves from stems and reserve each separately. Tie stems together with string or cheesecloth. Chop leaves.

Pat chicken pieces dry and season lightly with salt and pepper on all sides. Heat oil and butter in large heavy skillet over medium-high heat. Add chicken pieces in batches and brown well on all sides. Using tongs or a slotted spoon, remove to a plate. Discard fat from skillet.

Return chicken pieces to skillet. If they do not fit in one layer, arrange breast and wing pieces on top. Add chicken juices from plate, tomatoes, stock, and tarragon stems, pushing them under chicken, and bring to a simmer. Cover and simmer over low heat about 15 minutes, or until breast pieces are tender. Transfer to a platter with a slotted spoon, cover, and keep warm. Cook remaining chicken pieces about 5 minutes more, or until all are tender. Add leg and thigh pieces to platter and keep warm. Discard back pieces, neck, and wing tips. (Chicken can be kept in sauce, covered, 1 day in refrigerator.)

Skim as much fat as possible from juices in skillet, tilting skillet to make skimming easier. Add cream to skillet and bring to a boil, skimming often. Strain sauce into a sauté pan or shallow saucepan, pressing on tomatoes. Simmer, stirring and skimming often, until sauce is thick enough to coat a spoon. Add chopped tarragon; taste and adjust seasoning. Use paper towels to blot fat from chicken platter. Pour sauce over chicken and serve.

❧ COUNTRY CHICKEN WITH CABBAGE AND CARROTS
Poulet au chou et aux carottes

Chicken with cabbage might seem an unlikely pair, but cooks in northern France have popularized it by developing tasty entrées like this one, in which the cabbage strips are briefly blanched, then gently braised with the chicken and carrots to absorb their flavors. Rustic dishes of this type have a timeless appeal, and are currently enjoying tremendous popularity on restaurant menus. Serve the chicken with steamed or boiled potatoes.   MAKES 4 SERVINGS

*3 medium-size carrots, scraped and
    cut in 2-inch lengths*
*1 1/2 cups Chicken Stock (see recipe)
    or packaged broth*
1/4 teaspoon sugar
Salt and freshly ground pepper
*1/2 medium-size head green cabbage
    (about 1 1/2 pounds), cored
    and rinsed*

*1 chicken (3 pounds), cut in
    serving pieces, or 2 1/2 pounds
    chicken pieces*
1 tablespoon vegetable oil
2 tablespoons butter
1 onion, thinly sliced

Cut thick carrot pieces in quarters lengthwise; cut thin pieces in half lengthwise. In a medium saucepan, combine carrot pieces, chicken stock, sugar, and salt and pepper to taste and bring stock to a boil. Simmer, covered, over medium-low heat for 30 minutes, or until tender. Cook over high heat, uncovered, until stock is reduced to about 3/4 cup. Drain carrots, reserving cooking liquid.

Cut cabbage in strips. In a large pan of boiling salted water, boil cabbage for 5 minutes. Drain, rinse under running cold water, and squeeze out excess liquid.

Pat chicken dry and season with salt and pepper. In a stainless-steel or enameled skillet large enough to hold chicken in one layer, heat oil and 1 tablespoon butter over medium-high heat. Add chicken and brown it. Using tongs, transfer it to a plate.

Add onion to skillet and cook over low heat, stirring, for 7 minutes, or until softened. Add cabbage and salt and pepper and cook over low heat, stirring, for 3 minutes. Return chicken pieces to skillet and add chicken juices from plate and half of carrot-cooking liquid. Cover and cook over low heat for 15 minutes, or until breasts are just tender. With a slotted spoon, transfer breasts to a platter, cover, and keep warm. Cook legs and wings over low heat, covered, for 5 minutes more, or until they are tender; transfer them to platter, cover, and keep warm.

Drain remaining carrot cooking liquid into skillet and boil until it is absorbed by cabbage. Taste and adjust seasoning. Stir in remaining butter. Transfer chicken pieces to heated plates, spoon cabbage alongside chicken, and set carrot pieces on top.

CHICKEN WITH EGGPLANT AND COUSCOUS
Poulet à l'aubergine et au couscous

In this easy Mediterranean-style entrée, the chicken is braised with tomatoes, onion, and eggplant. It is paired with couscous, which is enhanced with the chicken's cooking juices. MAKES 4 SERVINGS

*1 chicken (3 1/2 pounds), cut in 8
    serving pieces, or 3 pounds
    chicken pieces*
Salt and freshly ground pepper
*2 tablespoons olive oil or vegetable
    oil*
1 large onion, cut in thin slices
2 garlic cloves, chopped
1 small eggplant, peeled and diced

*3 ripe tomatoes, peeled, seeded, and
    chopped*
1 bay leaf
*1 teaspoon fresh thyme leaves, or
    1/4 teaspoon dried leaf thyme,
    crumbled*
*1/3 cup Chicken Stock (see recipe)
    or packaged broth*

QUICK COUSCOUS

5 tablespoons butter, room	*Pinch of salt*
temperature	*1 cup hot Chicken Stock (see recipe)*
1 1/4 cups couscous	*or packaged broth*

1 tablespoon chopped fresh parsley

Season chicken lightly with salt and pepper. Heat oil in a very large, deep skillet or sauté pan. Add chicken in several batches and brown lightly on all sides. Remove to a plate. Add onion and cook over low heat until soft but not brown. Add garlic and cook about 30 seconds. Stir in eggplant, then tomatoes, and add bay leaf and thyme. Cook 2 or 3 minutes, stirring often. Return chicken to pan and add stock. Cover and simmer over low heat 30 to 35 minutes, or until tender. (Chicken can be kept, covered, 1 day in refrigerator.)

QUICK COUSCOUS

Heat 1 tablespoon butter in a heavy-based small saucepan. Add couscous and cook over low heat, stirring with a fork, about 1 minute, or until it absorbs the butter. Add salt and hot chicken stock and cover. Set over low heat for 1 minute, turn off heat, and leave for 5 minutes. Fluff gently with a fork. Add remaining 4 tablespoons butter in pieces, cover, and leave 1 minute. Toss again with a fork until butter is absorbed. Taste and, if couscous is not yet tender, add 2 tablespoons very hot water or cooking liquid from chicken, cover, and leave another 2 minutes until absorbed. Toss again with a fork, cover, and keep warm.

When chicken is tender, remove pieces of chicken and eggplant; don't worry if a few eggplant pieces remain in sauce. Discard bay leaf. Boil sauce for 2 or 3 minutes to thicken it slightly and concentrate flavors. Taste and adjust seasoning. Return chicken and eggplant pieces to sauce, cover, and keep warm.

Spoon couscous onto center of a large platter. Arrange chicken and eggplant around it, moisten them with sauce, and sprinkle with chopped parsley. Serve remaining sauce separately.

Grilled Chicken

Though some modern chefs act as if they have "invented" grilling, the technique is ancient and its delicious results have been appreciated for thousands of years. The appetizing aroma and flavor of chicken grilled over an open fire cannot be achieved by any other cooking method. It is a superb way to enjoy high-quality poultry.

All the flavors of chicken are highlighted by grilling. Browned crisp skin hides tender juicy meat. During grilling, the skin and outer layer of meat is seared from the heat of the grill so it protects the inner part of the meat and helps keep in the juices.

To help keep the chicken moist, French cooks like to brush it with an oil-based marinade, particularly one that combines olive oil, garlic, and herbs. Mustard is also a popular seasoning for grilled chicken; it is often spread on the chicken pieces, which are then rolled lightly in bread crumbs and sprinkled with melted butter before being grilled. As the bird grills, some cooks like to use branches of rosemary as a basting brush.

In France, grilled chicken is frequently prepared on a ridged stove-top grill. This is a useful implement for indoor grilling, and the nonstick versions are easy to use. Use of the stove-top grill produces more of a smoky grilled taste than the broiler does. (The broiler tends to produce a steamed effect.)

Traditional French partners for grilled chicken are usually simple: a sauce of lightly cooked fresh tomatoes, a zesty tartar sauce, or sometimes a vinegar-accented *sauce diable* as in Deviled Duck with Brussels Sprouts. Often there is no sauce at all, but rather a few lemon wedges, or a flavored butter, as in Grilled Chicken with Cilantro-Lime Butter and Green Beans. Grilled mushroom caps and grilled tomatoes are favorite accompaniments, as are French fried potatoes and fried onions. But you can also serve baked potatoes, fresh corn, or any lightly cooked vegetable in season. Or follow the example of many French cooks and make the grilled chicken the star ingredient in a main-course salad.

Hints

- Be careful when grilling chicken: if it is too close to the coals or other heat source, it will burn on the outside and remain raw inside.
- Boneless chicken pieces are easiest to grill because they cook quickly.
- When time allows, bring the poultry to room temperature before grilling or broiling so it cooks quickly and evenly.
- Preheat the broiler with its rack and pan inside for about 10 minutes. A hot rack or grill is essential for searing the poultry properly. If it is not hot enough, the meat will stick.
- Leave a little room between the pieces of poultry on the grill; crowding lowers the temperature and can cause the meat to steam.

GRILLED CHICKEN WITH CILANTRO-LIME BUTTER AND GREEN BEANS
Poulet grillé au beurre de coriandre et aux haricots verts

Simple dishes are often the most delicious and this is certainly a good example—sizzling hot chicken with a tangy herb butter and crisp-tender green beans. A light marinade flavors the chicken and helps keep it moist during grilling. The seasoned butter is heated with the green beans and is also spooned onto the chicken at the serving time, melting in contact with the meat's hot surface and forming a simple sauce.   MAKES 4 SERVINGS

2 tablespoons olive or vegetable oil
2 tablespoons strained fresh lime
    juice
Salt and pepper to taste
1 tablespoon coarsely chopped
    cilantro (fresh coriander)

1/2 onion, sliced
4 boneless chicken breast halves or
    thighs, with skin (total about
    1 1/2 pounds)

CILANTRO-LIME BUTTER

6 tablespoons butter, softened
1 1/2 teaspoons strained fresh lime
    juice

3 tablespoons chopped cilantro
    (fresh coriander)
Salt and freshly ground pepper

1 pound green beans, ends trimmed
Lime wedges and cilantro sprigs for
    garnish (optional)

Mix oil, lime juice, salt and pepper, cilantro, and onion in shallow dish. Add chicken and turn until coated with mixture. Cover and marinate at room temperature 1 hour or in refrigerator up to 6 hours, turning from time to time.

CILANTRO-LIME BUTTER

Beat butter until very soft, and gradually beat in lime juice. Stir in cilantro. Season with salt and pepper to taste. Cover and refrigerate 1 or 2 hours so flavors blend. (Seasoned butter can be kept, covered, 1 day in refrigerator.) Bring to room temperature before using.

Remove chicken from marinade, removing any pieces of onion from chicken. Discard onion, reserving remaining marinade.

Cook beans in a medium saucepan of boiling salted water until just tender, about 5 minutes. Drain, rinse with cold water, and drain well.

Heat a ridged stove-top grill pan over medium-high heat, prepare a charcoal grill, or preheat broiler with rack about 4 inches from heat source. Pat chicken dry and sprinkle chicken with salt and pepper on both sides. Set chicken on broiler rack or on grill or on an oiled rack over glowing coals, skin side down. Grill or broil, brushing once or twice with marinade, for 3 minutes. Turn chicken with tongs and broil or grill, brushing once with marinade, until meat feels springy, about 3 to 6 minutes, depending on thickness. To check whether chicken is done, cut into thickest part with tip of a sharp knife; color should no longer be pink, but white. Remove and keep warm.

Meanwhile, heat 2 tablespoons cilantro butter in saucepan, add beans, salt and pepper, and toss until combined.

Transfer chicken and beans to plates. Garnish with lime wedges and cilantro sprigs. Serve immediately, with cilantro butter.

❦ GRILLED CHICKEN WITH ASPARAGUS, FETTUCCINE, AND MALTAISE CREAM
Poulet grillé aux asperges, aux fettuccine et à la crème maltaise

The well-known Maltaise sauce, or orange hollandaise, the traditional partner for asparagus, reappears here in a new, lighter guise—an essence of white wine simmered with shallots that is enriched with cream and flavored with orange zest and juice. Fettuccine tossed with asparagus and the luscious sauce makes a delectable bed for the grilled chicken breasts.   MAKES 4 SERVINGS

3/4 pound thin asparagus
5 tablespoons butter
5 teaspoons minced shallots
1/2 cup dry white wine
1 1/4 cups heavy cream
Salt and freshly ground pepper
1 pound boneless chicken breasts, with skin, patted dry
1 tablespoon vegetable oil
8 ounces fresh fettuccine, or 6 ounces dried

2 1/2 teaspoons finely grated orange zest
2 1/2 teaspoons strained fresh orange juice
1 1/4 teaspoons strained fresh lemon juice
Thin strips of orange zest for garnish (optional)

Cut off asparagus tips and cut stalks in 1-inch pieces, discarding about 1 1/2 inches of bases. Refrigerate 2 tablespoons butter.

Melt 2 tablespoons butter in a medium saucepan over low heat. Add shallots and cook about 2 minutes, or until softened. Add wine and bring to a boil, stirring. Simmer over medium heat until liquid is reduced to about 1/4 cup, about 3 minutes. Stir in cream and bring to a boil. Simmer over medium heat, stirring occasionally, until mixture is thick enough to lightly coat a spoon, about 4 minutes. Season sauce lightly with salt and pepper. (Sauce can be kept, covered, 1 day in refrigerator.)

Heat a ridged stove-top grill pan over medium-high heat, prepare a charcoal grill, or preheat broiler with rack about 4 inches from heat source. Rub meat side of chicken with 1 tablespoon oil and season with a pinch of salt and pepper. Set chicken on ridged grill pan or broiler rack or on an oiled rack over glowing coals, skin side down. Grill or broil about 7 minutes per side, pressing occasionally on thickest part of chicken with a spatula. To check whether chicken is done, cut into thickest part with tip of a sharp knife; color should no longer be pink, but white. Transfer chicken to a plate and keep warm.

Boil asparagus in a saucepan of boiling salted water for 2 minutes. Drain, rinse under cold water, and drain thoroughly. Melt 1 tablespoon butter in a skillet over medium-low heat. Add asparagus, salt, and pepper, and sauté until tender, about 2 minutes.

Cook pasta in a large pan of boiling salted water over high heat, stirring occasionally, until it is al dente, about 30 seconds to 2 minutes for fresh pasta, 5 minutes for dried. Drain well, and transfer to a bowl. While pasta is cooking, reheat sauce over medium heat, stirring. Add 2 tablespoons cold butter to sauce and stir over low heat just until blended. Add orange zest and juice and lemon juice. Taste and adjust seasoning.

Toss pasta with all but ¼ cup sauce, add asparagus, and transfer mixture to heated plates. Set chicken breasts on top, spoon remaining sauce over them, and garnish top of chicken with orange zest, if desired.

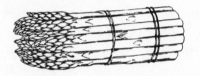

CHICKEN BREAST PAILLARDES WITH SPICED TOMATO SAUCE
Paillardes de poulet, sauce tomate épicée

Chicken *paillardes* are most often sautéed, as in Chicken Paillardes with Tricolored Peppers and Basil, but they can also be grilled, as in this entrée. They should be watched carefully so they do not overcook. Here the chicken is set on a bed of tangy tomato sauce, flavored with cumin and cilantro, an influence of the many North African cooks in France. For a light summer dinner, rice pilaf makes an excellent accompaniment. MAKES 4 SERVINGS

SPICED TOMATO SAUCE

2 tablespoons vegetable oil
1/2 onion, minced
2 garlic cloves, minced
1 teaspoon ground cumin
1/4 teaspoon turmeric
2 pounds ripe tomatoes, peeled,
     seeded, and finely chopped, or
     two 28-ounce cans whole plum
     tomatoes, drained and chopped

Salt and freshly ground pepper
Pinch of cayenne pepper
2 teaspoons tomato paste (optional)
2 1/2 teaspoons minced cilantro
     (fresh coriander) or fresh
     parsley

4 whole boneless chicken breasts
     from small chickens (6 to 7
     ounces each), skinned
Salt and freshly ground pepper

2 tablespoons vegetable oil
4 small sprigs cilantro or parsley
     for garnish

SPICED TOMATO SAUCE

Heat oil in large saucepan over low heat. Add onion and cook, stirring occasionally, until soft but not brown. Add garlic and cook, stirring, 30 seconds. Add cumin and turmeric and cook, stirring, 30 seconds. Add tomatoes, salt, pepper, and cayenne and stir well. Bring to boil over medium-high heat. Reduce heat to low and cook, uncovered, stirring occasionally, until tomatoes are very soft, about 30 minutes. Sauce will be chunky. Add tomato paste if a brighter color is desired. (Sauce can be kept, covered, 1 day in refrigerator.)

Trim chicken breasts of excess fat and cartilage. Pound them individually between 2 pieces of plastic wrap or wax paper to 1/4-inch thickness, using flat meat pounder or rolling pin. Preheat oven to 275°F.

Reheat sauce and add minced cilantro. Taste and adjust seasoning. Cover sauce and keep warm.

Heat ridged grill pan over medium-high heat until very hot; when one end of chicken breast is touched to grill, it should make sizzling noise. Pat *paillardes* dry, season with salt and pepper, and brush with oil. Put 1 or 2 *paillardes* on grill, depending on its size. Cook 1 1/2 minutes per side, brushing lightly with oil before turning. Use 2 wide spatulas to turn chicken. Chicken is done when no longer pink inside; cut to check. Transfer chicken to ovenproof platter or plates, cover, and keep warm in oven while grilling remaining *pail-lardes.*

Divide sauce among 4 plates and set *paillardes* on top, letting sauce show from sides. Garnish with cilantro or parsley sprigs.

⚜ GRILLED CHICKEN AND AVOCADO SALAD WITH OLIVES, TOMATOES, AND MINT
Salade de poulet grillé aux avocats, aux olives, aux tomates, et à la menthe

Grilling chicken, then seasoning it with vinaigrette, is a marvelous way to prepare chicken salad. Avocado adds richness, while tomatoes and mint give the salad a fresh touch. Serve this salad as a colorful buffet platter, or as a light main course.

MAKES 4 SERVINGS

1 ½ *pounds boneless chicken breast,* · *with skin, patted dry*
1 *tablespoon olive oil*

½ *teaspoon dried oregano, crumbled*
Salt and freshly ground pepper

LEMON DRESSING
1 *tablespoon plus 1 teaspoon strained fresh lemon juice*
5 *tablespoons extra-virgin olive oil*
Pinch of cayenne pepper, or ¼ *teaspoon hot pepper sauce*

½ *teaspoon dried oregano, crumbled*
Salt and freshly ground pepper
¼ *cup chopped red onion*

½ *cup Niçoise or other oil-cured black olives, cut in half and pitted*
¼ *cup chopped fresh mint*
3 *tablespoons chopped Italian parsley*
1 *medium-size or 2 small ripe tomatoes (about 6 ounces), diced*

2 *medium-size ripe California avocados (about 1* ¼ *pounds), preferably Haas*
12 *to 16 leaves Boston or butter lettuce (optional)*

Heat a ridged stove-top grill pan over medium-high heat, prepare a charcoal grill, or preheat broiler with rack about 4 inches from heat source. Rub meat side of chicken with oil and sprinkle with oregano and a pinch of salt and pepper. Set chicken on ridged grill pan or broiler rack or on an oiled rack over glowing coals, skin side down. Grill or broil about 7 minutes per side, pressing occasionally on thickest part of chicken with a spatula. To check whether chicken is done, cut into thickest part with tip of a sharp knife; color should no longer be pink, but white. Transfer chicken to a plate, let cool to room temperature, and discard any juices that escape from it. Remove skin. Cut chicken in about ¾-inch cubes.

LEMON DRESSING

In a medium bowl, combine lemon juice, oil, cayenne or hot pepper sauce, oregano, and salt and pepper to taste, and whisk until blended. Stir in onion.

Add chicken cubes to dressing, and taste and adjust seasoning. Let marinate for 1 hour at room temperature, stirring occasionally. Add olives, mint, parsley, and tomatoes. A short time before serving, cut avocados in half and remove pits. Using a small melon-ball cutter, shape avocado pulp into balls and add them to salad. Toss salad gently, and taste and adjust seasoning. (Salad can be kept, covered tightly, 1 hour in refrigerator.)

If desired, put 3 or 4 lettuce leaves on each plate. To serve, spoon salad onto center of lettuce or into salad bowls.

NOTE: Oil-cured black olives are available at specialty foods shops.

SEE PHOTOGRAPH.

Sautéed Turkey

Brillat Savarin, the famous French food writer of the early nineteenth century, called turkey "one of the finest gifts that the New World gave the Old." The Old World's cooks returned the favor by developing techniques and sauces that we enjoy using for our turkeys.

Today turkey is the second most popular type of poultry for home cooking in France and the United States, and roasting is the customary way to prepare it in both countries. For small gatherings, however, a whole turkey is sometimes just too large. And since several hours are required to roast a whole turkey, the breast meat tends to dry out if it is not basted often.

The solution to these problems is to plan festive meals around turkey breasts, using an easy formula: The briefly cooked meat is accompanied by a smooth, quick-to-prepare sauce and colorful fresh vegetables in season. Each plate is arranged attractively, with the turkey slices coated with sauce in the center, or set atop the sauce, and the vegetables encircling them.

The French treat turkey breast slices much like veal scallops. In many Paris markets *escalopes de dinde* or turkey breast slices are a relatively new item that is now sold alongside the *escalopes de veau* or thin veal slices. Sautéing is the best cooking technique because it enables the turkey breast to cook quickly and remain moist.

Turkey breasts are very lean, and so are an ideal companion for the wonderful, modern French cream-reduction sauces and butter sauces. Although rich, these marvelous sauces are more light-textured than traditional sauces because no flour is used. They are a delight to the cook in a hurry, since most are ready in just a few minutes.

Hints

• The sauces in the recipes in this section also make great accompaniments to briefly reheated slices of roast turkey, and turn these leftovers into a feast.

• All the recipes prepared with turkey breast slices can also be made with boned, skinned chicken breasts.

🐚 TURKEY SLICES WITH BEER BEURRE BLANC, CHARD, AND CARROTS
Escalopes de dinde au beurre blanc à la bière, aux blettes, et aux carottes

In this special-occasion dish, the lean turkey breast meat is complemented by the creamy beer beurre blanc, a new variation of the classic sauce. If Swiss chard is not available, substitute spinach, or choose another green vegetable such as broccoli florets, green beans, or sautéed zucchini sticks.   MAKES 4 SERVINGS

2 pounds Swiss chard

BEER BEURRE BLANC

2 medium-size shallots, minced
½ cup beer
¼ cup heavy cream

Salt and freshly ground pepper
½ cup cold butter, cut in 8 pieces

¾ pound large carrots, cut in ¼-inch slices
4 to 5 tablespoons butter
Salt and freshly ground pepper

1 to 1¼ pounds turkey breast slices (³⁄₈-inch thick), patted dry
2 tablespoons vegetable oil

Remove chard stalks and thick white veins and discard or reserve for other uses. Rinse leaves thoroughly. Pile chard leaves and cut them crosswise in ½-inch-wide strips.

BEER BEURRE BLANC

In a small saucepan, cook shallots in beer over medium-high heat until about 3 tablespoons liquid remain, about 5 minutes. Add cream and bring to a boil. Simmer 1 minute, and add a pinch of salt and pepper. (Sauce can be kept, covered, several hours at room temperature. Keep butter in refrigerator.)

Put carrots in a saucepan, cover with water, and add a pinch of salt. Bring to a boil, reduce heat to low, cover, and simmer about 7 minutes, or until just tender. Drain all but a few tablespoons water. Cover and keep warm.

Heat 3 tablespoons butter in a large skillet or sauté pan over medium-low heat. Add about half the chard and a pinch of salt and pepper. Cook, stirring often, about 6 minutes, or until tender. Transfer to a plate with a slotted spoon. Add 1 tablespoon butter to skillet, if needed, and heat over low heat. Cook remaining chard in same way. Return all of chard to pan and remove from heat.

Season turkey with salt and pepper on both sides. Heat oil and 1 tablespoon butter in a large heavy skillet over medium-high heat. Add half the turkey slices and sauté about 1 ½ minutes per side, or until they just change color inside; cut to check. Transfer to a plate and keep warm. Repeat with remaining turkey and transfer to plate.

Reheat chard, stirring, then taste and adjust seasoning. Reheat carrots in their covered saucepan; drain water.

To finish sauce, bring shallot mixture to a simmer. Set pan over low heat and add cold butter pieces, 1 at a time, whisking, adding each after previous one is incorporated. Remove from heat and taste and adjust seasoning.

Remove turkey from plate, discarding any liquid that has accumulated. Make a ring of chard on each serving plate and set turkey in center. Put carrot slices on opposite sides of turkey. Pour a little sauce over turkey, and serve remaining sauce separately.

SAUTÉED TURKEY WITH BASIL AND SUMMER VEGETABLES
Escalopes de dinde au basilic et aux légumes d'été

Green and yellow zucchini and red and green peppers are spooned around the turkey for this quick Mediterranean-style entrée. Diced tomatoes, a hint of garlic, and plenty of basil give the fresh finishing touch. The basil is cut in chiffonnade, or thin strips—a quick and easy alternative to chopping, and the basil keeps its color better.

Chicken breast halves are also superb prepared this way. The only accompaniment this colorful dish needs is crusty French or Italian bread, or saffron-flavored rice or pasta.   MAKES 4 SERVINGS

1 pound boneless turkey breast
    (turkey tenderloins)
1 medium-size green bell pepper
1 medium-size red bell pepper
2 medium-size green zucchini
    (about 1/2 pound)
2 medium-size yellow zucchini or
    yellow squash (about 1/2
    pound)
1 large ripe tomato (about 3/4
    pound), peeled and seeded

6 tablespoons olive oil
1 1/2 teaspoons fresh thyme leaves,
    or 1/2 teaspoon dried leaf
    thyme, crumbled
Salt and freshly ground pepper
1/4 cup chicken stock
2 teaspoons strained fresh lemon
    juice
1/2 cup thin strips of basil leaves
1 large garlic clove, minced

Cut turkey in thin diagonal slices about 1/4 inch thick, and pat dry. Cut bell peppers, both types zucchini, and tomato in small (about 1/2-inch) dice; keep separately at room temperature.

Heat 3 tablespoons oil in a large heavy deep skillet or sauté pan over medium heat. Add peppers and sauté about 2 minutes. Add green and yellow zucchini, thyme, and salt and pepper. Cover and cook about 4 minutes, stirring occasionally, or until vegetables are just tender. Remove from heat.

Meanwhile, season turkey with salt and pepper on both sides. Heat remaining 3 tablespoons oil in a large heavy skillet over medium-high heat. Add turkey and sauté 1 1/2 to 2 minutes per side, or until just tender and no longer pink inside; cut to check. Transfer to a plate, cover, and keep warm. Leave oil in skillet.

Add stock to skillet and bring to a boil, stirring. Add liquid from plate of turkey. Remove from heat and add lemon juice, then taste and adjust seasoning. Add half the basil strips.

Quickly reheat vegetables over high heat. Remove from heat and stir in garlic, then tomato and remaining basil strips. Spoon sauce over turkey and serve vegetables on the side.

NOTES: If boned and skinned chicken breasts are substituted for turkey, sauté them, pressing on them with a spatula, about 3 minutes per side.

If desired, use a decorative cutter to cut some of the zucchini in fluted strips.

SEE PHOTOGRAPH.

TURKEY BREASTS WITH MUSTARD SAUCE AND SNOW PEAS
Escalopes de dinde à la dijonnaise aux pois gourmands

Steamed new potatoes or beets are fine accompaniments for this turkey and its creamy, zesty sauce. Always taste mustard sauces to decide whether to add more mustard, because the different brands vary in strength. If you like, substitute Brussels sprouts for the snow peas.   MAKES 4 SERVINGS

3 tablespoons butter
½ onion, chopped
2 tablespoons white wine vinegar
¼ cup dry white wine
Pinch of dried leaf thyme
1 small bay leaf
Salt
1 cup heavy cream

½ teaspoon tomato paste
¼ pound snow peas, ends removed
Freshly ground pepper
1 ½ pounds turkey breast slices
*   (¼- to ½-inch thick), patted*
*   dry*
3 tablespoons vegetable oil
2 to 3 teaspoons Dijon mustard

Melt 1 tablespoon butter in a medium saucepan. Add onion and cook over low heat, stirring often, about 10 minutes, or until soft but not brown. Add vinegar, wine, thyme, bay leaf, and a pinch of salt and simmer until nearly all liquid evaporates. Stir in cream and bring to a boil, stirring. Simmer over low heat 5 minutes, stirring often, then stir in tomato paste. Continue simmering, stirring often, 5 minutes more, or until thickened. Strain into another saucepan, pressing hard on onion. (Sauce can be kept, covered, 1 day in refrigerator.)

Cook snow peas in a medium saucepan of boiling salted water, uncovered, over high heat 1 minute, or until crisp-tender. Drain, rinse with cold water, and drain well.

Heat 1 tablespoon butter in a skillet or sauté pan over medium heat. Add snow peas and salt and pepper and sauté until heated. Cover and keep warm.

Season turkey with salt and pepper on both sides. Heat oil and remaining tablespoon butter in a large skillet or sauté pan. Add enough turkey slices to make one layer. Sauté over medium-high heat about 2 minutes on each side, or until just tender when pierced with a sharp knife; do not overcook or meat will be dry. Remove turkey slices. Sauté remaining slices and remove them.

Meanwhile, reheat sauce over low heat, stirring often. Whisk in 2 teaspoons mustard, then taste and adjust seasoning. Add more mustard, if desired.

To serve, put turkey breasts on plates and coat with sauce. Serve with snow peas on the side.

CRISP TURKEY PAILLARDES WITH CAPERS
Paillardes de dinde aux câpres

I find this one of the best ways to prepare turkey breasts. An egg–and–bread crumb coating keeps the lean turkey meat juicy and helps hold any fragile slices together in a neat shape, in a way similar to the veal in the Austrian *wiener schnitzel* and the Italian *costolette alla milanese*. In France, the sautéed turkey is moistened with nut-brown butter. For a zesty garnish, the turkey slices are topped with tiny lemon dice, capers, and parsley.   MAKES 4 SERVINGS

1 1/4 pounds turkey breast slices (about 8 slices), about 1/4 inch thick
1 lemon
1/3 cup all-purpose flour
3/4 cup unseasoned dry bread crumbs

2 eggs
Salt and freshly ground pepper
3 tablespoons vegetable oil
7 tablespoons butter
2 tablespoons capers, drained
2 tablespoons minced fresh parsley

If any of the turkey slices is thicker than 1/4 inch, pound it between 2 pieces of plastic wrap or wax paper to even thickness of 1/4 inch, using flat meat pounder or rolling pin.

Cut peel from lemon, cutting away any white pith. Section lemon by cutting inward to center of fruit on each side of the white membrane that divides sections; hold lemon over bowl to catch juice.

(Reserve lemon juice for other recipes.) Discard membranes and any seeds, and cut lemon sections in ¼-inch dice. Set aside.

Spread flour on a large plate. Spread bread crumbs on a second plate. Beat eggs in a shallow bowl. Season turkey with salt and pepper on both sides. Lightly coat turkey slice with flour on both sides, tapping and shaking to remove excess. Dip slice in egg, then dip in bread crumbs so turkey is completely coated; pat and press lightly so crumbs adhere. Repeat with remaining slices. As each slice is dipped, transfer to tray or large plate and arrange slices side by side. Handle turkey gently at all stages so coating does not come off.

Heat oil and 3 tablespoons butter in large heavy skillet over medium-high heat. Add enough turkey to make one layer in skillet. Sauté until golden brown on both sides, about 1 minute per side. Turn carefully using 2 wide spatulas. If fat in skillet begins to brown, reduce heat to medium. Transfer turkey slices to ovenproof platter, arrange them side by side, and keep warm in a 275°F. oven while sautéing remaining slices.

To serve, sprinkle turkey with capers, parsley, and lemon dice. Heat remaining 4 tablespoons butter in medium, heavy saucepan (preferably with a light-colored interior) over medium-low heat, shaking pan often, just until butter is light brown. Pour immediately over turkey and serve.

TURKEY BREAST SLICES WITH CURRY SAUCE AND BROCCOLI
Dinde à la sauce curry et aux brocolis

When I taught cooking classes on new ways to prepare turkey, this dish was a favorite of my students. It is delicious, practical, and quick. The light curry sauce can be made ahead and reheated before serving. At mealtime the turkey is briefly sautéed, the broccoli is lightly cooked, and your dinner is ready in minutes.

MAKES 4 SERVINGS

3 tablespoons vegetable oil

3 tablespoons butter

1 large onion, finely chopped

1 tablespoon curry powder

2 cups Chicken Stock (see recipe) or
    packaged broth

1 cup heavy cream

1 1/2 pounds turkey breast slices
    (1/4 to 1/2 inch thick), patted
    dry

Salt and freshly ground pepper

3 bunches broccoli, divided into
    medium florets

Heat 1 tablespoon oil and 1 tablespoon butter in a large skillet or sauté pan. Add onion and cook, stirring often, about 10 minutes, or until soft. Stir in curry powder and cook 2 minutes, stirring. Stir in 1 1/2 cups stock, add a pinch of salt, and bring to a boil. Simmer, stirring often, until about 1 cup mixture remains. Stir in cream and bring to a boil. Simmer 5 minutes, or until sauce is thick enough to coat spoon. (Sauce can be kept, covered, 1 day in refrigerator.)

Season turkey with salt and pepper on both sides. Heat 2 tablespoons oil and 2 tablespoons butter in a large skillet or sauté pan. Add enough turkey slices to make one layer. Sauté over medium-high heat about 2 minutes on each side, or until just tender when pierced with a sharp knife; do not overcook or meat will be dry. Remove turkey slices. Sauté remaining slices and remove them.

Meanwhile, add broccoli florets to a large pan of boiling salted water and boil, uncovered, about 5 minutes, or until just tender. Drain thoroughly.

Reheat sauce gently. Discard excess fat from turkey pan, add remaining 1/2 cup stock, and bring to a boil, scraping up any browned bits. Boil until reduced to about 1/4 cup. Add to sauce and simmer again until thick enough to coat a spoon. Taste and adjust seasoning.

Return turkey breasts to sauce and reheat gently, turning slices to coat them with sauce; do not boil. To serve, put turkey breasts in center of plates or a platter and spoon sauce over them. Arrange broccoli around turkey.

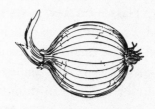

🌿 RICE PILAF WITH TURKEY, ROQUEFORT, AND GREEN ONIONS
Riz pilaf à la dinde, au roquefort et aux oignons nouveaux

This is a very contemporary entrée in that it consists mainly of a grain with a relatively small amount of meat. The rice is combined with lightly sautéed nuggets of turkey. This makes a delightful lunch or light meal, accompanied by a tomato salad. If you have extra cooked turkey or chicken, this recipe is a great way to use it.

MAKES 2 TO 3 LIGHT MAIN-COURSE SERVINGS,
OR 4 TO 6 FIRST-COURSE SERVINGS

10 ounces boneless turkey breasts (turkey breast tenderloins)
4 tablespoons butter
1/2 cup minced onion
1 cup long-grain white rice
2 cups hot Chicken Stock (see recipe) or packaged broth
1/4 teaspoon dried leaf thyme, crumbled

1 bay leaf
1/4 teaspoon salt
Freshly ground pepper
1/3 cup crumbled Roquefort cheese
2 tablespoons vegetable oil
1/2 cup packed, thinly sliced green onions (green and white parts)

Position rack in lower third of oven and preheat to 350°F. Cut round of parchment paper to diameter of pan to be used for cooking rice (8 to 9 1/2 inches), and butter paper.

Cut turkey breasts diagonally in slices about 1/2 inch wide, then in pieces measuring about 1 1/2 inches by 3/4 inch by 1/2 inch. Pat dry on paper towels.

Melt 3 tablespoons butter in 8- to 9 1/2-inch ovenproof sauté pan or deep skillet over low heat. Add onion and cook, stirring, until soft but not brown, about 7 minutes. Add rice and sauté over medium heat, stirring, until grains begin to turn milky white, about 4 minutes.

In a saucepan, bring stock, thyme, and bay leaf to a boil over high heat. Pour over rice and stir once. Add salt and pepper and bring to a boil. Press round of buttered paper onto rice, buttered side down, and cover with tight lid. Bake in oven, without stirring, 18 minutes. Taste rice; if it is too chewy or if liquid is not absorbed, bake 2 minutes more. Discard bay leaf. Scatter Roquefort over pilaf and cover.

Heat oil and remaining tablespoon butter in large skillet over medium-high heat. Add turkey pieces, sprinkle with pepper, and sauté, tossing with 2 slotted spatulas, until turkey is just tender and lightly browned, about 2 minutes. Remove with slotted spatula to plate and keep warm. Add green onions to skillet and sauté over medium heat 30 seconds. Sprinkle green onions over rice.

Fluff rice with fork and toss until Roquefort is thoroughly mixed into rice. Add turkey pieces, discarding any liquid on plate, and toss lightly. Taste and adjust seasoning. Gently transfer pilaf to serving dish and serve.

TURKEY TENDERLOINS WITH BÉARNAISE SAUCE
Blanc de dinde, sauce béarnaise

Rich béarnaise sauce is a classic partner for tournedos, or steak of beef tenderloins, but I like it with turkey, which is leaner. This dish is also delicious made with chicken breasts or salmon fillets.

MAKES 4 SERVINGS

BÉARNAISE SAUCE

3/4 cup butter, preferably unsalted
2 tablespoons tarragon vinegar or white wine vinegar
1/4 cup dry white wine
1/4 teaspoon coarsely cracked black pepper (in pepper mill)
2 shallots, chopped
1 tablespoon coarsely chopped fresh tarragon

3 egg yolks, room temperature
Salt and white pepper or cayenne pepper
1 tablespoon minced fresh tarragon
1 tablespoon minced fresh chervil or fresh parsley

1 1/4 pounds turkey tenderloins, sliced about 1/4 inch thick
Salt and freshly ground pepper
1 tablespoon vegetable oil
1 tablespoon butter

1/2 cup dry white wine
1 medium-size ripe tomato, peeled, seeded, and finely diced
Tarragon sprigs for garnish

BÉARNAISE SAUCE

Melt butter in a small heavy saucepan over low heat. To clarify, pour into measuring cup and skim off white foam from surface. Pour remaining clear butter into a bowl, leaving white sediment behind in measuring cup. Let cool to lukewarm.

In a small heavy-based nonaluminum saucepan, combine vinegar, wine, cracked pepper, shallots, and coarsely chopped tarragon. Simmer over medium heat until only about 2 tablespoons liquid remain. Strain, pushing hard on shallots. Return wine mixture to saucepan and let cool to room temperature. Discard solids.

Whisk egg yolks and a pinch of salt into wine mixture. Set pan over low heat and cook, whisking vigorously and constantly, until mixture is creamy and thick enough so whisk leaves a clear trail as it crosses base of pan. Remove pan occasionally from heat; it should not become so hot that you can't touch the sides with your hands. Be careful not to let mixture become too hot or egg yolks will curdle. When yolk mixture becomes thick enough, remove it immediately from heat. Continue to whisk for about 30 seconds.

Gradually whisk in clarified butter, drop by drop. After sauce has absorbed about 2 or 3 tablespoons butter, add rest of butter in a very thin stream, whisking vigorously and constantly. Add a pinch of white pepper or cayenne, minced tarragon, and chervil or parsley. Taste and adjust seasoning. Serve as soon as possible. (Sauce can be kept warm for about 15 minutes in its bowl set on a rack above warm water, but it must be whisked frequently. It can also be kept warm in a thermos.)

Season turkey with salt and pepper. Heat oil and butter in a large skillet over medium-high heat. Add enough turkey to make one layer and sauté about 1 to 1½ minutes per side, or until just tender and no longer pink inside. Remove. Repeat with remaining turkey.

Discard fat. Add ½ cup wine to pan and boil, stirring, until only about 3 tablespoons liquid remain. Gradually whisk wine into béarnaise sauce.

Spoon a little sauce over center of each turkey slice, sprinkle with diced tomato, and garnish with tarragon sprigs. Serve remaining sauce separately.

TURKEY TENDERLOINS WITH QUICK BÉARNAISE SAUCE

Follow first two paragraphs above. Instead of third paragraph, proceed thus: In a blender or food processor, process egg yolks with pinch of salt and strained wine mixture until they are lightened in color and very well blended. Reheat clarified butter to just bubbling. With machine running, gradually incorporate hot butter, drop by drop, into yolks. After 2 or 3 tablespoons butter have been added, pour remaining butter through in a fine stream, with machine still running.

Transfer to bowl. Add a pinch of white pepper or cayenne, minced tarragon, and chervil or parsley. Taste and adjust seasoning. Serve as soon as possible.

NOTE: When making this version, do *not* add the ½ cup wine to skillet after sautéing turkey for incorporation into sauce. Quick béarnaise is thinner than classic béarnaise and cannot absorb the extra liquid.

TURKEY BREASTS WITH GARLIC CREAM AND GREEN BEANS
Escalopes de dinde à la crème d'ail et aux haricots verts

Whole garlic cloves simmer in the light creamy sauce and are then removed, leaving a subtle taste. Accompany the turkey with corn on the cob, and round out the meal with a salad of tomatoes or of roasted peppers. 　　　　　　　　　　MAKES 4 SERVINGS

6 large garlic cloves, cut in half
1 bay leaf
5 parsley stems
¼ cup white wine vinegar
⅓ cup chicken stock or water
1 cup heavy cream
Pinch of cayenne pepper
1½ pounds turkey breast slices
  (¼ to ½ inch thick), patted
  dry

Salt and freshly ground pepper
2 tablespoons vegetable oil
2 tablespoons butter
½ pound tiny French green beans
  (haricots verts) or regular
  green beans, ends removed

Combine garlic, bay leaf, parsley stems, vinegar, and stock or water in a medium saucepan. Bring to a boil and simmer until reduced to about ¼ cup. Add ½ cup cream and bring to a boil. Strain, return to saucepan, and bring to a boil, stirring. Add remaining cream and simmer, stirring often, about 5 minutes, or until sauce is thick enough to coat a spoon. Add cayenne, and taste and adjust seasoning.

Season turkey with salt and pepper on both sides. Heat oil and butter in a large skillet or sauté pan. Add enough turkey slices to make one layer. Sauté over medium-high heat about 2 minutes on each side, or until just tender when pierced with a sharp knife; do not overcook or meat will be dry. Remove turkey slices. Sauté remaining slices and remove.

Meanwhile, add green beans to a large pan of boiling salted water and boil, uncovered, about 5 minutes, or until just tender. Drain thoroughly.

To serve, put turkey breasts in center of plates and coat with sauce. Arrange green beans around turkey, or scatter a few green beans over each portion of turkey and serve remaining beans separately.

Roast and Braised Turkey

Turkey is the choice entrée for many holiday dinners in France, especially Christmas and New Year's. French turkeys are much smaller than American ones; French cooks prefer them this way because the smaller birds cook fairly quickly and remain moist.

Like our holiday birds, the French turkey is traditionally served stuffed, often with sumptuous, even luxurious, stuffings. One lavish old-time recipe calls for stuffing the turkey with whole black truffles; chopped truffles are still used in stuffing as a flavoring ingredient. In contrast to our bread stuffings, French stuffings are usually based on sausage meat or other ground meat, although they may contain some bread as well. Of course, these moist delicious stuffings gain more richness from the roasting juices as they bake in the turkey.

Originally developed as an economical way to stretch meat, stuffing has become the highlight of a roast poultry dinner for many people, especially a dinner planned around turkey. In fact, a roast turkey menu without stuffing is almost unthinkable. Yet stuffing has other uses—it can be baked in a separate dish and served as a delectable accompaniment for roast turkey breasts or any roast or grilled meat.

Besides stuffing, braised chestnuts are the most popular partner for the holiday turkey, partly because they are in season in fall and winter. Sometimes chestnuts are added to the stuffing as well. A side dish frequently served with the holiday turkey is buttered Brussels sprouts, but fresh peas, glazed carrots, or any selection of seasonal vegetables are equally good.

Although whole turkeys are too large to be braised, braising is an ideal method for keeping turkey pieces moist, as in Braised Turkey Breast with Madeira, Mushrooms, and Olives. The braising liquid not only flavors the turkey, but also becomes an aromatic sauce.

Hints

• If using a frozen turkey, allow enough time for it to thaw in the refrigerator; a medium-size frozen turkey requires about 2 days.

• Generally ½ cup stuffing per pound of poultry will fill the bird without leaving any extra, but for most people's taste this does not allow enough stuffing for each serving. I like to allow about ¾ to 1 cup stuffing per pound of poultry and to bake the extra stuffing separately.

• Although the stuffing mixture can be prepared ahead, it should not be spooned into the poultry until just before roasting.

• Stuffing is much softer and moister when baked inside a bird, and is dryer and crisper when baked separately. If desired, bake some of the stuffing each way to enjoy both textures.

• If you are pressed for time, remember that an unstuffed bird roasts faster; bake the stuffing in a separate dish and baste it occasionally with the roasting juices.

• Remove any extra stuffing from the bird after dinner and store it in a container, not in the bird.

• To reheat leftover stuffing, spoon it into a buttered baking dish, or, for individual portions, into buttered ramekins. Dot with butter, sprinkle with a little stock, and bake at 350°F. until hot, about 30 to 45 minutes, depending on the size of the baking dish.

ROAST TURKEY WITH CALVADOS SAUCE
Dinde rôtie, sauce au calvados

The main problem in roasting turkey is keeping the breast meat moist during the long time required for the bird to cook. The French solve this by covering the bird's breast with a thin layer of pork fat, called barding fat. Since barding fat is not readily available here, a piece of butter-moistened cheesecloth is used instead to achieve a similar result.   MAKES 8 SERVINGS

*Apple, Calvados, and Turkey
    Stuffing (see following recipe)*
3/4 cup butter
*1 fresh or thawed frozen turkey
    (10 to 12 pounds)*

Salt and freshly ground pepper
*3 cups Turkey Stock (see below) or
    3 1/4 cups Chicken Stock (see
    recipe) or packaged broth*

FOR TURKEY STOCK (OPTIONAL)
*Neck and giblets of turkey (except
    liver)*
1/4 onion
1 bay leaf

2 cups water
*About 3 cups Chicken Stock (see
    recipe) or packaged broth*

*1/4 cup plus 2 to 3 teaspoons
    Calvados*

1/4 cup all-purpose flour
Salt and freshly ground pepper

Prepare stuffing. Soften 1/2 cup butter. Preheat oven to 425°F. Remove top rack. Reserve turkey neck and giblets. Season turkey inside and out with salt and pepper. Spoon some stuffing into neck cavity. Fold neck skin under body and fasten with a skewer. Pack body cavity loosely with some stuffing and cover opening with a crumpled piece of foil. If desired, truss turkey with a trussing string and needle or by closing it with skewers. Spoon remaining stuffing into a buttered 4- to 6-cup baking dish.

Spread turkey with 1/2 cup softened butter and put it breast side up on a rack in a large roasting pan. Roast 30 minutes, basting twice. Meanwhile, melt remaining 1/4 cup butter in a medium saucepan, and put a large double piece of cheesecloth in saucepan of melted butter.

Reduce oven temperature to 350°F. Cover turkey breast with butter-soaked cheesecloth. Roast turkey 1½ hours, basting with pan juices every 15 minutes. If pan becomes dry, add ¼ cup stock or water.

FOR TURKEY STOCK (OPTIONAL)

While turkey is roasting, make turkey stock, if desired. In medium saucepan combine turkey neck and giblets (except liver), onion, bay leaf, 2 cups water, and 2 cups chicken stock. Bring to a boil. Cover and simmer over low heat for 1½ hours. Strain, and add enough chicken stock to make 3 cups.

Put dish of extra stuffing in oven and baste with a little of the turkey juices. Cover with foil and bake about 45 minutes. Meanwhile, continue roasting turkey, basting every 15 minutes, until juices run clear when leg is pricked, or meat thermometer inserted into thickest part of thigh registers 180°F., about 20 to 45 minutes more.

Carefully transfer turkey to platter or large board; discard strings, skewers, and cheesecloth. Baste once with pan juices, and cover.

Pour roasting juices into measuring cup; pour off fat and reserve. Return juices to pan, add ¼ cup Calvados and ¾ cup chicken or turkey stock, and bring to a boil, stirring and scraping to dissolve any brown bits in pan. Strain into a bowl.

Heat ⅓ cup reserved fat in a saucepan over low heat. Add flour and cook, whisking over low heat, about 4 minutes, or until bubbling. Add remaining 2¼ cups stock and liquid used to deglaze roasting pan and bring to a boil, whisking. Simmer, whisking occasionally, about 5 minutes, or until thick enough to coat a spoon. Add 2 to 3 teaspoons Calvados to taste. Taste and adjust seasoning.

Carve turkey and arrange on platter. Spoon stuffing onto platter or into a serving dish. Reheat sauce briefly, pour into a sauceboat, and serve alongside turkey.

APPLE, CALVADOS, AND TURKEY STUFFING
Farce de dinde aux pommes et au calvados

French stuffings are usually made with ground pork for richness, and lean ground veal for flavor. This recipe substitutes the more easily found ground turkey for the veal, adds toasted walnuts for a little crunch, and fresh ginger for zip. It makes enough stuffing for a 10- to 12-pound turkey or two 4-pound chickens. Double the recipe for a large turkey (16 to 20 pounds). If roasting only 1 chicken, prepare half the recipe, using a medium skillet, and bake any extra stuffing in a baking dish. MAKES ABOUT 8 CUPS; ABOUT 6 TO 8 SERVINGS

1 1/4 cups walnuts

About 8 to 10 ounces day-old or stale white bread (preferably good-quality French or Italian bread), enough to yield 4 cups crumbs

1/2 pound fresh pork sausage meat, such as mild Italian sausage (1 cup)

3/4 pound ground turkey (1 1/2 cups)

6 tablespoons butter

2 onions, finely chopped (about 2 cups)

4 cups peeled, finely diced tart green apples, such as Granny Smith (about 1 1/2 pounds, or 3 medium-size apples)

Salt and freshly ground pepper

2 tablespoons minced fresh ginger

1/8 teaspoon ground cloves

2 teaspoons minced fresh thyme, or 1/2 teaspoon dried leaf thyme, crumbled

1/2 cup Calvados

Preheat oven to 350°F. Toast nuts in oven until lightly browned, about 5 minutes. Cool and chop coarsely.

Slice bread and put it, a few slices at a time, in food processor to make crumbs. Transfer to a large bowl.

Cook sausage and ground turkey in a large heavy skillet over medium-high heat, breaking up meat with wooden spoon, until it is no longer pink, about 7 minutes. Transfer to a bowl.

Add butter to skillet and melt over medium heat. Add onions, apples, and a pinch of salt and pepper. Cook, stirring occasionally, until onion is soft but not brown, about 10 minutes. Add ginger and cook 2 minutes. Add sausage mixture, cloves, and thyme and cook, stirring, 1 minute. Remove from heat.

Add apple-sausage mixture and nuts to bread crumbs and toss lightly until blended. Add Calvados and toss again. Mixture may appear dry, but will become much moister from juices in bird. Taste and adjust seasoning. (Stuffing can be refrigerated up to 1 day in covered container. Do not stuff turkey in advance.)

ROAST TURKEY BREAST WITH FRESH CRANBERRIES
Blanc de dinde aux airelles

Choosing a boneless turkey breast is an easy way to serve roast turkey to a small number of people. Because the breast cooks more quickly than the rest of the turkey, cooking it separately helps to ensure moist meat. Whole fresh cranberries give the sauce a beautiful color, and actually are an American addition to the French red wine sauce. Our variety of cranberries are not available in France, although there are small cranberrylike berries called *airelles*.

MAKES 4 SERVINGS

1 piece boneless turkey breast with skin (2 pounds), room temperature

Salt and freshly ground pepper
1/4 cup butter, softened

CRANBERRY AND RED WINE SAUCE

1 1/2 cups dry red wine
1/2 cup plus 2 tablespoons water
10 tablespoons sugar
1 cinnamon stick
12 ounces (3 cups) fresh or frozen cranberries, rinsed

A few drops of lemon juice
Salt and freshly ground pepper
1 tablespoon cornstarch, potato starch, or arrowroot dissolved in 2 tablespoons water

Preheat oven to 400°F. Pat turkey dry. Tie in a compact shape. Season with salt and pepper, and rub it all over with softened butter. Set in a small roasting pan and roast 30 minutes, basting occasionally. Turn over and roast for 15 to 20 minutes more, until a meat thermometer inserted into center of turkey registers 170°F., or until tender when pierced with a skewer.

CRANBERRY AND RED WINE SAUCE
To prepare cranberries, combine wine, water, sugar, and cinnamon stick in a medium saucepan. Bring to a boil, stirring. Add cranberries, then cover and simmer over low heat 6 or 7 minutes, or until tender. Discard cinnamon stick. Drain liquid from cranberries and reserve separately.

When turkey is tender, transfer to a board and keep warm. Add reserved cranberry liquid to roasting pan. Bring to a boil, scraping in browned bits from pan. Strain into a saucepan. Add a few drops of lemon juice and season to taste with salt and pepper. Return to a simmer.

Whisk cornstarch or potato starch or arrowroot mixture to blend, then gradually whisk half into simmering sauce. Return to a boil, whisking. If sauce is too thin, gradually whisk in remaining starch mixture and return to a boil. Reduce heat to low, add cranberries, and reheat gently.

Cut turkey in slices and set on a platter. Garnish with a few spoonfuls of whole cranberries from sauce. Serve remaining cranberries in sauce in a bowl.

BRAISED TURKEY BREAST WITH MADEIRA, MUSHROOMS, AND OLIVES
Blanc de dinde braisé au madère, aux champignons, et aux olives

Braising is an excellent method for cooking turkey because the meat does not dry out and because the aromatic braising liquid becomes a flavorful base for the sauce. The combination of mushrooms and olives is a classic addition. Light potato fritters called potatoes Dauphine (set on a separate plate to keep them crisp) or rice pilaf accompany this dish well. MAKES 4 SERVINGS

MADEIRA-BRAISED TURKEY

1 piece boneless turkey breast with skin (2 pounds)
1 tablespoon vegetable oil
3 tablespoons butter
1 onion, diced or coarsely chopped
1 carrot, diced or coarsely chopped
1 large garlic clove, crushed

3 tablespoons cold water
2 teaspoons tomato paste
1 tablespoon cornstarch, potato starch, or arrowroot

2 cups Chicken Stock (see recipe) or packaged broth
Pinch of dried leaf thyme
1 bay leaf
5 parsley stems
Salt and freshly ground pepper
2 tablespoons Madeira

6 ounces mushrooms, cut in quarters
1 cup pitted black olives, drained
1 to 2 tablespoons Madeira

MADEIRA-BRAISED TURKEY

Pat turkey dry with paper towels and tie in a compact shape. Heat oil and butter in a heavy casserole, add turkey, and brown it lightly on all sides over medium-high heat. Remove to a plate. Add onion and carrot to casserole and sauté over medium-high heat, stirring often, until well browned. Be careful not to let mixture burn. Stir in garlic.

Add ½ cup chicken stock, thyme, bay leaf, parsley stems, and salt and pepper, and bring to a boil. Add turkey and simmer over medium heat until most of liquid has evaporated, turning turkey once. Add another ½ cup chicken stock and simmer again over medium heat until liquid has reduced to about ¼ cup. Add remaining 1 cup stock and 2 tablespoons Madeira and bring to a simmer. Cover and simmer over low heat, basting occasionally, for about 1 hour, or until turkey is tender when pierced with a skewer or a sharp knife. Remove meat to a carving board and keep warm.

Whisk cold water into tomato paste in a small bowl. Add cornstarch or potato starch or arrowroot and whisk until smooth. Gradually pour into simmering sauce, whisking constantly. Return to a boil, whisking, then strain sauce into a medium saucepan, pressing on vegetables. Add mushrooms and simmer 5 minutes, or until tender. Add olives and 1 or 2 tablespoons more Madeira and simmer for 1 to 2 minutes. Taste and adjust seasoning.

Cut meat in slices with a long flexible knife and arrange them to overlap on a platter. Spoon mushrooms and olives with a little sauce around turkey, and spoon some sauce over slices. Serve remaining sauce separately.

LANGUEDOC TURKEY WING STEW WITH RICE AND COLORFUL VEGETABLES
Ragoût d'ailes de dinde à la languedocienne

Turkey wings benefit from long slow cooking, as in this colorful meal-in-one-pot from Languedoc in southern France, a region known for its good-quality poultry. French cooks finish the dish with Bayonne ham, but prosciutto is a fine substitute. MAKES 6 SERVINGS

5 ½ pounds small turkey wings, patted dry

6 tablespoons vegetable oil

2 onions, chopped

¾ pound carrots, diced

2 large garlic cloves, chopped

1 pound ripe tomatoes, peeled, seeded, and chopped, or one 28-ounce can whole plum tomatoes, drained and chopped

¼ cup Cognac or brandy

5 cups water

2 bay leaves

½ teaspoon dried leaf thyme, crumbled

Salt and freshly ground pepper

½ pound green beans, broken into 1-inch pieces

1 ½ pounds fresh peas (about 1 ½ cups shelled), or 1 ½ cups frozen

1 ½ cups long-grain rice

2 ounces prosciutto, cut in thin strips

Cut each turkey wing in 2 pieces at joints, or in 3 pieces if wing tips are still attached. In a large heavy stainless-steel or enameled casserole, heat 3 tablespoons oil over medium-high heat. Add turkey wings in batches and brown them, transferring them with a slotted spoon to a plate as they are browned.

Add 1 tablespoon oil to casserole and heat. Add onions and carrots and cook over low heat, stirring, about 10 minutes, or until onions are soft but not brown. Add garlic and cook 30 seconds, stirring. Add tomatoes and cook 1 minute. Return wings to pan, pour Cognac or brandy over them, and bring to a boil. Add water, bay leaves, thyme, and salt and pepper and return to a boil. Reduce heat, cover, and simmer, turning turkey pieces over once or twice, for 2 hours, or until they are tender.

Discard bay leaves and any wing tips. Remove smaller (middle) wing sections; leave large sections in cooking liquid. Remove meat from bones of middle wing sections and tear or cut meat in thin strips about 1½ inches long. Measure 3 cups of cooking liquid through a strainer and reserve for cooking rice; return vegetables in strainer to casserole. Simmer turkey and vegetable mixture, uncovered, for 10 minutes to reduce liquid slightly. Add green beans to casserole, push them into liquid, and simmer, uncovered, 15 minutes. Add peas, pushing them into liquid; simmer fresh peas 15 minutes or frozen peas 5 minutes, or until beans and peas are tender. (Stew can be kept, covered, 1 day in refrigerator. Reheat it over low heat, covered.)

In a heavy saucepan, sauté rice in 2 tablespoons oil over low heat, stirring, until rice is transparent. Add reserved 3 cups cooking liquid and bring mixture to a boil. Reduce heat to low, cover, and cook, without stirring, 18 minutes, or until rice is tender. Stir in turkey strips and prosciutto. Let stand, covered, 10 minutes off heat. Taste and adjust seasoning.

Serve turkey wing pieces and vegetables from enameled casserole or from a heated deep serving dish and rice from another heated serving dish. To serve, spoon rice onto each heated plate and set a turkey wing piece on top. Spoon vegetables around rice and a little cooking liquid over each turkey piece.

Duck and Goose

Window shopping for food is one of the delights of life in Paris. Store owners display their enticing delicacies in windows facing the sidewalk. Fauchon's, the most famous specialty food shop in France, displays beautiful glazed ducks garnished with seasonal fruit for the admiration of passersby.

The meaty taste, tender flesh, and fabulous aroma of duck make it a favorite restaurant entrée. The same people who find duck so appealing at restaurants, though, rarely—if ever—prepare it at home. Most, I imagine, are reluctant because they believe it is complicated. Yet a duck is almost as easy to roast as a chicken. And roasting is the ideal technique for cooking duck, as it highlights the bird's natural flavor, gives it a crisp, golden skin, and makes for moist meat.

Roast duck is a marvelous main course for an intimate dinner for two. As an added bonus, any leftovers can be enjoyed hot or cold the next day. You might experiment with a duck salad, adding greens, rice, pasta, or mixed vegetables, and moistening it with a light vinaigrette.

Duck with fruit has become a classic not only in the West, but also in the Orient. The rich flesh of duck is complemented by both sweetness and acidity, and for this reason benefits greatly from being combined with fruits, especially those that possess both these attributes. The renowned French *canard à l'orange* is made with oranges, while plum sauce is such a frequent Chinese accompaniment that it is some-times called duck sauce. Other fresh and dried fruits, such as peaches, cherries, pineapple, pears, apples, cranberries, and mangoes are also fine matches, as are sweet vegetables such as carrots and turnips. When the natural tartness of the fruit does not balance its sweetness, the adjustment is provided by the addition of wine, citrus juice, or vinegar.

Spirits that match the fruit can add to the harmony of flavors. For example, a small amount of Grand Marnier or Cointreau provides the finishing touch to the sauce for duck with oranges. In Normandy, roast duck is served with sautéed apples and Calvados, the Norman apple brandy. Sharp condiments like mustard are also good with duck, as in Deviled Duck with Brussels Sprouts, and so are spices such as curry, saffron, cayenne, ginger, and garlic.

For the purpose of cooking, goose can be thought of as a very large duck, except that due to its size it is roasted at a lower tempera-ture. Its rich meat makes it a poultry of choice in certain regions of France, notably Alsace. Roast goose is one of the most festive poultry dishes and is especially suited to a holiday dinner.

The meat of a perfectly roasted duck or goose is succulent enough to serve on its own, but a quick pan sauce can be made using the roasting juices, stock, and a little dry white wine. The sauce will have ample character without any addition of cream or large amounts of butter.

In fact, it is the bird's own fat that adds to the richness of the sauce and the juiciness of the meat. Before roasting, the skin is pierced all over—a procedure used only for duck and goose. This allows the fat to drain while the bird cooks. As a result, the meat is continually basted in its own juices and what remains in the pan can serve as the foundation for a delicious sauce.

Sauces for roast duck or goose need not be complicated. Al-though the prestigious creations of haute cuisine require long-sim-mered brown sauce, there are plenty of simple traditional dishes also. One French recipe calls for roasting a duck, then adding a chopped shallot and the juice of an orange to the pan juices. Another directs the cook to serve a plain roasted duck without sauce and to garnish it with lemons, so each diner can squeeze a little lemon juice on his or her portion.

The French generally prefer "pink" or rare duck. At the Tour d'Argent, one of the most illustrious restaurants in the French capital, duck breasts are served extremely rare for the restaurant's celebrated specialty, Pressed Duck. The owners were so proud of this entrée that in 1890 they began numbering their ducks; this custom still continues. Each diner receives a card with the number of his duck. (My duck's number in August 1980 was 580,147!) While the duck breast is being served, the legs are grilled so they finish cooking, because they take longer to cook than the breast, and they are served as a second duck course, accompanied by a green salad.

A roast duck or goose is beautiful served whole, but is easiest to carve in the kitchen. Combine dramatic effect with practicality and present the whole bird on a platter, then take it back to the kitchen to carve it. Then return the pieces to the platter with the sauce and garnish.

Hints

- Thaw frozen duck or goose at least 24 hours in the refrigerator. If absolutely necessary, it can be thawed in its wrapping in a large bowl under cool running water; it will require several hours.
- If a bird has any pinfeathers, singe them briefly over a direct flame and pull them out before roasting.
- A special procedure used for duck and geese, and not for other poultry, is to prick the skin in order to help the fat melt and escape as it cooks. This fat can be strained, saved in jars in the refrigerator, and used for sautéing; it is especially good with onions and potatoes.
- Trussing a duck before roasting keeps it in a neat, compact shape, holds the neck skin over the breast meat to protect this meat, and prevents the legs and wings from drying out. To truss in a simple manner, tie two pieces of kitchen string around the duck crosswise, so one holds the wings tightly to the body and the other holds the legs. If you prefer not to truss the duck, push the tail section into the body and catch the neck-skin flap with the wing tips, so that they hold the neck skin over the breast meat.
- Use paper towels and pot holders to turn duck during roasting.
- Turn the roasting pan around once or twice in the oven to brown the duck evenly.
- A duck can be easily carved in two steps: (1) Remove the leg and thigh piece from each side; (2) with a boning knife, cut down the

center of the breast section, dividing it in two, then cut under each breast half to separate it from the breast bone and remove the meat. The breast meat can then be cut in pieces on a cutting board.

- After a duck is carved, the pieces can be broiled briefly to reheat them. Arrange them skin side up in the broiler pan and broil them until the skin is brown and slightly crisp; or reheat them briefly in the oven.

- To reheat leftover meat, remove it from the bones, cut in pieces, and sauté briefly in a skillet. Do not try to reheat meat on the carcass; the heat will take too long to reach the interior and the meat will dry out.

- Cold or reheated roast duck or goose makes a delicious addition to salads; or the sautéed meat can be added to hot rice pilaf or pasta.

FRENCH ROAST DUCK
Canard rôti à la française

Roast duck is succulent on its own, accompanied by fresh vegetables, but when a quick pan sauce is desired, French cooks simply take advantage of the savory duck roasting juices and combine them with duck or chicken stock and a little wine. The pan sauce can be flavored at the last moment with 1 to 1½ tablespoons chopped fresh herbs: chives, tarragon, parsley, basil, dill, or cilantro.

In addition to salt and pepper, other fragrant ingredients can be added to the duck before cooking for extra zest. Fresh herbs, especially thyme or rosemary sprigs or sage leaves, an onion, or a few orange sections or apple wedges can be placed inside its cavity, then removed before the duck is carved.

If you like, roast the duck only until the breast is rare, and serve it with the pan sauce. Then grill the legs, and accompany them with a salad of lettuce, diced mushrooms, and a mustardy vinaigrette, as they do at the Tour d'Argent, and imagine you are there, enjoying the splendid view of Notre Dame and the Seine.

MAKES 2 TO 4 SERVINGS

1 duck with giblets (about 4 1/2 to
　　5 pounds), thawed if frozen,
　　patted dry

Salt and freshly ground pepper

DUCK PAN SAUCE (OPTIONAL)

1/2 cup dry white wine
2 cups Rich or Simple Duck Stock
　　or Chicken Stock (see recipes)
　　or packaged broth

3/4 teaspoon cornstarch, potato
　　starch, or arrowroot dissolved
　　in 1 1/2 teaspoons water
1 tablespoon butter

Position rack in center of oven and preheat to 450°F. Remove fat from inside duck near tail and under neck skin. Remove giblets and neck from inside duck and reserve for stock (except for liver, which can be reserved for sautéing). Cut off wing tips and reserve for stock. For easier carving, remove wishbone: Set duck on its back and lift neck skin. First bone above neck is V-shaped wishbone. Outline it carefully with boning knife and pull; add to giblets for stock.

Season duck inside and out with salt and pepper. Using trussing needle or skewer, pierce skin all over, including thighs, back, and lower part of breast, where fat is thickest, at intervals of about 1/2 inch; do not pierce meat. Truss duck, if desired.

Set duck on its side on rack in medium, heavy roasting pan and roast 10 minutes. Turn duck onto other side and roast 10 minutes. Using a bulb baster, remove fat from pan. Set duck on its breast and roast 10 minutes. Again, discard fat from pan. Set duck on its back and roast 10 minutes.

Reduce oven temperature to 400°F. Continue roasting duck, discarding fat occasionally, about 20 to 40 minutes. To check whether duck is done, use trussing needle, skewer, or carving fork to prick thigh meat in plumpest part: if juices that escape are still red, duck is not done; if they are slightly pink, duck is rare; if they are clear, duck is well-done. (If browner skin is desired, transfer duck to broiler pan and broil about 5 inches from heat source until skin is deep brown.)

Transfer duck to platter, draining juices from inside duck into roasting pan. Discard any trussing strings. Cover loosely and keep duck warm. (Duck can be prepared 30 minutes ahead, covered loosely, and kept warm in oven with heat turned off and door ajar.)

DUCK PAN SAUCE (OPTIONAL)

Pour off fat from roasting pan but leave in darker-colored duck juices. Reheat juices in roasting pan over medium-high heat. Add wine and bring to a boil, stirring and scraping up any browned bits and moving pan back and forth over burner to heat evenly. Strain mixture into medium saucepan. Boil until reduced to 1/4 cup. Add stock and boil, skimming occasionally, until mixture is reduced to 3/4 cup, about 5 minutes. Remove from heat. Skim excess fat from surface of sauce.

Bring sauce to a simmer over medium heat. Whisk cornstarch or potato starch or arrowroot mixture to blend, then gradually whisk half of it into simmering sauce. Return to boil, whisking. If sauce is too thin, gradually whisk in remaining starch mixture and return to a boil. Remove from heat. Whisk in butter, and taste and adjust seasoning.

Carve duck as described on page 82. If meat becomes cold during carving, cover platter with foil and reheat briefly in 350°F. oven. If using sauce, reheat gently, if necessary, and serve it separately.

ROAST DUCK WITH MADEIRA AND DRIED FRUIT
Canard rôti au madère et aux fruits secs

Poached dried peaches and prunes provide a colorful, sweet accompaniment to the rich duck meat and to the Madeira sauce. Serve the duck with rice and with a sweet vegetable, such as sugar snap peas, green peas, or carrots.   MAKES 2 TO 4 SERVINGS

6 dried peach halves (about 3 ounces), each cut in 2 pieces
3/4 cup plus 1 tablespoon Madeira
Water
8 pitted prunes (about 3 ounces)
1 duck with giblets (about 4 1/2 to 5 pounds), thawed if frozen, patted dry

1 cup Rich or Simple Duck Stock or Chicken Stock (see recipes) or packaged broth
3/4 teaspoon cornstarch, potato starch, or arrowroot, dissolved in 1 1/2 teaspoons water
Salt and freshly ground pepper

Combine peaches, ¼ cup Madeira, and ½ cup water in small deep bowl or cup and cover. Combine prunes, ½ cup Madeira, and ¼ cup water in small deep bowl or cup and cover. Soak fruit for 2 hours.

Roast duck as in first five paragraphs in French Roast Duck (page 84).

When duck is nearly done, transfer each fruit with its soaking liquid to a separate small saucepan. Add enough water to each fruit to barely cover, if necessary. Bring mixtures to a simmer. Cover and cook over low heat until fruit is just tender, about 3 or 4 minutes. Pour liquids into bowl. Set fruit aside.

Pour off fat from roasting pan but leave in darker-colored duck juices. Reheat juices in roasting pan over medium-high heat. Add ½ cup stock and bring to a boil, stirring and scraping up any browned bits and moving pan back and forth over burner to heat evenly. Strain into medium saucepan. Add peach and prune liquids and remaining ½ cup stock. Boil, skimming occasionally, until sauce is reduced to ¾ cup, about 5 minutes. Remove from heat and skim excess fat from surface.

Bring sauce to a simmer over medium heat. Whisk cornstarch or potato starch or arrowroot mixture to blend, then gradually whisk half of it into simmering sauce. Return to a boil, whisking. If sauce is too thin, gradually whisk in remaining starch mixture and return to a boil. Add remaining tablespoon Madeira and cook over low heat, whisking, 1 minute. Add salt and pepper to taste. Add fruit, cover, and let stand 2 minutes.

Transfer duck to platter. Spoon fruit around duck, spoon a little sauce over fruit, and serve remaining sauce separately.

To carve duck, see page 82.

ROAST DUCK WITH CHESTNUTS
Canard rôti aux marrons

A roast bird with braised chestnuts is probably the most popular holiday dish in France. Here the chestnuts are braised in duck stock, which is then combined with red wine and shallots to make a sauce for the duck. If you would like an additional accompaniment, glazed pearl onions, sautéed mushrooms, or cooked carrots are good choices.   MAKES 3 TO 4 SERVINGS

¾ pound fresh chestnuts

2½ cups Rich or Simple Duck
    Stock or Chicken Stock (see
    recipes) or packaged broth

1 small celery stalk, broken into 2
    pieces

Salt and freshly ground pepper

1 duck with giblets (about 4½ to
    5 pounds), thawed if frozen,
    patted dry

1¼ cups dry red wine

2 tablespoons minced shallots

Pinch of dried leaf thyme, crumbled

¾ teaspoon cornstarch, potato
    starch, or arrowroot dissolved
    in 1½ teaspoons water

Put chestnuts in medium saucepan and add enough water to cover by about 1 inch. Bring to a full boil over high heat and boil 1 minute. Remove from heat. Remove 1 chestnut with a slotted spoon and cover pan. Cut into chestnut peel at base and pull off outer skin. Using a paring knife, scrape off inner skin. Repeat with remaining chestnuts, removing them 1 at a time.

Put peeled chestnuts in medium saucepan with 1½ cups stock, celery, and salt and pepper. Bring to a boil. Reduce heat to low, cover, and simmer until chestnuts are just tender when pierced with point of sharp knife, about 15 minutes; do not overcook or they may fall apart. Uncover and leave in liquid until ready to use. (Chestnuts can be kept in their liquid, covered, up to 2 days in refrigerator.)

Roast duck as in first five paragraphs in French Roast Duck (page 84).

In a medium, heavy saucepan bring ¾ cup wine, shallots, and thyme to a boil. Boil over medium heat, stirring occasionally, until wine is reduced to about 3 tablespoons. Cover and reserve.

When duck is nearly done, cover chestnuts and reheat in their cooking liquid over low heat. Discard celery. Drain chestnut liquid and reserve. Cover chestnuts and keep warm.

Pour off fat from roasting pan but leave darker-colored duck juices. Reheat juices in roasting pan over medium-high heat. Add remaining ½ cup wine and bring to a boil, stirring and scraping up any browned bits and moving pan back and forth over burner to heat evenly. Strain into shallot mixture. Boil over medium-high heat until reduced to ⅓ cup. Add remaining 1 cup stock and chestnut cooking liquid. Boil, skimming occasionally, until sauce is reduced to 1 cup. Remove from heat. Skim excess fat from surface of sauce.

Bring sauce to a simmer over medium heat. Whisk cornstarch or potato starch or arrowroot mixture to blend, then gradually whisk half of it into simmering sauce. Return to a boil, whisking. If sauce is too thin, gradually whisk in remaining starch mixture and return to a boil. Taste and adjust seasoning.

Add ¼ cup sauce to hot chestnuts and mix gently. Transfer duck to platter, spoon chestnuts around duck, and serve sauce separately.

To carve duck, see page 82.

❧ HOME-STYLE ROAST DUCK WITH ORANGE SAUCE
Canard à l'orange maison

Most restaurant versions of this entrée call for brown sauce, which requires long hours of simmering, and for a special caramel of sugar and vinegar. Yet the tastes of the duck roasting juices, oranges, and Grand Marnier, combined with a quick duck stock, produces a delicious sauce as well. Instead of orange sections, other fresh fruit such as poached cherries, poached apricot halves, or fresh grapes can be added to the sauce.   MAKES 2 TO 4 SERVINGS

4 large navel oranges
1 duck with giblets (about 4½ to
    5 pounds), thawed if frozen,
    patted dry
1 onion
1 carrot
1½ cups Simple Duck Stock or
    Chicken Stock (see recipes) or
    packaged broth

1 teaspoon tomato paste
1 tablespoon water
Salt and freshly ground pepper
1 tablespoon cornstarch, potato
    starch, or arrowroot dissolved
    in 2 tablespoons water
¼ cup strained fresh orange juice
1 tablespoon Grand Marnier
A few drops of lemon juice

Peel 1 orange down to flesh, removing as much white pith as possible. Separate into segments and put them inside duck. Cut onion and carrot in half and put in roasting pan that will be used for roasting duck.

Roast duck as in first five paragraphs for French Roast Duck (page 84).

Meanwhile, prepare orange sauce. Using a vegetable peeler, remove zest of 1 orange, being careful not to remove any of bitter white pith with it. Cut zest in very thin needlelike strips. Put in a saucepan and cover generously with water. Boil 5 minutes, rinse with cold water, and drain thoroughly.

Remove white pith from peeled orange. Peel another orange down to flesh, removing as much pith as possible. Cut both oranges carefully in segments, cutting on both sides of membranes between segments to remove. Cut last orange in half, preferably in a zigzag pattern.

Bring 1 cup stock to a boil. In a small bowl, whisk tomato paste with water until smooth. Whisk mixture into stock and simmer 2 minutes until blended. Stir in blanched orange zest and remove from heat.

When duck is cooked, transfer to a platter. Discard any trussing strings and keep warm. Discard fat from roasting pan but leave layer of darker-colored duck juices underneath, carrot, and onion. Add remaining 1/2 cup stock to pan and bring to a boil, scraping in brown bits from pan. Boil 2 to 3 minutes, or until liquid is reduced by half. Strain into sauce, and season to taste with salt and pepper.

Whisk cornstarch or potato starch or arrowroot mixture to blend, then gradually whisk it into simmering sauce. Return to a boil, whisking. Reduce heat to low, whisk in orange juice and Grand Marnier, and heat without boiling. Add a few drops of lemon juice, and taste and adjust seasoning. Add orange segments and heat very gently.

To serve, spoon a little sauce over duck. Garnish platter with orange segments and orange halves, and serve remaining sauce separately.

To carve duck, see page 82.

DEVILED DUCK WITH BRUSSELS SPROUTS
Canard aux choux de Bruxelles, sauce diable

The name of this dish comes from the pungent *sauce diable* or "devil sauce," flavored with mustard, cayenne, and wine vinegar, that provides a lively foil for the duck's richness.

MAKES 2 TO 4 SERVINGS

1 duck with giblets (about 4 1/2 to
    5 pounds), thawed if frozen,
    patted dry

Salt and freshly ground pepper
3/4 pound small Brussels sprouts

DEVIL SAUCE

2 tablespoons minced shallots
1 tablespoon white wine vinegar
3/4 cup dry white wine
1 cup Rich or Simple Duck Stock
    or Chicken Stock (see recipes)
    or packaged broth

1 tablespoon Dijon mustard
Salt and freshly ground pepper
Pinch of cayenne pepper

Roast duck as in first five paragraphs in French Roast Duck (page 84), reserving 4 tablespoons of duck fat removed from roasting pan.

While duck is roasting, trim Brussels sprouts, removing any tough bases and yellow leaves. Cook sprouts uncovered in large pan of boiling salted water over high heat until just tender but still bright green, about 7 minutes. Drain, rinse with cold water until completely cooled, and drain thoroughly.

DEVIL SAUCE

In a small saucepan, heat 1 tablespoon reserved duck fat, add shallots and cook over low heat, stirring, for 2 minutes. Add vinegar and 1/4 cup wine and bring to a simmer. Cook over medium-low heat until liquid is reduced to about 2 tablespoons. Cover and reserve.

Pour off fat from roasting pan but leave in darker-colored duck juices. Reheat juices in roasting pan over medium-high heat. Add remaining 1/2 cup wine and bring to a boil, stirring and scraping up any browned bits and moving pan back and forth over burner to heat evenly. Strain into shallot mixture and boil over medium heat until mixture is reduced to 1/4 cup. Add stock and boil, skimming occasionally, until mixture is reduced to 3/4 cup, about 5 minutes. Remove from heat and skim excess fat from surface of sauce. Whisk in mustard and heat over low heat, whisking constantly, for 1 minute. Add salt, pepper, and cayenne to taste.

Heat 3 tablespoons reserved duck fat in a medium skillet. Add Brussels sprouts, season with salt and pepper, and heat over medium-low heat, tossing or stirring gently until hot.

Either serve duck whole or carved (see page 82). Using a slotted spoon, transfer sprouts to platter around duck, and serve sauce separately.

🌿 DUCK WITH PEARS AND PORT
Canard aux poires au porto

For this simple but elegant entrée, the pears are poached in spiced port, which is then used as the basis for a sauce for both duck and pears. Onion or Leek Compote (page 104 or 208) makes a wonderful side dish. MAKES 2 TO 4 SERVINGS

1 duck (about 4½ to 5 pounds), thawed if frozen, patted dry	4 ripe but firm pears
1½ cups port	A few drops of lemon juice
1½ cups water	Salt and freshly ground pepper
2 tablespoons sugar	1½ teaspoons cornstarch, potato starch, or arrowroot dissolved in 1 tablespoon water
2 whole cloves	

Roast duck as in first five paragraphs of French Roast Duck (page 84).

Meanwhile, prepare pears. Combine port, water, sugar, and cloves in a medium saucepan. Bring to a boil, stirring, then remove from heat. Peel pears, cut in half, and core them; then cut each piece in half lengthwise. Return port mixture to a boil. Add pears, cover, and simmer over low heat 12 to 15 minutes, or until tender. Discard cloves. Remove pears from heat, leaving them in their liquid.

When duck is tender, transfer to a platter, discard any trussing strings, and keep warm. Discard fat from roasting pan but leave in layer of darker-colored duck juices underneath. Drain poaching liquid from pears and add it to roasting pan. Bring to a boil, scraping in browned bits from pan. Strain into a saucepan. Add a few drops of lemon juice, and season to taste with salt and pepper. Return to a simmer.

Whisk cornstarch or potato starch or arrowroot mixture to blend, then gradually whisk half of it into simmering sauce. Return to a boil, whisking. If sauce is too thin, gradually whisk in remaining starch mixture and return to a boil. Reduce heat to low, add pears, and heat gently.

Carve duck (see page 82) and set pieces on a platter. Garnish platter with pears, and spoon a little sauce over duck and pears. Serve remaining pears and sauce in a bowl.

CASSOULET WITH ROAST DUCK
Cassoulet au canard rôti

Traditional cassoulet often features *confit* of duck or goose, or salted poultry pieces cooked slowly in their own fat. Making *confit* is a lengthy process, however, and roast duck is a fine substitute. Duck or goose *confit* can be purchased at some specialty markets; if you find it, you can use 4 pieces of *confit* in this recipe instead of the roast duck.   MAKES 6 TO 8 SERVINGS

COOKED BEANS

1 pound dried white beans, such as Great Northern (about 2 1/3 cups)

1 onion, peeled and studded with 2 whole cloves

1 carrot, peeled

1 bay leaf

2 whole garlic cloves, peeled

1 sprig fresh thyme, or a pinch of dried leaf thyme

Pinch of salt

8 ounces thick-sliced bacon, cut in thin strips

2 1/2 pounds boned lamb shoulder, cut in 2-inch cubes, or 2 1/2 pounds lamb for stew

1 large onion, chopped

3 cloves garlic, chopped

1 pound tomatoes, peeled, seeded, and chopped, or one 28-ounce can whole plum tomatoes, drained and chopped

Salt and freshly ground pepper

1 sprig fresh thyme, or 1/4 teaspoon dried leaf thyme, crumbled

1 bay leaf

5 parsley stems

1 tablespoon chopped fresh basil, or 1 teaspoon dried basil, crumbled

1 duck (about 4 1/2 to 5 pounds), thawed if frozen, patted dry

1/2 pound smoked Polish sausage or other sausage

1/4 cup unseasoned bread crumbs

COOKED BEANS

Sort beans; discard any broken beans or stones. Soak beans in cold water to cover generously for 8 hours or overnight. Rinse beans, drain, and put them in a large saucepan. Add enough water to cover them by at least 2 inches. Add clove-studded onion and carrot and push them into beans. Tie bay leaf, whole garlic cloves, and thyme in a piece of cheesecloth, and add to pan. Cover and bring to a boil over medium heat. Reduce heat to low and simmer about 30 minutes; add a pinch of salt and continue simmering about 1 hour more, or until just tender, adding hot water if necessary so beans remain covered. Keep beans in their cooking liquid. (Beans can be cooked 1 day ahead and refrigerated.)

Heat bacon in a large heavy casserole until fat begins to run. Fry until lightly browned; remove with a slotted spoon and drain on paper towels. Pour off all but 2 tablespoons fat. Add lamb cubes to pan in 2 batches and brown them on all sides over medium-high heat. Remove them, add chopped onion, and cook over low heat until softened. Add garlic and cook 30 seconds. Stir in tomatoes and cook 2 minutes.

Return lamb to pan. After beans have cooked at least 30 minutes, add 1 cup bean liquid, 1 1/2 cups water, and a little salt and pepper. Tie thyme, bay leaf, and parsley stems together with string or in cheesecloth, and add. Bring to a boil, reduce heat, cover, and simmer 1 to 1 1/2 hours, or until tender. Discard herb bundle. Add bacon to pan and simmer 1 minute. Add basil, taste, and adjust seasoning. Skim off excess fat.

Preheat oven to 400°F. Pull out fat from inside duck. Season duck inside and out with salt and pepper. Using trussing needle or skewer, pierce skin all over at intervals of about 1/2 inch; do not pierce meat. Roast duck on a rack in a roasting pan for 1 hour. Cut it in 8 pieces.

Meanwhile, put sausage in a pan, cover with water, and bring just to a simmer. Cook over low heat 15 minutes. Drain, discard casing, and slice.

Discard onion, carrot, and cheesecloth bag from beans. With a slotted spoon, put half the beans in a 10-cup gratin dish in an even layer. With the slotted spoon, arrange lamb and bacon in dish, and top with duck pieces and sausage slices. Spoon remaining beans on top. Reserve remaining bean liquid. Ladle enough of lamb cooking liquid into gratin dish to come nearly to top of beans; if there isn't enough, add a little of reserved bean cooking liquid. (Cassoulet can be prepared ahead up to this point, covered, and kept 3 days in refrigerator; if any lamb cooking liquid remains, reserve it and add to refrigerated cassoulet before baking, to compensate for slight drying in refrigerator.)

Sprinkle cassoulet with bread crumbs and bake about 30 to 40 minutes, or until hot and golden brown. Serve from baking dish.

DUCK BREAST WITH MANGO SAUCE
Magret de canard aux mangues

Duck breast is a delightful cut to cook on its own—it's like eating tender steak with a duck flavor! Mango provides an attractive garnish and is the basis for the light sweet-and-sour sauce.

MAKES 4 SERVINGS

Breast of 2 ducks (about 1 3/4 to 2 pounds total), thawed if frozen (see note)

2 ripe mangoes, peeled (1 1/4 pounds total)

1 1/2 cups Rich or Simple Duck Stock or Chicken Stock (see recipes) or packaged broth

1 tablespoon chopped peeled fresh ginger

2 medium-size shallots, minced

1/3 cup dry red wine

2 tablespoons red wine vinegar

Salt and freshly ground pepper

2 tablespoons vegetable oil

1 to 2 teaspoons sugar (optional)

Pinch of cayenne

1 tablespoon butter (optional)

1 ripe mango, sliced thin, for garnish

Using a paring knife, remove skin and fat from duck, and pat dry.

Purée mangoes in blender or food processor, add 3/4 cup stock, and blend until smooth.

In small saucepan, simmer ginger with shallots, wine, and vinegar over medium heat until mixture is reduced to about 3 tablespoons. Add 1/4 cup stock, bring to a boil, and strain, pressing on shallot mixture. Return to pan. Add puréed mango mixture and bring to a boil. Remove from heat.

Season duck with salt and pepper. Heat oil in a heavy skillet over medium-high heat. Add duck and sauté about 3 minutes per side, or until medium-rare; it should be pink when cut. Remove duck, cover, and let stand 5 minutes.

Pour off fat from skillet. Add remaining ½ cup stock to skillet. Boil, stirring, until reduced to ¼ cup. Add mango sauce and simmer until sauce is thick enough to coat a spoon. Taste, add sugar if desired, and simmer briefly to dissolve it. Add cayenne. Off heat, stir in butter, if desired. Taste and adjust seasoning.

To serve, cut duck in thin lengthwise slices. Add carving juices to sauce. Spoon sauce onto plate and set duck slices on top, fanning out from the center. Garnish with mango slices, alternating them with duck slices on the plate.

NOTE: Duck breasts can be purchased at fine butcher shops and specialty stores. Or you can cut them from the ducks, as on page 82.

DUCK RAGOÛT WITH TOMATOES, WHITE WINE, AND PEAS
Ragoût de canard à la marseillaise

Ducks can be cut in pieces and made into delectable ragoûts like this one, which enables you to cook the duck ahead and reheat it, and saves the trouble of last-minute carving. If you are saving the duck breasts for another dish, such as Duck Breasts with Mango (preceding recipe), you can make this ragoût with duck legs only. The rich duck meat is matched with a fresh tomato sauce and a variety of colorful vegetables, making this a complete main course.

MAKES 3 SERVINGS

1 duck (about 4 1/2 to 5 pounds),
   thawed if frozen, patted dry
3 sprigs marjoram
3 large sprigs thyme
1 bay leaf
2 tablespoons olive oil
1 onion, minced
3 large garlic cloves, minced
2 pounds ripe tomatoes, peeled,
   seeded, and chopped, or two
   28-ounce cans whole plum
   tomatoes, drained and chopped

1/2 cup dry white wine
Salt and freshly ground pepper
1/4 pound pearl onions
1/4 pound baby carrots or large
   carrots
1/2 cup Rich or Simple Duck Stock
   or Chicken Stock (see recipes)
   or packaged broth
1 pound fresh peas (about 1 cup
   shelled), or 1 cup frozen
Pinch of cayenne pepper

Set duck on its side, slit skin between leg and body and cut off leg and thigh piece at thigh joint by cutting between thigh bone and body. Repeat on other side. Cut each leg piece in 2 pieces at joint (follow line of fat to locate it). Cut off excess fat. Cut off wing and reserve for stock. Cut breast off bone and cut into 2 pieces. Reserve back and bones for stock. Tie marjoram, thyme, and bay leaf together with string or in cheesecloth to make a bouquet garni.

Heat olive oil in a large sauté pan or deep skillet over medium-high heat. Add leg and thigh pieces and brown, taking about 7 minutes on skin side and about 3 minutes on meat side. Remove pieces. Add breast pieces and brown them about 3 minutes on skin side and 1 minute on meat side. Reduce heat to medium, if necessary, to prevent burning. Remove pieces and pour off fat into a bowl.

Return 2 tablespoons fat to pan and heat over medium-low heat. Add minced onion and cook, stirring occasionally, about 8 minutes, or until softened. Add garlic, then tomatoes and bouquet garni and bring to a boil. Return duck pieces to pan, add wine and salt and pepper, and bring to a simmer. Cover and simmer over low heat, turning duck pieces occasionally, until tender when pierced with a knife, about 10 minutes for breast pieces and about 20 minutes for legs. Remove duck pieces from pan.

Meanwhile, prepare vegetables. Put pearl onions in a small saucepan, cover with water, bring to a boil, and boil 1 minute. Drain, rinse under cold water, and drain well. Peel with a paring knife. (If using large carrots, cut them in 1 1/2-inch lengths, then cut each in quarters lengthwise.)

After removing duck pieces from pan, add pearl onions, carrots, and stock. Cover and simmer 20 minutes, or until vegetables are tender. Discard bouquet garni. If necessary, cook sauce, uncovered, a few minutes more until it is thick.

Cook fresh or frozen peas in a medium saucepan of boiling salted water about 2 minutes, or until just tender. Drain, rinse with cold water, and drain well.

Skim fat from sauce. Add a pinch of cayenne pepper, then taste and adjust seasoning. Remove skin from duck pieces, if desired, and return duck to sauce. (Duck ragoût can be kept, covered, up to 2 days in refrigerator.)

Reheat ragoût gently, add peas, and heat slowly. Taste again, adjust seasoning if necessary, and serve.

ROAST GOOSE STUFFED WITH FIGS, PINE NUTS, AND RICE
Oie farcie aux figues, aux pignons, et au riz

Although goose is traditionally a winter delicacy, it is available frozen all year. Choose one that weighs 9 pounds or less; larger geese may not be tender enough for roasting. The lean Mediterranean rice stuffing, flavored with lemon peel and juice in addition to the toasted nuts and dried fruit, is perfect with the goose.

MAKES 6 TO 8 SERVINGS

FIG, PINE NUT, AND RICE STUFFING

2 tablespoons olive oil

1 onion, minced

1½ cups long-grain white rice

3 cups hot water

2 teaspoons fresh thyme leaves, or
    ¾ teaspoon dried leaf thyme,
    crumbled

1 bay leaf

Salt and freshly ground pepper

¾ cup pine nuts

4 teaspoons grated lemon peel

1¼ cups (8 ounces) dried small
    dark figs (Mission figs), stems
    removed, quartered

Cayenne pepper to taste

1 young goose (about 8 to 9
    pounds), thawed if frozen

Salt and freshly ground pepper

¼ cup dry white wine

1½ cups Simple Goose Stock or
    Chicken Stock (see recipes) or
    packaged broth

2 teaspoons cornstarch, potato
    starch, or arrowroot dissolved
    in 2 tablespoons water

3 to 4 small dark figs, cut in half
    lengthwise, for garnish

FIG, PINE NUT, AND RICE STUFFING

Preheat oven to 350°F.

Heat oil in large sauté pan or deep skillet over low heat. Add onion and cook, stirring, until soft but not brown, about 7 minutes. Add rice and sauté over medium heat, stirring, until grains begin to turn milky white, about 4 minutes.

Pour 3 cups hot water over rice and stir once. Add thyme, bay leaf, and salt and pepper. Bring to boil over high heat. Reduce heat to low, cover with tight lid, and simmer without stirring, 18 minutes. Taste rice; if it is very chewy or if liquid is not absorbed, cook 2 minutes more. Discard bay leaf.

Toast pine nuts on a small baking sheet in oven 3 to 5 minutes, or until light brown. Transfer to a plate.

Fluff rice with fork. Gently stir in grated lemon peel, pine nuts, and figs. Add cayenne; taste and adjust seasoning, making sure to season stuffing well. Let cool.

Increase oven temperature to 450°F. Remove excess fat from goose, and pat dry. Cut off fatty flap of skin near tail. Prick goose skin a few times with a fork or skewer; do not pierce meat. Season goose inside and outside with salt and pepper. Spoon stuffing gently into goose without packing. Put goose on its back on rack in roasting pan. Put a piece of foil at tail to secure stuffing.

Roast goose 30 minutes, or until it begins to brown, basting occasionally. Remove fat with bulb baster as it accumulates.

Reduce oven temperature to 350°F. and roast 1 hour and 15 minutes, basting occasionally. Cover goose with foil and continue roasting, pouring off fat from time to time and basting once or twice, about 45 minutes, or until meat in thickest part of drumstick no longer looks pink when pierced.

Spoon stuffing out of goose. Cover goose and keep warm. Heat any remaining stuffing in a skillet over low heat, stirring with fork. Add stuffing from goose and lightly combine. Add 2 tablespoons goose fat from pan to stuffing mixture, if desired.

Discard remaining fat from pan. Deglaze pan with wine and ½ cup stock. Bring to a boil, stirring and scraping. (If roasting pan is large, place it over 2 burners.) Strain deglazing mixture into a small saucepan. Add remaining stock and bring to a boil. Season lightly with salt and pepper and reduce heat to low.

Whisk cornstarch or potato starch or arrowroot mixture to blend, then gradually whisk half of it into simmering sauce. Return to a boil, whisking. If sauce is too thin, gradually whisk in remaining starch mixture and return to a boil. Taste and adjust seasoning.

To carve goose, cut off breast and legs. Carve breast in thin slices. Serve with stuffing, garnishing each serving with a fig half. Serve sauce separately.

GOOSE WITH GRAPES, ORANGES, AND KIWIS
Oie aux raisins, à l'orange, et aux kiwis

Goose is a favorite for those who prefer dark meat—that's all it has! This roast goose, with its colorful fruit garnish and exquisite port sauce, makes a lovely, festive main course. Serve it with wild rice, white rice, or steamed potatoes. MAKES 6 TO 8 SERVINGS

1 young goose (about 8 to 9
    pounds), thawed if frozen,
    patted dry
Salt and freshly ground pepper
1 onion, quartered
1 large navel orange
2 kiwis
1 1/2 cups Simple Goose Stock or
    Chicken Stock (see recipes) or
    packaged broth

1/4 cup port
1 tablespoon cornstarch, potato
    starch, or arrowroot dissolved
    in 2 tablespoons port
2 tablespoons strained fresh orange
    juice
2 teaspoons Cognac
A few drops of lemon juice
    (optional)
1/2 cup red seedless grapes

Preheat oven to 450°F. Remove excess fat from goose. Cut off fatty flap of skin near tail. Prick goose skin a few times with a fork or skewer; do not pierce meat. Season goose inside and outside with salt and pepper. Put quartered onion inside goose. Put goose on its back on rack in roasting pan.

Roast goose 30 minutes, or until it begins to brown, basting occasionally. Remove fat with a bulb baster as it accumulates.

Reduce oven temperature to 350°F. Turn goose over onto its breast. Roast 1 hour and 15 minutes. Cover goose with foil and continue roasting, removing fat from time to time and basting once or twice, about 45 minutes more. To check, pierce thickest part of drumstick deeply with thin knife; meat should no longer look pink.

Peel orange and remove pith. Cut orange in segments carefully, removing as much as possible of membrane between them. Cut each segment in half. Peel kiwis; cut 1 in half-slices and 1 in rounds.

When goose is cooked, discard fat from pan. Deglaze pan with 1/2 cup goose stock and the port. Bring to a boil, stirring and scraping. (If roasting pan is large, place it over 2 burners.)

Strain deglazing mixture into a medium saucepan. Add remaining goose stock and bring to a boil. Season lightly with salt and pepper and reduce heat to low.

Whisk cornstarch or potato starch or arrowroot mixture to blend, then gradually whisk half of it into simmering stock. Return to a boil, whisking. If sauce is too thin, gradually whisk in remaining starch mixture and return to a boil. Whisk in orange juice and Cognac and heat without boiling. Add lemon juice, if desired; taste and adjust seasoning. Add grapes, kiwi half-slices, and half the orange segments. Let stand 30 seconds to heat fruit.

To carve goose, cut off breast and legs; discard onion. Carve breast in thin slices. Spoon sauce over portions of goose, and garnish with kiwi rounds and remaining orange segments.

SEE PHOTOGRAPH.

Game Birds

A famous classic preparation, which illustrates how esteemed game birds are in France, is stuffing them with foie gras and truffles. More common and more affordable matches are fresh vegetables, mushrooms of all types, and often fruit, especially grapes.

We are lucky that game birds are becoming more available to us as well. Birds with dark, tasty meat such as quail and squab, as well as birds like pheasant, which have delicate meat, can now be found at fine markets and butcher shops. Today these birds are raised, rather than being caught in the wild, and this makes it easier to control their quality.

Cornish game hens, more like small chickens than game, have long been easy to find in our markets. Although they are not available in France, they work well in French recipes that call for pheasant or baby chickens.

Game is usually reserved for a somewhat festive occasion rather than for everyday cooking because it is more expensive, not because it is complicated to cook. The main thing to remember is that the meat of game birds is lean and should not be overcooked or it will be dry. With this in mind, all the traditional poultry cooking methods can be used for them. Roasting *en cocotte* and sautéing are especially suitable because the birds cook quickly and remain moist. (For more about these cooking techniques, see "Chicken en Cocotte" and "Chicken Sautés.")

Sauces for game can be simple cooking juices deglazed with a flavored vinegar, as in Quail with Raspberry Vinegar and Onion Compote, or enriched with wine or spirits and a little butter, as in

Pheasant with Armagnac and Vegetable Julienne. Game birds are also good in tomato sauces, as in Braised Squab in Tomato-Saffron Sauce on a Bed of Pasta.

Hints

• An easy alternative to trussing squab, since they are so small, is to leave the wing tips on and to use them to pin the neck skin to the back of the bird.

• To serve Cornish hens, cut the cooked bird in half with poultry shears, cutting through the breast, then along the backbone. If desired, cut out the backbone when serving.

• Quail and squab are sometimes available boneless; their cooking time is shorter and they are much easier to eat.

QUAIL WITH WILD MUSHROOMS
Cailles à la forestière

It is hard to find a more irresistible combination than this one, with its superb sauce that blends the tastes of mushrooms, quail, and white wine. Serve this entrée to people who feel comfortable with one another; it's not easy to avoid using your fingers to eat the quail! You might want to provide finger bowls of water with lemon slices.

MAKES 4 SERVINGS

8 ounces fresh wild or exotic
    mushrooms, such as
    chanterelles, cèpes, or shiitake
    mushrooms
3 tablespoons vegetable oil
3 tablespoons plus 1 1/2 teaspoons
    butter
8 quail (about 1/4 pound each),
    thawed if frozen, patted dry
Salt and freshly ground pepper

12 ounces button mushrooms,
    quartered
2 shallots, minced
1 1/2 cups Chicken Stock (see recipe)
    or packaged broth
1/3 cup dry white wine
1 1/2 teaspoons all-purpose flour
2 tablespoons chopped fresh Italian
    parsley or regular parsley

Wipe wild mushrooms very gently with damp paper towel. If using shiitake mushrooms, cut off their tough stems. If mushrooms are large, cut in bite-size pieces.

Heat 2 tablespoons oil and 1 tablespoon butter in a large heavy sauté pan over medium-high heat. Season 4 quail with salt and pepper and add to pan. Brown birds on all sides for 6 to 7 minutes total, turning with tongs and covering with a splatter screen. If juices darken, reduce heat to low; do not let them burn. Remove to a plate. Repeat with remaining quail. Pour off about half the fat from pan.

Add button mushrooms and salt and pepper and brown lightly over medium heat. Leave mushrooms in pan.

Reduce heat to low, add shallots, and stir. Add quail with liquid from plate and ¼ cup stock. Cover and cook about 5 minutes on each side, or until quail legs are tender. To check, make a slit in plump part—meat near bone should be pink, not red. When quail are done, transfer to a platter and keep warm. Leave button mushrooms in pan.

Meanwhile, in a large skillet heat remaining 1 tablespoon oil and 2 tablespoons butter over medium-high heat. Add wild mushrooms and salt and pepper and sauté until tender, about 5 minutes.

Add wine to pan with button mushrooms and bring to a boil, stirring. Add remaining 1¼ cups stock and boil until mixture is reduced to about 1¼ cups. Taste and adjust seasoning.

Make kneaded butter by mashing 1½ teaspoons soft butter in a small bowl, then stirring in flour. Bring sauce to a simmer and push mushrooms to side of pan. Whisk in kneaded butter in 2 pieces. Return to a simmer, whisking. Add parsley, and taste and adjust seasoning.

Reheat wild mushrooms, if necessary. Cut quail in half, and serve with wild mushrooms on the side and mushroom sauce spooned over quail.

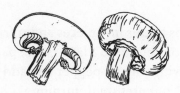

QUAIL WITH RASPBERRY VINEGAR AND ONION COMPOTE
Cailles au vinaigre de framboise et à la compote d'oignons

Raspberries might seem surprising with quail, but the berries and the raspberry vinegar sauce taste fabulous with the succulent quail meat. Although this is a new recipe, it is based on the time-honored French practice of making game sauces with wine vinegar and balancing the vinegar's acidity with currant jelly; this sauce uses a hint of raspberry preserves as the counterpoint.   MAKES 4 SERVINGS

ONION COMPOTE
4 to 6 tablespoons butter
2 pounds onions, cut in half and
*   sliced thin*

Salt and freshly ground pepper

6 tablespoons butter
2 tablespoons vegetable oil
8 quail (about ¼ pound each),
*   thawed if frozen, patted dry*
Salt and freshly ground pepper
2 shallots, minced

1 cup Chicken Stock (see recipe) or
*   packaged broth*
¼ cup raspberry vinegar
1 ½ teaspoons raspberry preserves
24 raspberries for garnish

ONION COMPOTE
   Melt butter in a large heavy casserole or sauté pan over low heat. Add onions and salt and pepper. Cover and cook, stirring often, 45 minutes. Uncover and cook, stirring very often, about 15 minutes, or until onions can be crushed easily with a wooden spoon; be careful not to let them burn. (Compote can be kept, covered, 1 day in refrigerator; reheat in saucepan over low heat.) Taste and adjust seasoning.

   Cut 4 tablespoons butter in 4 pieces and refrigerate. Heat oil and remaining 2 tablespoons butter in a large sauté pan over medium-high heat. Season 4 quail with salt and pepper and add to pan. Brown birds on all sides for 6 to 7 minutes total, turning with tongs and covering with a splatter screen. If juices darken, reduce heat to low; do not let them burn. Remove to a plate. Repeat with remaining quail.

Pour off all but a thin film of fat from pan. Reduce heat to low and stir in shallots. Add quail with liquid from plate and ¼ cup stock. Cover and cook about 5 minutes on each side, or until quail legs are tender. To check, make a slit in plump part of leg—meat should be pink, not red. Transfer to a platter and keep warm.

Add raspberry vinegar and remaining ¾ cup stock to pan and bring to a boil, stirring and scraping to dissolve pan juices. Boil until reduced to about ¾ cup. With pan over low heat, add 1 piece cold butter, shaking pan to swirl butter into sauce. Add remaining butter pieces in same way. Remove from heat. Stir in raspberry preserves. Taste and adjust seasoning.

Spoon onion compote on center of each plate. Set 2 quail on opposite sides of compote, and pour some sauce over quail. Garnish each plate with 6 fresh raspberries.

SQUAB EN COCOTTE WITH ROSEMARY AND ZUCCHINI
Pigeonneaux en cocotte au romarin et aux courgettes

The flavorful meat of squab is well complemented by assertive herbs like fresh rosemary. Steamed rice, moistened with some of the light sauce made from the squab cooking juices, is the best accompaniment.
MAKES 4 SERVINGS

4 squab (about 12 to 14 ounces each), room temperature
Salt and freshly ground pepper
3 tablespoons olive oil
3 medium-size zucchini (1 pound total)

4 medium-size garlic cloves, minced
2 tablespoons minced fresh rosemary, or 2 teaspoons dried, crumbled
⅓ cup dry white wine

Preheat oven to 400°F. Remove neck and giblets from squab. Pull out fat from inside squab on both sides near tail, and cut off tail. Pat squab dry. Season evenly inside and outside with salt and pepper. Use wing tips to hold squab neck skin in place.

Heat oil in heavy 4- to 5-quart oval enamel-lined cast-iron casserole over medium-high heat. Set squab on their sides in casserole. Cover pan with large splatter screen, if desired, and brown, about 2 minutes. (If fat begins to turn dark brown at any time, reduce heat to medium.) Using 2 wooden spoons to prevent squab skin from tearing (and standing back to avoid splatters), gently turn squab onto breasts and brown about 2 minutes. Turn onto other sides and brown 2 minutes more. Turn squab on backs and brown 2 minutes. Baste squab with pan juices, then cover casserole and bake squab in oven 20 minutes.

Meanwhile, cut each zucchini crosswise in 3 equal pieces, then in lengthwise strips about 1/4 inch wide and 1/4 inch thick.

Stir garlic and half the rosemary into pan juices. Baste squab with juices and cover. Reduce oven temperature to 350°F. and bake squab until meat is still pink when thickest part of leg is pierced with a thin knife, about 5 minutes. Transfer squab to platter, reserving pan juices. Cover squab with foil and keep warm.

Bring pan juices to a boil over medium heat. Add zucchini and season with salt and pepper. Cook, stirring occasionally, until crisp-tender, about 3 minutes. Discard any squab juices on platter. Using slotted spoon, arrange zucchini around squab. Cover with foil.

Skim as much fat as possible from juices in casserole, then bring to a boil. Add wine and boil again, skimming fat frequently and scraping up any browned bits on bottom and sides of casserole. Boil until slightly thickened, about 2 minutes. Add remaining rosemary and simmer over low heat for 2 minutes, stirring often. Taste and adjust seasoning. Pour sauce into sauceboat and serve alongside platter of squab and zucchini.

BRAISED SQUAB IN TOMATO-SAFFRON SAUCE ON A BED OF PASTA
Pigeonneaux braisés à la provençale

This recipe takes the trouble out of eating squab; after it is braised, the meat is cut in strips and returned to the sauce. Thus it can be reheated and there are no bones to contend with at the table. The exuberant Provençal sauce of tomatoes, saffron, and garlic gains extra flavor because the squab simmers in it. If squab is not available, substitute Cornish hens or chicken pieces, but keep in mind that their cooking times will be longer.   MAKES 4 TO 6 SERVINGS

4 squabs (about 12 to 14 ounces each), thawed if frozen
Salt and freshly ground pepper
3 tablespoons olive oil
2 onions, cut in half and sliced thin
1 medium-size carrot, cut in half and sliced thin
3 pounds ripe tomatoes, cut in large dice, or three 28-ounce cans whole plum tomatoes, drained and diced
6 medium-size garlic cloves, minced

1/2 cup Chicken Stock (see recipe) or packaged broth
2 sprigs fresh thyme, or 1/2 teaspoon dried leaf thyme, crumbled
1 bay leaf
5 parsley stems (optional)
1/4 teaspoon saffron threads, crumbled
Cayenne pepper to taste
1 pound fresh fettuccine, or 12 to 14 ounces dried
Thyme sprigs for garnish

Remove neck and giblets from squab. Pull out fat from inside squab on both sides near tail. Cut off tail and wing tips, and pat dry. Season evenly inside and outside with salt and pepper.

Heat 2 tablespoons oil in heavy enamel-lined cast-iron casserole over medium-high heat. Add squab and brown lightly on all sides, taking about 2 minutes per side. Remove to a plate.

Add onions and carrot to casserole and cook over medium-low heat, stirring often, until onions just begin to brown, about 10 minutes. Add tomatoes, garlic, stock, thyme, bay leaf, parsley stems (if desired), saffron, and salt and pepper, and bring to a boil, stirring. Reduce heat to low, cover, and simmer 30 minutes.

Return squab to pan and add any juices from plate. Cover and simmer over low heat 8 minutes. Turn squab over and simmer 7 minutes, or until just tender; when thickest part of leg is pierced with a knife, meat should look pink.

Remove squab and cool until easy to handle. Remove legs; leave leg meat on bones. Cut remaining meat from bones and discard skin. Save breast meat in large pieces and cut remaining meat in strips.

Remove bay leaf and parsley stems from sauce. Purée sauce in a food mill; or purée in food processor and then push through a strainer. Return sauce to casserole and reheat. If sauce is too thin, boil uncovered, stirring often, until thickened, about 5 to 7 minutes. Add cayenne and taste and adjust seasoning.

Reheat sauce and stir in small squab pieces, then larger pieces. Turn large pieces over and keep warm over very low heat.

Cook pasta in a large pot of boiling salted water uncovered over high heat about 2 minutes for fresh or 5 minutes for dried, or until just tender (al dente). Drain, transfer to a large bowl, and toss with remaining tablespoon olive oil. To serve, spoon pasta onto plates and top with squab and sauce; set larger pieces of meat on top. Garnish with thyme sprig.

PHEASANT WITH COGNAC, BRAISED SHALLOTS, AND GRAPES
Faisan au cognac, aux échalotes, et aux raisins

Grapes and game birds are a popular combination in France; the juicy fruit beautifully complements the lean meat. Besides pheasant, squab and quail are also served with grapes. Old-fashioned recipes call for the tedious process of peeling and seeding the grapes, but seedless grapes, which don't have tough skins, turn this into an easy dish. For a pretty presentation, use both green and red grapes when they are available. MAKES 2 OR 3 SERVINGS

1/4 pound shallots (8 or 9 medium), peeled
1 young pheasant (about 2 1/2 pounds), thawed if frozen, room temperature
Salt and freshly ground pepper
2 tablespoons vegetable oil
1 tablespoon butter
5 tablespoons Cognac or brandy

2/3 cup Chicken Stock (see recipe) or packaged broth
1 teaspoon potato starch dissolved in 2 teaspoons water
1/3 cup small green seedless grapes, room temperature
1/3 cup small red seedless grapes, room temperature

Preheat oven to 400°F. Cut shallots in half lengthwise, pulling them apart by their natural division where possible. Cover shallots with water in a small saucepan, bring to a boil, and boil 2 minutes. Drain thoroughly.

Remove giblets from pheasant; cut off neck, tail, and wing tips. Pull out fat from inside on both sides near tail and from neck end. Pat pheasant dry. Season evenly inside and outside with salt and pepper.

Heat oil and butter in heavy 4- to 5-quart oval enamel-lined cast-iron casserole over medium-high heat. Set pheasant on its side in casserole, cover pan with large splatter screen, if desired, and brown about 2 minutes. (If fat begins to turn dark brown at any time, reduce heat to medium.) Using 2 wooden spoons to prevent pheasant skin from tearing (and standing back to avoid splatters), gently turn onto its breast and brown about 2 minutes. Turn pheasant onto other side and brown 2 minutes more, then turn on its back and brown 2 minutes.

Baste pheasant with pan juices. Using bulb baster, remove most of fat from pan. Add shallots to pan and pour 4 tablespoons Cognac or brandy over pheasant; cover and let stand 5 minutes. Bake, covered, about 15 minutes, or until meat is white with just a touch of pink near the bone; check by piercing breast meat with a knife. Do not overcook or pheasant will be dry. (Pheasant can be kept warm in casserole, covered, for 15 minutes.)

Meanwhile, in small saucepan bring stock to a boil. Reduce heat to low. Whisk potato starch mixture to blend, then gradually whisk it into stock. Simmer over low heat 1 minute; mixture will be thick.

When pheasant is done, pour cooking juices into a glass measuring cup, leaving shallots in pan. Pour off lighter layer of fat, leaving dark juices (at bottom) behind. Return juices to casserole and bring to a simmer. Add thickened stock mixture and grapes. Cover and cook over low heat 2 minutes. Remove from heat and stir in remaining tablespoon Cognac. Taste and adjust seasoning.

Carve pheasant, removing excess fat. Serve breast and thigh meat; drumsticks are full of sinews and difficult to eat. (Meat can be scraped off and used in rice or pasta dishes, or used for stock.) Spoon grapes and shallots around pheasant, and spoon sauce over it.

❧ PHEASANT WITH ARMAGNAC AND VEGETABLE JULIENNE
Faisan à l'armagnac à la julienne de légumes

Pheasant should be cooked only briefly because its lean delicate meat can overcook easily. Here the pheasant pieces are served on a bed of vegetable julienne and topped with the aromatic, Armagnac-scented juices.   MAKES 2 OR 3 SERVINGS

1 young pheasant (about 2 1/2 pounds)

1 1/2 to 2 1/2 cups Chicken Stock (see recipe) or unsalted packaged broth

1 medium-size leek (about 7 ounces), split and cleaned

3 medium-size carrots (about 7 ounces total)

2 celery stalks, peeled to remove strings

7 tablespoons butter

1/4 pound mushrooms, cut in half and sliced thin

Salt and freshly ground pepper

1 tablespoon vegetable oil

2 tablespoons plus 2 teaspoons Armagnac, Cognac, or brandy

Cut pheasant in 8 pieces as you would cut a chicken (see page 313). After cutting wing with some of breast meat, cut remaining breast meat off bone in 2 pieces. Reserve back, neck, and wing tips for stock, along with any meat scraps.

Make pheasant stock, if desired. Put pheasant back, neck, and other bones and scraps in 2 1/2 cups chicken stock in a medium saucepan and bring to a boil. Cover and cook over low heat 45 minutes. Strain stock, return to saucepan, and boil until reduced to 3/4 cup.

If not making pheasant stock, boil 1 1/2 cups chicken stock until reduced to 3/4 cup.

Cut leek in 2-inch pieces, press with hand to flatten, and cut lengthwise in 1/4-inch slices. Cut carrots in about 2-inch pieces. Cut each piece lengthwise in slices 1/4 inch thick, then each slice in lengthwise strips 1/4 inch thick. Cut celery in pieces about same size as carrots.

Cut 4 tablespoons butter in 4 pieces and refrigerate. Melt 2 tablespoons butter in a sauté pan or shallow casserole. Add carrots, celery, mushrooms, leeks, and salt and pepper and stir. Cover and cook over low heat, stirring occasionally, 15 minutes, or until tender, and reserve.

Pat pheasant pieces dry. Heat oil and 1 tablespoon butter in another sauté pan or shallow casserole over medium-high heat. Add pheasant pieces and salt and pepper to taste and brown on all sides, a total of about 5 minutes. Add 2 tablespoons Armagnac and ¼ cup pheasant or chicken stock and bring to a simmer. Cover and simmer about 5 minutes for breast pieces, and about 12 to 15 minutes for leg and thigh pieces, or until tender when pierced with a thin knife or skewer. Remove pheasant to platter and keep warm.

Reheat vegetables. Add remaining ½ cup stock to sauce from the pheasant pan. Boil to reduce to ½ cup. With pan on and off heat, swirl in cold butter, 1 piece at a time, until incorporated. Pour into a small bowl and add 2 teaspoons Armagnac. Taste and adjust seasoning. Serve pheasant breast and thigh meat on top of vegetables. (Drumsticks are full of sinews and are difficult to eat.) Serve sauce separately.

CORNISH HENS WITH POTATOES, LEEKS, AND DILL
Coquelets en cocotte aux poireaux et aux pommes de terre

Cornish hens are not available in France, but they are wonderfully moist when baked French style, *en cocotte.* In this dish, leeks are sautéed in the tasty cooking juices, which are then accented with dill and cream to form a delicate sauce for the birds.

MAKES 4 SERVINGS

2 Cornish hens (about 1½ pounds each), thawed if frozen, room temperature
Salt and freshly ground pepper
2 tablespoons vegetable oil
1 tablespoon butter
2 large leeks (about 1 pound total), white and light green parts only, split and cleaned

6 medium-size oval potatoes (about 1½ pounds total)
2 sprigs fresh dill
2 tablespoons dry white wine
½ cup heavy cream
2 tablespoons snipped fresh dill

Preheat oven to 400°F. Remove neck and giblets from hens. Pull out fat from inside on both sides near tail. Cut off tail and wing tips and pat hens dry. Season hens evenly inside and outside with salt and pepper, and truss, if desired.

Heat oil and butter in heavy 4- to 5-quart oval enamel-lined cast-iron casserole over medium-high heat. Set hens on their sides in casserole. Cover pan with large splatter screen, if desired, and brown, about 3 minutes. (If fat begins to turn dark brown at any time, reduce heat to medium.) Using 2 wooden spoons to prevent skin from tearing (and standing back to avoid splatters), gently turn hens onto their breasts and brown about 3 minutes. Turn hens onto other sides and brown 3 minutes more, then turn hens on their backs and brown 2 minutes.

Baste hens with pan juices. Cover casserole and bake until juices run clear when thickest part of leg is pierced with a thin knife or skewer, about 30 minutes; if juices are still pink, bake a few more minutes and test again. (Hens can be kept warm in casserole, covered, for 15 minutes.) Lift hens, draining their juices back into casserole, and transfer to a platter. Discard trussing strings, if used. Cover hens with foil and keep warm.

Cut leeks in 2-inch pieces, press with hand to flatten, and cut lengthwise in 1/4-inch slices; reserve. Peel potatoes and cut in half lengthwise. Trim each half to an oval shape, using a paring knife to round out any sharp angles. Keep potatoes in bowl of cold water until ready to cook.

In large saucepan, cover potatoes with water and bring to a boil. Add salt, cover, and simmer over medium heat until nearly tender, about 10 minutes. Drain thoroughly.

Bring pan juices in casserole to a boil. Add potatoes, dill sprigs, and salt and pepper to taste. Cook over low heat, carefully turning potatoes often, until they are light brown and just tender, about 10 minutes. Using slotted spoon, transfer potatoes to dish and keep warm. Discard dill sprigs.

Add leeks to casserole and sprinkle with salt and pepper. Cover and cook over low heat, stirring occasionally, until just tender, about 5 minutes. Meanwhile, cut hens in half with poultry shears, cutting through breastbone, then along back. Discard any juices on platter. Using slotted spoon, arrange leeks around hens. Arrange potatoes atop leeks; cover.

Skim as much fat as possible from juices in casserole and bring to a boil. Add wine and bring to a boil, stirring and scraping up any browned bits on bottom and sides of casserole. Add cream and bring to a boil, stirring. Reduce heat to medium and simmer, stirring often, until sauce is thick enough to lightly coat a spoon, about 3 minutes. Strain into sauceboat. Sprinkle potatoes with 1 teaspoon snipped dill, and stir remaining dill into sauce. Taste sauce and adjust seasoning. Serve sauce alongside platter of hens.

CORNISH HENS WITH GARBANZO BEANS AND RAISINS
Coquelets aux pois chiches et aux raisins secs

An American bird, French flavors, and a Moroccan presentation give this entrée an intriguing character. The hens are paired with couscous, which is topped, Moroccan-style, with raisins and garbanzo beans, and moistened with a Madeira butter sauce.

MAKES 4 SERVINGS

1/2 cup dried garbanzo beans (chick-peas), sorted and rinsed, or 1 1/2 cups canned garbanzos
Salt and freshly ground pepper
2 Cornish hens (about 1 1/2 pounds each), thawed if frozen
2 tablespoons vegetable oil
6 to 7 tablespoons butter

1 large onion (about 1/2 pound), minced
1/2 cup dark raisins
1 cup couscous
1 cup boiling water
5 tablespoons Madeira
6 tablespoons cold butter, cut in 6 pieces

Soak dried garbanzo beans in bowl of 1 1/2 cups cold water in cool place 8 hours or overnight. Drain beans and rinse. Put in medium saucepan, add 2 cups water, and bring to a boil. Reduce heat to low, cover, and simmer 45 minutes. Add pinch of salt and simmer until tender, about 30 minutes more. (Cooked beans can be kept in their cooking liquid, covered, 2 days in refrigerator.)

Preheat oven to 400°F. Remove neck and giblets from hens. Pull out fat from inside on both sides near tail. Cut off tail and wing tips, and pat hens dry. Season inside and outside with salt and pepper, and truss, if desired.

Heat oil and 1 tablespoon butter in heavy 4- to 5-quart enamel-lined cast-iron casserole over medium-high heat. Set hens on their sides in casserole. Cover with large splatter screen, if desired, and brown about 3 minutes. (If fat begins to turn dark brown, reduce heat to medium.) Using 2 wooden spoons to prevent skin from tearing (and standing back to avoid splatters), gently turn hens onto their breasts and brown about 3 minutes. Turn hens onto other sides and brown 3 minutes more, then turn on their backs and brown 2 minutes.

Baste hens with pan juices. Cover casserole and bake until juices run clear when thickest part of leg is pierced with a thin knife or skewer, about 30 minutes; if juices are still pink, bake a few more minutes and test again.

While hens are cooking, melt 2 tablespoons butter in large heavy skillet over low heat. Add onion and cook, stirring often, until soft but not brown, about 10 minutes.

When hens are tender, lift them, draining their juices back into casserole, and transfer them to a platter. Discard trussing strings, if used. Cut hens in half with poultry shears, cutting through breastbone, then along back. Cover and keep warm.

Drain cooked beans or canned beans and add to pan juices. Add raisins, cover, and simmer over low heat until raisins are tender, about 7 minutes. Using a slotted spoon, transfer beans and raisins to bowl. Cover and keep warm. Reserve juices in casserole.

Add 1 tablespoon butter to onion in skillet and melt over low heat. Using fork, mix in couscous. Season with salt and pepper. Remove from heat and shake skillet to spread couscous in even layer. Pour boiling water over couscous and add 1 tablespoon pan juices. Immediately cover skillet tightly. Let couscous stand 5 minutes. Cut 2 or 3 tablespoons butter in 6 pieces and let stand at room temperature.

Skim as much fat as possible from juices in casserole, and bring to a boil. Add 4 tablespoons Madeira and boil 1 minute, scraping up any browned bits from bottom and sides of casserole. Pour Madeira sauce into small heavy saucepan. If any fat remains, remove by quickly running paper towel over surface of sauce. Cover and reserve.

Scatter room-temperature butter pieces over couscous, cover, and let stand 2 minutes. Toss couscous with fork to distribute butter evenly. Taste and adjust seasoning. Lightly spoon couscous in a mound on platter, spoon garbanzo beans and raisins around outer edge of couscous, and place hens alongside. Cover and keep warm.

Add remaining tablespoon Madeira to sauce and bring to boil. Reduce heat to low. Whisk in 2 pieces of cold butter. Whisk in remaining butter, 1 piece at a time, removing pan from heat briefly if drops of melted butter appear on surface of sauce. Do not let sauce become too hot or it will separate. (If sauce breaks down at any time, remove from heat and whisk in 2 more tablespoons cold butter.) Remove from heat, and taste and adjust seasoning. Pour into sauceboat and serve separately alongside platter with hens, beans, and couscous.

CORNISH HENS WITH BRANDY-PORT SAUCE AND PEAS
Coquelets au porto aux petits pois

Sautéing is one of the best ways to prepare Cornish hens—they cook quickly and become very tender and succulent. The creamy sauce here gains a delicate sweetness from the port and the peas.

MAKES 4 SERVINGS

2 large Cornish hens (1 1/4 to 1 1/2 pounds each), thawed if frozen
Salt and freshly ground pepper
2 tablespoons butter
1 1/2 pounds fresh peas (about 1 1/2 cups shelled), or 1 1/2 cups frozen, thawed

3/4 cup Chicken Stock (see recipe) or packaged broth
1/3 cup Cognac or brandy
1/3 cup port
1 cup heavy cream

Cut each hen in 4 pieces: First cut off 2 leg-and-thigh pieces at thigh joint, then 2 breast-and-wing pieces. Cut off backs and wing tips and reserve for stock. Pat hen pieces dry, and season with salt and pepper. Melt butter in heavy sauté pan or deep skillet over medium-high heat. Add hen pieces and brown well on each side, about 3 minutes. Cover and cook over low heat about 15 minutes, or until tender. Remove hen pieces to a platter and keep warm, covered, in 275°F. oven.

Meanwhile, cook fresh peas in a medium saucepan of boiling salted water, uncovered, 2 or 3 minutes, or until just tender. Drain, rinse with cold water, and drain well.

Reheat hen pan juices, add stock, and bring to a boil. Add Cognac, port, and cream and cook over medium heat until sauce is thick enough to coat a spoon, about 6 minutes. Add cooked fresh or thawed frozen peas and heat gently. Taste and adjust seasoning. Spoon sauce with peas over hens and serve.

Meat

VEAL

BEEF

LAMB

PORK

RABBIT

VENISON

Much is made of the richness of the French diet. Yet the portions of meat are usually much smaller than ours and are accompanied by a generous amount of vegetables. French chef manuals call for cutting five-ounce steaks, while books for home cooks often specify even more diminutive pieces. Our steaks of eight ounces would seem enormous to a Frenchman.

Buying meat at a market in France is a pleasure because the butchers are so knowledgeable. Like chefs, they go through an apprenticeship program to thoroughly learn their *métier,* and only after several years of work experience does someone have the right to call himself a butcher. Butchers treat their profession as an art, too, arraying daintily tied roasts and other meats in an appealing manner. And butchers are glad to give advice on how to cook the various cuts of meat and what to serve with them.

"Color themes" help cooks remember the methods of French meat cookery; these serve as basic outlines for summarizing their essence. The "red-and-white" theme describes types of meats and the "brown-and-white" theme refers to types of culinary preparations.

The red-and-white theme relates to the meat's color. For the purpose of cooking, meats are divided into red—beef, lamb, and venison—and white—veal and pork and sometimes very young lamb. In broadest terms, red meats are cooked over highest heat and are often served rare, while white meats are cooked more gently and are usually served well-done.

The brown-and-white theme relates to the style of all sorts of entrées in traditional French cuisine, from sautés to braised dishes, and from ragoûts to sauces. For a brown dish, the meat is well browned and moistened with brown stock and often red wine. For a white dish, a light stock and usually white wine are used, and the sauce is frequently enhanced with cream. To this I feel a third category should be added, one which originated in Provençal cooking but now is popular throughout France—red dishes, in which tomatoes are prominent in the sauce or cooking liquid.

The themes come together in that red meats are often cooked in the brown style and white meats in the white style. Any type of meat can be cooked as a tomato-flavored dish.

Within this framework, chefs created hundreds of recipes by varying the vegetables and flavorings. For example, Escoffier in his *Guide Culinaire,* considered to be the bible of fine cuisine of this century, gives ninety-five variations on entrées made with tenderloin steaks alone. Here are just a few examples: Tournedos Dubarry, sautéed steaks surrounded by browned cheese-topped cauliflower florets and topped with a sauce of veal stock finished with butter; Tournedos La Vallière, steaks coated with tomato-mushroom sauce finished with julienne of truffles; Tournedos à la moelle, grilled steaks topped with a slice of marrow and served with a butter-enriched red wine sauce; and Tournedos parisienne, steaks topped with stuffed artichoke hearts, surrounded by butter-sautéed potato balls and served with a rich brown sauce.

Veal Scallops and Chops

Scallops and chops, the most luxurious cuts of veal, are ideal for an elegant meal that is ready in a short time. Because of their delicate taste, French cooks traditionally pair them with subtle sauces, as in Veal Paillardes with Light Tarragon Cream, but they also excel in matching them with the zesty flavors of olive oil, light tomato sauces, and Mediterranean vegetables.

Scallops are thin tender slices of veal. When they are pounded even thinner, they are called *paillardes.* Both slices and chops are lean cuts of veal that must be handled with care and should not be allowed to overcook, or they will be dry.

Veal scallops and *paillardes* are sautéed so that their outer surface browns slightly and forms a light crust that keeps the meat moist and succulent. By the time this has occurred, the interior of these thin meat slices is already sufficiently cooked.

Since veal chops are thicker than scallops, they finish cooking over lower heat after browning, occasionally with the addition of a little liquid. Chops can also be grilled, but should first be marinated so they remain moist.

To further prevent sticking and to protect the delicate flesh of the veal, it is often lightly floured before sautéing. Or it can be dipped in flour, egg, and bread crumbs, like the turkey in Crisp Turkey Paillardes with Capers. Coatings also brown more easily than uncoated meat would and give veal slices an appetizing appearance. If using a heavy pan with a nonstick surface, however, veal can be sautéed without being floured.

It is important to buy veal scallops from a good butcher, because some veal can be disappointingly watery and tasteless. Veal is best when it is very light pink; it should never be red or brownish. The cut of veal suitable for scallops and *paillardes* is sold under several names: veal cutlets, boneless veal slices, scallops, scaloppine, and escalopes.

A quick pan sauce is often prepared with the meat juices that caramelize on the bottom of the skillet during sautéing. It is made directly in the pan by deglazing, or dissolving the browned meat essences in a small amount of liquid, such as white wine, alcoholic cider, Madeira, port, veal or chicken stock, or a combination of these. The sauce is reduced by boiling until it thickens slightly and its flavor intensifies. Sometimes the wine and stock are reduced before the veal is sautéed so the cooked meat will not have to wait long. For a finishing touch, fresh herbs, and sometimes cream or butter, are added.

Mushrooms, both regular and wild, are a favorite accompaniment for veal scallops and chops, but these can also be served with any seasonal vegetables, especially the noble ones like asparagus and artichoke bottoms.

Hints

• When buying veal scallops, try to choose pieces of meat that are cut from one muscle, rather than two muscles connected by a membrane, so the scallops will not curl up during cooking.

• Flour veal pieces when ready to sauté them. If they sit even for a few minutes, the flour becomes moistened by juices from the meat and may stick to the pan.

• When sautéing or grilling veal, do not crowd the skillet or grill; this reduces the temperature of the pan and causes the meat to stew. For the same reason, bring the meat to room temperature if possible before cooking, so it will not cool the pan too much.

• Keep sautéed meat hot in a warming drawer or a low oven while finishing the sauce. Cover uncoated meat to prevent it from drying out. Do not cover coated meat or the crust will become soggy.

• When sautéing veal scallops or *paillardes* for more than four people, use several skillets to avoid keeping the meat warm for too long.

• Before deglazing the pan after sautéing flour-coated meat, scrape the pan clean if any large bits of coating are stuck to it.

✿ VEAL PAILLARDES WITH LIGHT TARRAGON CREAM
Paillardes de veau à la crème d'estragon

"A meal in minutes" might be one definition for *paillardes,* or thin cuts of fine meat that are grilled or sautéed. This easy but elegant sautéed veal is a favorite of my students. Any seasonal vegetable makes a fine partner for the veal, but I prefer asparagus, steamed potatoes, or sautéed mushrooms, which are wonderful with the fresh-tasting creamy sauce.   MAKES 4 SERVINGS

4 veal cutlets or scallops (4 ounces each)
1/4 cup all-purpose flour
Salt and freshly ground pepper
2 tablespoons vegetable oil
4 tablespoons butter
2 medium-size shallots, minced
1/2 cup dry white wine

1/2 cup White Veal Stock or Chicken Stock (see recipe) or packaged broth
1 cup heavy cream
1 1/2 to 2 tablespoons chopped fresh tarragon
1 tablespoon chopped fresh parsley (optional)

Pound veal cutlets, 1 at a time, between 2 pieces of plastic wrap or wax paper to thickness of 1/4 inch, using flat meat pounder or rolling pin.

Spread flour in a large plate. Season veal with salt and pepper on both sides. Heat oil and 2 tablespoons butter in large heavy skillet over medium-high heat. Lightly coat 2 pieces of veal with flour on both sides, and tap and shake to remove excess. Add coated veal pieces to skillet. Sauté until lightly browned on both sides, about 1 1/2 minutes per side. Turn using 2 wide spatulas. Transfer veal to oven-proof platter, arrange it side by side, and keep warm in a 250°F. oven. Repeat flouring and sautéing with remaining veal. If fat in skillet begins to brown, reduce heat to medium.

Discard fat from skillet. Add remaining 2 tablespoons butter and melt over low heat. Stir in shallots. Pour in wine and bring to a boil, stirring and scraping browned bits from base of pan. Boil, stirring, until wine is reduced to about 1/4 cup. Add stock and boil until mixture is again reduced to about ¼ cup. Stir in cream and a pinch of salt and pepper. Simmer over medium heat, stirring, until sauce is thick enough to coat a spoon, about 7 minutes.

Stir in tarragon and parsley, and taste and adjust seasoning. Transfer veal to plates, discarding any liquid that escaped from veal. Spoon sauce over veal and serve immediately.

VEAL SCALLOPS WITH MEDITERRANEAN VEGETABLES
Escalopes de veau aux légumes méditerranéens

Preparing this dish will transport you to the sunny Mediterranean. The lightly cooked veal served with eggplant, red pepper, and a five-minute tomato sauce is a perfect summertime entrée. Steamed white or brown rice or couscous are excellent accompaniments.

MAKES 4 SERVINGS

1 small eggplant (about ¾ pound)
3 small zucchini
1 large red bell pepper
10 to 12 tablespoons olive oil
Salt and freshly ground pepper
4 veal scallops (each about 4 ounces and ¼ inch thick), patted dry

1 pound ripe tomatoes, peeled, seeded, and finely chopped, or one 28-ounce can whole plum tomatoes, drained and chopped
2 teaspoons chopped fresh thyme, or ¾ teaspoon dried leaf thyme
1 medium-size garlic clove, very finely minced
1 tablespoon chopped fresh parsley

Cut eggplant in half lengthwise, then slice in half-moons about ¼ inch thick. Slice zucchini in rounds about ¼ inch thick. Core pepper and cut in lengthwise strips about ¼ inch wide.

Heat 2 tablespoons olive oil in a large heavy skillet over medium-high heat. Quickly add enough eggplant slices to make one layer. Season with salt and pepper, and sauté about 2 or 3 minutes per side, or until tender. Using slotted spatula, transfer to paper towels. Continue with remaining eggplant in 2 or 3 more batches, adding about 2 tablespoons oil between batches.

Add 1 tablespoon oil to skillet. Add zucchini, season with salt and pepper, and sauté over medium-high heat about 1 or 2 minutes per side, or until tender. Remove with slotted spoon.

Add 1 tablespoon oil if skillet is dry. Add pepper and sauté about 5 minutes, or until tender. Return eggplant and zucchini to skillet and cover.

Heat 2 tablespoons olive oil in large skillet over high heat. Add veal, season with salt and pepper, and sauté about 1 minute per side, or until lightly browned and just tender. Transfer to a platter in one layer, cover, and keep warm in 250°F. oven.

Add tomatoes and salt and pepper to pan used to cook veal and cook over high heat about 5 minutes, or until thickened. Meanwhile, heat vegetables over medium heat. Pour any juices from veal platter into tomatoes and bring to a simmer. Remove from heat and add thyme and garlic. Taste and adjust seasoning.

To serve, divide vegetables among plates, set veal on top, and place one spoonful of tomato sauce onto the center of each veal piece. Sprinkle chopped parsley on sauce.

❧ VEAL CHOPS WITH CIDER AND PEARL ONIONS
Côtes de veau au cidre et aux petits oignons

This is one of the dishes I love best—it is delicious, quick, and easy and has very few ingredients. I first tasted it in Normandy, where cider is used in cooking much like wine is in other regions. Be sure to purchase dry, or alcoholic cider; regular apple cider will be too sweet. Potato purée is a traditional accompaniment in the region, but I like to serve the veal with asparagus or broccoli as well.

MAKES 4 SERVINGS

4 small veal loin chops (about ½ pound each), approximately 1 inch thick
20 pearl onions (about 4 to 5 ounces)

Salt and freshly ground pepper
2 tablespoons butter
½ cup hard cider
⅔ cup heavy cream
2 teaspoons snipped chives

Trim excess fat from veal chops and pat dry. Put pearl onions in a saucepan, cover with water, and boil 1 minute. Drain, rinse with cold water, and peel with a paring knife.

Season veal on both sides with salt and pepper. Melt butter in a large heavy sauté pan or skillet over medium-high heat. Add veal chops and brown on both sides, about 2 or 3 minutes per side. Transfer veal to a plate. Add onions to pan and sauté over medium-high heat about 3 minutes, or until they begin to brown. Push onions to side of pan.

Return veal chops to skillet. Add cider and veal juices from plate and bring to a simmer. Cover and cook over low heat about 4 or 5 minutes per side, or until veal is tender; meat should be light pink or white. Remove veal from pan. Continue cooking onions about 10 minutes, or until tender. Remove with slotted spoon.

Bring cooking juices to a boil. Boil until reduced to about ½ cup. Add cream and cook until thick enough to coat a spoon, about 4 minutes. Taste and adjust seasoning. Return veal and onions to sauce and heat gently, uncovered; turn veal over to coat it with sauce.

Put chops on plates and onions next to them. Spoon sauce over chops and sprinkle with chives.

HERBED VEAL CHOPS WITH COGNAC
Côtes de veau aux herbes et au cognac

For this simple entrée, Cognac and fresh herbs lend a subtle accent to the cooking juices from the veal chops. Serve the chops with an assortment of colorful cooked vegetables, as in Roast Chicken with Spring Vegetables (see recipe), or, when time is short, with a fresh salad and best-quality French bread.   MAKES 4 SERVINGS

4 veal rib chops (about 8 or 9
*   ounces each), ¾ to 1 inch*
*   thick*
6 tablespoons butter
Salt and freshly ground pepper

6 tablespoons Cognac or brandy
2 tablespoons chopped fresh parsley
1 tablespoon snipped fresh chives
1 tablespoon chopped fresh tarragon

Pat veal chops dry. Melt 4 tablespoons butter in a large heavy skillet over medium-high heat. Add chops, season with salt and pepper, and sauté until brown, about 3 minutes per side. Reduce heat to low, add Cognac or brandy, and cover. Cook, turning veal over once or twice, until just tender, about 3 minutes; it should be just slightly pink when cut.

Add remaining 2 tablespoons butter and herbs and stir over low heat just until blended into juices. Taste juices and adjust seasoning. Turn veal chops over again to coat both sides with juices. Spoon juices over meat when serving.

MARINATED GRILLED VEAL CHOPS WITH WALNUT BUTTER
Côtes de veau grillées, beurre aux noix

Veal is generally marinated before it is grilled so it will not be dry. At serving time these chops are moistened with a seasoned butter as well. The walnut butter is softer than most flavored butters because walnut oil is substituted for part of the butter. When fresh basil is in season, prepare the variation that uses basil-garlic butter. Grilled mushrooms or peppers or sautéed zucchini make fine accompaniments.

MAKES 4 SERVINGS

4 veal loin chops, about 1 inch thick

2 tablespoons plus 2 teaspoons olive oil

1 tablespoon strained fresh lemon juice

1/2 teaspoon dried basil

Salt and freshly ground pepper

WALNUT BUTTER

3 tablespoons butter, softened

1 1/2 tablespoons ground or very finely chopped walnuts

1 tablespoon minced fresh parsley

3 tablespoons French walnut oil

Salt and freshly ground pepper

Put veal chops in a shallow dish in which they fit snugly in one layer. Mix olive oil, lemon juice, and basil, and pour over veal. Turn veal so both sides are well coated. Cover and let stand at room temperature about 2 hours; or refrigerate 4 to 8 hours.

WALNUT BUTTER

Mix softened butter with ground or finely chopped walnuts and parsley. With fork, gradually beat in walnut oil. Season with salt and pepper to taste. Cover and refrigerate 2 hours so flavors blend. Serve at room temperature.

Heat grill or broiler with rack 3 to 4 inches from heat. Lightly oil grill or broiler. Remove veal chops from marinade and season with salt and pepper. Put chops on hot grill or hot broiler rack and grill or broil (broil with door slightly open), brushing occasionally with remaining marinade, about 4 minutes per side, or until cooked to desired doneness; check by piercing with a knife—meat should be slightly pink or white.

Transfer to platter and top each chop with a spoonful of walnut butter.

GRILLED VEAL CHOPS WITH GARLIC-BASIL BUTTER

Prepare veal as above, substituting following garlic-basil butter for walnut butter: Soften ¼ cup butter and beat with 1 tablespoon finely chopped fresh basil and 1 small garlic clove, minced. Season with salt and pepper to taste. Cover and refrigerate 2 hours so flavors blend. Serve at room temperature.

VEAL SCALLOPS WITH CHANTERELLES AND GLAZED ONIONS
Escalopes de veau aux chanterelles et aux oignons glacés

When fresh bright orange chanterelles are in season, this veal entrée with its white wine–tomato sauce is a real treat. Other wild or exotic mushrooms, such as the more available shiitake mushrooms, can be used instead.   MAKES 4 SERVINGS

GLAZED PEARL ONIONS

24 pearl onions	*4 tablespoons butter*
Salt and freshly ground pepper	*1 teaspoon sugar*

FRESH TOMATO SAUCE

2 tablespoons butter

2½ pounds ripe tomatoes, peeled, seeded, and chopped

Pinch of thyme

1 bay leaf

Salt and freshly ground pepper

½ pound wild mushrooms, such as chanterelles or shiitake mushrooms

2 tablespoons vegetable oil

3 tablespoons butter

1 shallot, finely chopped

4 veal scallops (4 to 5 ounces each)

Salt and freshly ground pepper

½ cup dry white wine

Pinch of sugar (optional)

GLAZED PEARL ONIONS

Put onions in a heavy saucepan in which they can fit in one layer. Cover with water, bring to a boil, and boil 1 minute. Drain and rinse with cold water. Peel them with a paring knife.

Return onions to saucepan with a pinch of salt and pepper, butter, and 4 tablespoons water. Cover and cook over low heat, shaking pan occasionally, 15 to 20 minutes, or until tender. Sprinkle with sugar and cook, uncovered, over medium heat until onions are lightly glazed. Set aside.

FRESH TOMATO SAUCE

Melt butter in a large skillet and add tomatoes, thyme, bay leaf, and salt and pepper. Cook over medium heat, stirring often, about 20 minutes, or until tomatoes are soft and mixture is thick and smooth. Discard bay leaf. Purée tomatoes in a food processor or blender until very smooth.

Clean wild mushrooms very gently with damp paper towel. If using shiitake mushrooms, cut off their tough stems. If mushrooms are large, cut in bite-size pieces. Heat 1 tablespoon oil and 2 tablespoons butter in a skillet. Add shallot, stir, and add mushrooms and salt and pepper. Sauté over medium-high heat. When mushrooms render their liquid, raise heat to high and sauté, tossing often, until mushrooms are browned and tender and liquid has evaporated; total cooking time is about 6 or 7 minutes.

Just before serving, heat remaining oil and butter in a skillet. Lightly season veal with salt and pepper. Add enough veal to pan to make one layer and sauté over medium-high heat 1 or 2 minutes on each side, until lightly browned and tender. Transfer to a platter and keep warm in a low oven while sautéing remaining veal. Reheat onions and mushrooms uncovered, if necessary.

Add wine to skillet in which veal was cooked and bring to a boil, stirring. Add tomato sauce and simmer 2 to 3 minutes, stirring, until tomato sauce absorbs wine. Taste and adjust seasoning; if sauce is too acid, add a pinch of sugar.

To serve, spoon a little sauce on each of 4 plates and put veal on top, letting sauce show. Spoon wild mushrooms on top and onions around veal. Serve immediately with remaining sauce alongside.

VEAL SCALLOPS WITH WATERCRESS SAUCE
Escalopes de veau au cresson

Raw watercress is quite peppery, but brief cooking tames it and leaves just enough zip to flavor the creamy sauce. In my cooking classes, I like to serve this dish with carrot timbales and glazed pearl onions with zucchini.   MAKES 4 SERVINGS

4 veal cutlets (4 ounces each),
   about 1/4 inch thick
1 bunch watercress (about 5
   ounces)
1 cup heavy cream
Salt and freshly ground pepper
2 tablespoons vegetable oil

2 tablespoons butter
2 medium-size shallots, minced
1/2 cup dry white wine
1/2 cup White Veal Stock or
   Chicken Stock (see recipes) or
   packaged broth

If veal cutlets are thicker than 1/4 inch, pound them, 1 at a time, between 2 pieces of plastic wrap or wax paper, using flat meat pounder or rolling pin.

Cut off leafy sections of watercress; discard thick stems. Put watercress into a large saucepan of boiling salted water and return to a boil. Drain, rinse with cold water, and drain well, pressing hard to extract excess liquid.

Purée cooked watercress in a food processor or blender with 1/3 cup cream until mixture turns bright green. Push watercress purée through a strainer, pressing hard to make sure purée goes through.

Season veal with salt and pepper on both sides. Heat oil and butter in large heavy skillet over medium-high heat. Add veal pieces to skillet and sauté until lightly browned on both sides, about 1½ minutes per side. Use 2 wide spatulas to turn. Transfer veal to oven-proof platter, arrange it side by side, and keep warm in a 275°F. oven. Repeat with remaining veal. If fat in skillet begins to brown, reduce heat to medium.

Discard fat from skillet. Add shallots and wine and bring to a boil, stirring and scraping browned bits from base of pan. Boil, stirring, until wine is reduced to about ¼ cup. Add stock and boil until mixture is again reduced to about ¼ cup. Stir in remaining ⅔ cup cream and a pinch of salt and pepper. Simmer over medium heat, stirring, until sauce is thick enough to coat a spoon, about 7 minutes. Stir in watercress purée and simmer 1 minute. Taste and adjust seasoning.

Transfer veal to plates, discarding any liquid that escaped from veal. Coat veal with sauce and serve remaining sauce separately.

SAUTÉED CALF'S LIVER WITH CÈPES
Foie de veau sauté bordelaise

Sautéed liver with onions is a well-loved match throughout Europe, but in the Bordeaux region, the pair is embellished with aromatic cèpes as well. Potato-and-leek crêpes are an irresistible accompaniment.   MAKES 4 SERVINGS

1 ounce dried cèpes or porcini
　　mushrooms
4 or 5 tablespoons butter
2 onions, cut in half and sliced
　　thin
3 medium-size shallots, finely
　　chopped
Salt and freshly ground pepper

1 pound calf's liver slices, about ¼
　　inch thick
1 or 2 tablespoons vegetable oil
¼ cup dry white wine
¾ cup Quick Brown Sauce (see
　　recipe)
1 tablespoon minced fresh parsley

Soak mushrooms in enough hot water to cover for 30 minutes. Remove mushrooms and rinse. Cut any large pieces in half.

Heat 3 tablespoons butter in a large heavy skillet or sauté pan over medium heat. Add onions and cook, stirring often, until soft, about 15 minutes. Add cèpes, one-third of chopped shallot, and salt and pepper. Cover and cook 5 minutes. (Cèpe mixture can be kept, covered, 1 day in refrigerator.)

Pat liver dry. Heat 1 tablespoon oil and 1 tablespoon butter in another large skillet over high heat. Season liver with salt and pepper on both sides. Add to skillet and sauté about 1 to 1½ minutes per side, or until red juices appear on outside but liver is still pink inside. Remove to plate and keep warm. If skillet gets dry, add more oil and butter.

Reheat cèpe mixture. Discard fat from skillet in which liver was cooked. Add wine and remaining shallots and bring to a boil, stirring. Add brown sauce and simmer until thick enough to coat a spoon. Taste and adjust seasoning.

Serve liver on bed of cèpe mixture and coat liver with sauce. Sprinkle with parsley.

Braised Veal

Most people first think of scaloppine and chops when they want to cook veal, but the inexpensive cuts of veal can be equally good or even better, especially when braised the French way—the meat is browned lightly and then gently simmered with aromatic vegetables, herbs, wine, and stock. During the slow cooking, the meat remains moist and becomes very tender. Cuts of meat with some bone are preferred, so that the braising liquid becomes enriched by the natural gelatin in the bones. A marvelous sauce results.

Veal shanks are one of the best cuts for braising, and in France they are sometimes used whole and occasionally in cubes. From their Italian neighbors French cooks learned to prepare the famous *osso buco*, a hearty and beautiful entrée of veal shanks braised in slices, and made it part of their own repertoire.

The round bone in the center of veal shank slices gives them a unique, attractive appearance. In fact, both the cut of meat and the dish made from it have been named for this characteristic bone. *Osso buco* literally means "bone with a hole," or marrow bone. For many, the marrow in the bone is the best part. It has a soft buttery texture and is delicious when spread on French or Italian bread.

The French are the greatest consumers of veal in the world, and have developed wonderful recipes for all the different cuts. Veal stew, usually prepared from veal shoulder and breast, is known in France by various names, including *ragoût, fricassée,* and *blanquette.* The meat for these stews is cut in smaller pieces than veal for braising and is not always browned, but the cooking liquid and technique of slow simmering are the same.

A variety of vegetables lend character to braised or stewed veal when simmered in the sauce alongside the meat, as in Veal Shanks with Madeira, Carrots, and Peas. Mediterranean seasonings, especially garlic and citrus peel and juice, are favored, as are fresh herbs, particularly thyme and basil. Due to their richness, veal shanks also pair well with fresh and dried fruit and with sweet-and-sour combinations. The sweetness of the fruit is balanced by the acidity of wine or citrus juice added to the sauce.

Rice is a favorite accompaniment for braised and stewed veal, but pasta of all kinds and boiled, steamed, or puréed potatoes are a fine match, too. If green vegetables are not already included in the recipe, try crisp-tender broccoli, snow peas, or green beans for a pleasant contrast in texture.

Braised veal provides a multitude of advantages for contemporary cooks. Though inexpensive, it offers the benefits of succulent meat with a tasty sauce; it can also be made ahead and reheated. Serving is easy—no carving is necessary. And the cuts of veal for braising are readily available. These festive dishes deserve to appear on our tables more often.

Hints

• Veal shank slices are cut crosswise from the part of the hind leg below the thigh or the foreleg below the shoulder and above the knee. Although foreshanks can be used, hind shanks are preferable because they are meatier and the bone is relatively small and contains more marrow.

- Veal shanks can be simmered over low heat on top of the stove instead of in the oven. In this case, they should be turned over halfway through the cooking time so that they cook evenly.

FRENCH OSSO BUCO
Osso buco à la française

Osso buco is one of the best cuts of veal. It has more taste than most cuts and produces marvelous sauces with natural body. Although tomato-braised *osso buco* is of Italian origin, the dish is a favorite in France, especially in Provence, where cooks flavor it with an abundance of fresh herbs.　　　　　　　　　　　MAKES 4 SERVINGS

Four 2-inch-thick veal shank slices,
preferably from meaty part of
hind shanks (about 3 pounds
total) (see note)
Salt and freshly ground pepper

¼ cup all-purpose flour
2 tablespoons vegetable oil or olive
oil
2 tablespoons butter

WHITE WINE BRAISING SAUCE
1 onion, minced
1 medium-size carrot, finely chopped
1 medium-size celery stalk, finely
chopped
2 sprigs parsley
3 sprigs fresh thyme, or ¾
teaspoon dried leaf thyme,
crumbled

1 bay leaf
½ cup dry white wine
3 medium-size garlic cloves, minced
1½ cups Brown Veal Stock or
Chicken Stock (see recipes) or
packaged broth

2 tablespoons minced fresh tarragon
or basil or snipped chives

1 tablespoon minced fresh parsley

Preheat oven to 350°F. Pat veal dry. If desired, tie string around each slice to keep even round shape. Season both cut sides with salt and pepper. Spread flour on plate and dredge veal in flour, patting off excess. Set floured veal pieces on plate in single layer.

Heat oil and butter in large deep sauté pan or heavy wide casserole over medium-high heat. Add veal and brown on both cut sides in 1 or 2 batches, depending on size of pan, taking 3 to 4 minutes per side and using 2 wooden spoons to turn pieces. Regulate heat so fat does not burn. Transfer veal to large plate in one layer. Repeat with remaining veal, if necessary.

WHITE WINE BRAISING SAUCE

Immediately reduce heat to low. Add onion, carrot, and celery to pan and stir to scrape in browned bits from bottom. Cook, stirring, until vegetables soften, about 7 minutes. Meanwhile, tie parsley sprigs, thyme, and bay leaf in piece of cheesecloth to make a bouquet garni. Add bouquet garni, wine, and garlic to pan of vegetables. Boil, stirring, until most of liquid evaporates. Return veal pieces to pan with bone standing up. Add stock and bring to a boil. Push down bouquet garni so it is immersed in liquid.

Cover pan and braise veal in oven until tender when pierced with tip of sharp knife but slices are not falling apart, about 1½ hours.

Transfer veal pieces carefully with slotted skimmer or slotted spatula to plate. Discard bouquet garni. Strain braising sauce, pressing firmly on vegetables to extract as much liquid as possible, discard solids, and return strained sauce to pan. (Veal can be kept, covered, in its sauce up to 1 day in refrigerator. Reheat it, tightly covered, in sauté pan or casserole over low heat and transfer veal with slotted skimmer to plate.)

Boil sauce, stirring often, until it is thick enough to lightly coat a spoon and is reduced to about ¾ cup, about 7 minutes. Stir in fresh tarragon, basil, or chives. Taste and adjust seasoning. Discard any liquid from plate of veal. Spoon sauce over veal and sprinkle with minced parsley. Serve with small spoons for scooping out marrow from bone.

NOTE: The thickness of veal shank slices available varies from 1½ to 3 inches. Those that are 2 inches thick are the best serving size, but others can be used. The cooking time will be slightly less for slices 1½ inches thick and slightly more for 3-inch-thick pieces.

OSSO BUCO WITH TOMATO SAUCE

Peel, seed, and chop 1 ½ pounds ripe tomatoes, and add to pan with stock. After transferring meat to platter, discard bouquet garni. Do not strain sauce. Stir 1 tablespoon tomato paste into sauce and bring to a boil, stirring. Boil, stirring, until sauce lightly coats a spoon and is reduced to about 2 cups. Add pepper, and taste and adjust seasoning. Return veal shanks to pan and spoon sauce over to coat them. Cover pan and let veal stand until ready to serve, at least 5 minutes or up to 30 minutes. Bring veal to a simmer and serve.

BRAISED VEAL SHANKS WITH ORANGES, PRUNES, AND RED WINE
Jarrets de veau braisés à l'orange et aux pruneaux

In this new version of *osso buco,* the veal is braised with a red-wine-and-orange sauce instead of the usual tomato sauce, and is finished with fruit, which complements the rich meat. An entrée of *osso buco* with apricots served at a Parisian restaurant where I worked briefly gave me the idea. Onion or Leek Compote (pages 104 or 208) is an excellent accompaniment. If desired, garnish plate with oregano, marjoram, or parsley leaves.   MAKES 4 SERVINGS

Four 2-inch-thick veal shank slices, preferably from meaty part of hind shanks (about 3 pounds total)
Salt and freshly ground pepper

¼ cup all-purpose flour
2 tablespoons vegetable oil or olive oil
2 tablespoons butter

RED WINE BRAISING SAUCE

1 onion, minced

1 medium-size carrot, finely chopped

1 medium-size celery stalk, finely chopped

1 large navel orange

2 sprigs parsley

3 sprigs fresh thyme, or 3/4 teaspoon dried leaf thyme, crumbled

1 bay leaf

1/2 cup dry red wine

3 medium-size garlic cloves, minced

1 1/2 cups Brown Veal Stock or Chicken Stock (see recipes) or packaged broth

16 small pitted prunes (about 4 ounces)

4 ounces pearl onions

1 tablespoon minced fresh parsley

Preheat oven to 350°F. Pat veal dry. If desired, tie string around each slice to keep even round shape. Season both cut sides with salt and pepper. Spread flour on plate and dredge veal in flour, patting off excess. Set floured veal pieces on plate in single layer.

Heat oil and butter in large deep sauté pan or heavy wide casserole over medium-high heat. Add veal and brown on both cut sides in 1 or 2 batches, depending on size of pan, taking 3 to 4 minutes per side and using 2 wooden spoons to turn pieces. Regulate heat so fat does not burn. Transfer veal to large plate in one layer. Repeat with remaining veal, if necessary.

RED WINE BRAISING SAUCE

Immediately reduce heat to low. Add onion, carrot, and celery to pan and stir to scrape in browned bits from bottom. Cook, stirring, until vegetables soften, about 7 minutes. Meanwhile, using vegetable peeler, pare 2 1/2-by-3/4-inch strip of orange peel. Tie pared strip of orange rind, parsley sprigs, thyme, and bay leaf in piece of cheesecloth to make a bouquet garni. Add bouquet garni, wine, and garlic to pan of vegetables. Boil, stirring, until most of liquid evaporates. Return veal pieces to pan with bone standing up. Add stock and bring to a boil. Push down bouquet garni so it is immersed in liquid.

Cover pan and braise veal in oven until tender when pierced with tip of sharp knife but slices are not falling apart, about 1 1/2 hours.

Meanwhile, pour 1 1/2 cups hot water over prunes and let stand until softened, about 1 1/2 hours.

Pare about half the remaining orange peel (orange part only) in wide strips. Cut them in thin julienne about 1½ to 2 inches long and at most ⅛ inch wide. Measure 1 packed tablespoon of julienned orange peel. Put them in medium saucepan and cover with water. Bring to a boil and boil 3 minutes. Rinse and drain thoroughly. (Braised veal, prunes, and orange peel can be prepared up to 1 day ahead and refrigerated separately. Gently bring veal to simmer in braising liquid in covered pan before continuing.)

Add pearl onions to medium saucepan of boiling water and boil 1 minute. Drain, rinse with cold water, and peel with a paring knife.

Cut remaining peel from orange with very sharp knife or serrated knife, cutting away any white pith. Section orange by cutting inward to center of fruit on each side of white membrane that divides sections. (Hold orange over bowl to catch juice that escapes.) Discard membranes. Reserve orange segments at room temperature.

When veal is tender, transfer to a platter with a slotted skimmer and cover to keep warm. Strain veal braising sauce into a small saucepan, pressing firmly on vegetables in strainer to extract liquid. Drain prunes and add to strained braising sauce. Add pearl onions and bring to a boil. Reduce heat to low, cover, and simmer until onions are just tender, about 10 minutes. Remove onions and prunes carefully with slotted spoon and arrange around veal. Cover and keep warm.

Boil braising sauce, stirring often, until it is thick enough to lightly coat a spoon and is reduced to about ¾ cup. Stir in julienne of orange peel and simmer over low heat 1 minute. Add pepper, and taste and adjust seasoning. Spoon sauce over veal and sprinkle with parsley. Remove orange segments from juice and use them to garnish platter.

SEE PHOTOGRAPH.

❧ VEAL SHANKS WITH MADEIRA, CARROTS, AND PEAS
Jarrets de veau au madère, aux carottes, et aux petits pois

Serve this delicate dish with steamed new potatoes, baked potatoes, or rice pilaf, which are wonderful with the savory sauce. A creamy vegetable soup would make an ideal first course.

MAKES 4 SERVINGS

Four 2-inch-thick veal shank slices, preferably from meaty part of hind shanks (about 3 pounds total)
Salt and freshly ground pepper

¼ cup all-purpose flour
2 tablespoons vegetable oil or olive oil
2 tablespoons butter

WHITE WINE BRAISING SAUCE
1 onion, minced
1 medium-size celery stalk, finely chopped
2 sprigs parsley
3 sprigs fresh thyme, or ¾ teaspoon dried leaf thyme, crumbled

1 bay leaf
½ cup dry white wine
3 medium-size garlic cloves, minced
1½ cups Brown Veal Stock or Chicken Stock (see recipes) or packaged broth

4 tablespoons Madeira
7 ounces carrots, quartered lengthwise and cut crosswise in ¼-inch slices
1 pound fresh peas (about 1 cup shelled), or 1 cup frozen

¼ teaspoon strained fresh lemon juice, or to taste
1 tablespoon minced fresh parsley (optional)

Preheat oven to 350°F. Pat veal dry. If desired, tie string around each slice to keep even round shape. Season both cut sides with salt and pepper. Spread flour on plate and dredge veal in flour, patting off excess. Set floured veal pieces on plate in single layer.

Heat oil and butter in large deep sauté pan or heavy wide casserole over medium-high heat. Add veal and brown on both cut sides in 1 or 2 batches, depending on size of pan, taking 3 to 4 minutes per side and using 2 wooden spoons to turn pieces. Regulate heat so fat does not burn. Transfer veal to large plate in one layer. Repeat with remaining veal, if necessary.

WHITE WINE BRAISING SAUCE

Immediately reduce heat to low. Add onion and celery to pan and stir to scrape in browned bits from bottom. Cook, stirring, until vegetables soften, about 7 minutes. Meanwhile, tie parsley sprigs, thyme, and bay leaf in piece of cheesecloth to make a bouquet garni. Add bouquet garni, wine, and garlic to pan of vegetables. Boil, stirring, until most of liquid evaporates. Return veal pieces to pan with bone standing up. Add stock and bring to a boil. Push down bouquet garni so it is immersed in liquid.

Cover pan and bake veal 1 hour. Using a slotted spatula, transfer veal carefully to plate. Reserve bouquet garni. Strain braising sauce, pressing firmly on vegetables.

Return veal to pan. Add strained sauce, 3 tablespoons Madeira, reserved bouquet garni, and carrots. Push carrots into liquid. Cover and bake until veal and carrots are tender when pierced with tip of a sharp knife but veal slices are not falling apart, about 30 minutes. (Veal and carrots can be kept, covered, up to 1 day ahead in refrigerator. Gently bring veal and carrots to simmer in braising sauce in covered pan before continuing.)

Using a slotted spatula, transfer veal and carrots to plate. Cover and keep warm. Discard bouquet garni. Add peas to sauce, cover, and simmer over low heat until just tender, about 10 minutes for fresh peas or 3 minutes for frozen peas. Remove with a slotted spoon.

Boil sauce, stirring, until thick enough to lightly coat a spoon and reduced to about ⅔ cup, about 7 minutes. Return veal, carrots, and peas to sauce. Add remaining tablespoon Madeira and heat over low heat 1 minute. Add lemon juice and pepper. Taste and adjust seasoning. To serve, set veal on platter, spoon vegetables and sauce over veal, and sprinkle with parsley.

❧ VEAL FRICASSEE WITH SORREL
Fricassée de veau à l'oseille

For the French, veal stew is one of the symbols of good home cooking—moist tender meat utilizing relatively inexpensive cuts and a tasty sauce that is not overly rich. The two classic types of veal stew are *fricassée* and *blanquette.* For *fricassée* the meat is browned, while for *blanquette* it remains light in color. Both veal breast and shoulder are used; the breast contains bones, which give flavor and body to the sauce, while the shoulder is meaty. Here fresh sorrel leaves add a tangy touch to the sauce, but if sorrel is not available, add strips of fresh basil, chopped tarragon, or snipped chives. Serve this stew with rice or pasta.   MAKES 4 SERVINGS

*2 pounds veal breast or veal short
    ribs, including bones, cut in
    chunks*
*1 1/2 pounds boneless veal shoulder
    or veal stew meat, cut in 1 1/2-
    to 2-inch pieces*

2 tablespoons butter
Salt and freshly ground pepper

BRAISING SAUCE
1 onion, chopped
1 medium-size garlic clove, peeled
5 sprigs parsley
1 bay leaf
1 large sprig thyme
1 whole clove

2 tablespoons all-purpose flour
*3 cups White Veal Stock or
    Chicken Stock (see recipes) or
    packaged broth*
1 carrot, quartered
1 celery stalk

1/2 pound pearl onions
*1/2 pound mushrooms, quartered if
    large*
1/3 to 1/2 cup heavy cream, to taste
Freshly grated nutmeg

*2 cups sorrel leaves (1 ounce, or 2
    small bunches), cut in thin
    strips*
1 tablespoon chopped fresh parsley

Trim excess fat from veal breast or ribs, and pat all veal dry. Melt butter in a large flameproof casserole over medium heat. Add veal in batches, season with salt and pepper, and sauté until it changes color, about 4 minutes. Remove with a slotted spoon.

BRAISING SAUCE

Add onion to casserole and cook over medium-low heat, stirring often, until soft but not brown, about 7 minutes. Meanwhile, tie garlic clove, parsley sprigs, bay leaf, thyme sprig, and whole clove in a piece of cheesecloth. Sprinkle onion with flour and cook, stirring, 1 minute. Stir in stock. Add veal, carrot, celery, and cheesecloth bag, and bring to a simmer, stirring often so flour does not stick. Cover and cook, stirring occasionally, about 40 to 45 minutes, or until veal is tender.

Meanwhile, put pearl onions in a heavy saucepan in which they can fit in one layer. Cover with water and boil 1 minute. Drain, rinse with cold water, and peel with a paring knife.

When veal is tender, transfer to a bowl, using a slotted spoon. Discard carrot. Add pearl onions and mushrooms to cooking liquid, bring to a boil, then reduce heat to medium-low and simmer, uncovered, about 25 minutes, or until onions are just tender. Discard celery and cheesecloth bag. Remove onions and mushrooms and set aside.

Add cream to sauce and simmer over medium heat, stirring, until just thick enough to coat a spoon. Add liquid from bowl of veal and simmer again until thick enough to coat a spoon. Return veal and vegetables to sauce and heat gently. If sauce becomes thin, simmer a few minutes more to thicken. Season to taste with salt, pepper, and nutmeg. (Veal can be kept in sauce, covered, 2 days in refrigerator. Reheat before continuing.)

Remove veal fricassee from heat and stir in sorrel until it wilts; it will lose its bright-green color. Taste again and adjust seasoning. Sprinkle with parsley and serve.

SWEETBREADS WITH MORELS AND SPINACH
Ris de veau aux morilles et aux épinards

Whenever I find sweetbreads on the menu of a fine restaurant, I order them, especially if they are in a luscious sauce! This recipe combines sweetbreads with one of the best sauces of all, which is enhanced by the smoky-rich taste of morels. It is inspired by a dish I enjoyed in Perigord, the truffle center of France, where the sweet-breads were topped by—slices of black truffles, of course! Although sweetbreads can be sautéed, braising brings out their delightful creamy texture and provides a base for the sauce. Good accompaniments are fresh pasta, spaetzle, best-quality rice such as Basmati, or crusty French bread. Sweetbreads can be found in good markets, but sometimes must be ordered in advance.   MAKES 4 OR 5 SERVINGS

2 1/2 pounds veal sweetbreads, thawed if frozen

3/4 ounce dried morels (about 3/4 cup)

4 tablespoons butter

1 onion, chopped

1 small carrot, chopped

1/2 cup dry white wine

1 cup White Veal Stock or Chicken Stock (see recipes) or packaged broth

1/2 teaspoon dried leaf thyme

1 bay leaf

Salt and freshly ground pepper

1 cup heavy cream

3 pounds fresh spinach, stems removed, leaves rinsed well, or two 10-ounce packages frozen leaf spinach

Freshly grated nutmeg

Soak sweetbreads in cold water, changing water a few times, for 3 hours, to whiten. Drain, rinse, and put in a large saucepan. Cover with cold water and bring to a boil over medium heat. Simmer 3 minutes. Drain and rinse with cold water until completely cool. Gently pull off skin with a paring knife and remove any tubes, fat, and cartilage.

Put sweetbreads on a plate lined with a towel or paper towel, and cover with another towel and plate. Put a weight such as a 2-pound can on top. Refrigerate about 2 hours or overnight; pressing gives sweetbreads better texture.

Soak morels in hot water to cover for about 30 minutes, or until soft. Remove from liquid, reserving 4 tablespoons. Rinse morels and drain. Cut any large ones in half.

Melt 2 tablespoons butter in a large sauté pan or casserole over medium-low heat. Add onion and carrot and cook, stirring often, about 7 minutes, or until onion softens. Add sweetbreads and cook about 2 minutes on each side. Add wine, stock, 2 tablespoons morel liquid, thyme, bay leaf, and salt and pepper, and bring to a boil. Cover and cook over low heat about 30 minutes, turning after about 15 minutes, or until sweetbreads are very tender when pierced with a knife; taste if you're not sure how tender you like them.

Remove sweetbreads and cool slightly. Strain cooking liquid into a bowl, pressing well on vegetables, and return to sauté pan. Add morels and 2 remaining tablespoons of soaking liquid if it is not sandy. Bring to a boil. Reduce heat to medium and simmer, uncovered, about 5 minutes, or until liquid is reduced to about 1 cup.

Meanwhile, cut sweetbreads in 1-inch chunks, following their natural divisions. Stir cream into sauce and bring to a boil. Reduce heat to medium and simmer, stirring occasionally, for 10 minutes, or until sauce is thick enough to lightly coat a spoon. Taste and adjust seasoning. Put sweetbreads in sauce and shake pan. Heat over low heat, uncovered, stirring gently so they will not break up. Simmer about 10 minutes to coat sweetbreads with sauce. (Sweetbreads can be kept in sauce, covered, 1 day in refrigerator.)

Put fresh or frozen spinach in a large saucepan with enough boiling salted water to cover. Return to a boil. Boil, uncovered, about 2 minutes, or until just tender and wilted. Drain, rinse with cold running water until cool, and drain thoroughly. Squeeze spinach gently by handfuls.

Melt remaining 2 tablespoons butter in a sauté pan over medium heat. Add spinach, salt, pepper, and nutmeg and sauté over medium heat until hot.

To serve, spoon spinach in a ring on each plate, or on one side. Place sweetbread pieces in center of or next to spinach, and coat them with sauce.

Beef Paillardes and Steaks

Food fashions sometimes go from one extreme to the other. Until a few years ago, many Americans had steak several times a week—huge, thick slabs that nearly covered the plates. Now the same people are saying "I don't eat steak anymore." In France, however, the popularity of steaks has been more stable, probably because servings have always been relatively small.

Today smaller, thin steaks are appearing in our own markets as well. By serving smaller portions, we can still enjoy the advantages of steak—its superb flavor, satisfying quality, ease of preparation, and brief cooking time. An even thinner version of a steak is the *paillarde,* a boneless slice of fine-quality meat that is pounded and then sautéed or grilled to perfect succulence.

In classic cuisine, *paillardes* referred only to beef and veal, specifically to thin beef *entrecôtes* (rib-eye steaks) and veal *escalopes.* The term has been extended and now includes other meats prepared by the same procedure, such as chicken breasts, turkey breast slices, lamb steaks, and even fish fillets. Accounting for the current fancy for *paillardes* is simple when you consider our present-day devotion to uncomplicated meals, fresh and fast.

To make *paillardes,* the pieces of meat are flattened by pounding, which makes them uniformly thin and ensures that they cook quickly and evenly and hold their shape better than they would if they were simply sliced as thin. *Paillardes* are quite large in surface area and give the diner the satisfaction of eating a piece of meat that appears generous in size but actually weighs relatively little.

Sautéing, or pan-frying, is a perfect method for cooking small steaks and *paillardes.* A great number of celebrated French dishes make use of this technique, including *entrecôte bordelaise* (boneless rib steak with Bordeaux wine sauce) and tournedos with Madeira sauce. The meat is seared, which produces a tasty brown crust that seals in most of the juices. Sautéing is the fastest procedure, too; in the time it takes to sear the steak on both sides, it is usually cooked through.

A heavy skillet is required for sautéing steaks so that the fat, usually a mixture of oil and butter, heats evenly and the meat cooks without scorching. Butter adds a lovely aroma and oil helps prevent it from burning at the necessary high temperature. The meat is sautéed in just enough fat to keep it from sticking. Less fat is needed for sautéing the richer red meats than for lean white meats. Red meats are not floured because their fat helps to prevent them from sticking to the pan.

As the meat is sautéed, some of its juices collect in the pan. These provide the base for a quickly made pan sauce, or deglazing sauce. It is made in just minutes by adding wine and beef stock to the skillet, then boiling until the liquid reduces. Once the sauce has absorbed the flavors of the pan juices and has become concentrated, it is spooned over the steak. Presented with this easy sauce, steak goes to the head of the list as one of today's most delectable "fast foods."

Thin steaks and *paillardes* are also delicious when grilled, but to help control their brief cooking times, a ridged stove-top grill pan is best. The ridges elevate the meat, thus enabling it to cook in dry heat and preventing it from boiling in any juices that escape. In addition, they mark the meat with an attractive grill pattern.

Thick steaks are best when grilled or barbecued. This technique has the advantage of cooking the meat almost entirely without fat, while giving it a smoky taste that complements the richness of the meat.

Hints

- For sautéing, select a skillet just large enough to accommodate the steaks, with a little room between them. If the pan is too small, the meat steams, its juices begin to boil, and it does not brown; if it is too large, the juices burn. If necessary, use 2 skillets and divide the deglazing liquid between them.

- If using a new cast-iron grill pan, season it by brushing it with oil and baking it for 2 hours in a very low oven. Before grilling, heat the seasoned grill in the oven so it absorbs the heat evenly and finish heating it on the stove. If it is large, place it on 2 burners. After use, clean it with a metal brush, and then brush it lightly with oil. Grill pans with a nonstick surface do not require seasoning or heating in the oven and can be cleaned like any other nonstick pan.

- A hot pan or grill is essential so that the meat is properly seared. If it is not hot enough, the meat will stick and, in the case of sautéing, will begin to stew in its juices. To check, hold a piece of meat vertically and just let its tip touch the pan or grill. If it does not immediately make sizzling noises, it is not hot enough; wait 30 seconds and check again.

- To pound meat for *paillardes,* use a heavy, flat meat pounder, a flat-surfaced mallet, or a rolling pin. Do not use a mallet with pointed or jagged edges because it may tear the meat. Place 1 piece of meat between 2 pieces of plastic wrap or wax paper to protect it and pound with tapping motions, using even pressure and working from the center of the meat to the outer edge, until it is of even thickness. Do not pound too forcefully or the meat may tear. Carefully peel off the wrap or paper and repeat with the remaining pieces of meat.

• For making *paillardes,* many butchers will agree to pound the meat for you.

• Do not use a fork to turn the meat while cooking because pricking will puncture the seared crust, release the meat's juices, and leave it dry. It is best to use a flat utensil, such as a wide spatula or pancake turner.

• To gauge doneness, press steak quickly with your finger; if meat resists only slightly, it is rare. Juices will soon appear in the area you pressed and then you can check their color also: red indicates rare; pink, medium-rare. If you are still not sure how done the steak is, make a small cut in its thickest part and check the color of the interior.

• Prepare the ingredients for the sauce ahead and have them on hand so the sauce can be made quickly. If the meat is kept hot for too long, it will become dry.

• Unlike other sauces, pan sauces for steak are generally concentrated essences and should be served in small amounts. They should seem a bit too strong when tasted alone, so they will be flavorful enough to complement the steak.

BEEF PAILLARDES WITH BROCCOLI AND RED WINE SAUCE
Paillardes de boeuf aux brocolis et au vin rouge

It is no wonder that red wine sauce is a time-honored match for steak. This easy-to-prepare version is subtly tangy and light, a perfect complement for the flavorful elegant *paillarde,* or thin steak. When asparagus is in season, it can be substituted for the broccoli.

MAKES 4 SERVINGS

*1 1/2 pounds rib-eye steaks, cut
    about 1/3 inch thick
16 to 20 medium broccoli florets*

*Salt and freshly ground pepper
2 tablespoons vegetable oil*

RED WINE SAUCE

³/₄ cup dry red wine

1 shallot, minced

¹/₄ teaspoon dried leaf thyme, crumbled

¹/₂ bay leaf

1 cup Quick Brown Sauce (see recipe)

2 tablespoons cold butter, cut in 2 pieces

2 teaspoons finely snipped chives

1 ¹/₂ teaspoons minced fresh tarragon

2 teaspoons minced fresh parsley

Pinch of sugar (optional)

Pound steaks, 1 at a time, between 2 pieces of plastic wrap or wax paper to thickness of ¹/₄ inch, using flat meat pounder or rolling pin.

Add broccoli to medium saucepan of boiling salted water to generously cover and boil, uncovered, over high heat until barely crisp-tender, about 3 minutes. Let stand, off heat, until ready to serve.

Season steaks with salt and pepper. Heat oil in large heavy skillet over high heat. Add half the steaks and sauté until brown, about 45 seconds per side. Turn using 2 wide spatulas. Transfer steaks to oven-proof platter, arrange them side by side, cover, and keep warm in 275°F. oven while sautéing remaining steaks. Pour off fat from skillet.

RED WINE SAUCE

Reheat juices in skillet over medium-high heat 2 or 3 seconds. Add wine and bring to a boil, stirring and scraping any browned bits from base of pan. Add shallots, thyme, and bay leaf and boil, stirring occasionally, until wine is reduced to about ¹/₄ cup.

Strain wine into medium saucepan, pressing on shallots. Whisk in brown sauce and bring to a boil, whisking. Reduce heat to low and add butter pieces, 1 at a time. Remove from heat and stir in chives, tarragon, and parsley. Taste and adjust seasoning; if too tart, add pinch of sugar. Drain broccoli. Spoon sauce over beef, and garnish with broccoli.

🌿 GRILLED BEEF PAILLARDES WITH WILD MUSHROOMS AND MADEIRA
Paillardes de boeuf grillées aux champignons sauvages et au madère

Fresh shiitake mushrooms combine with white mushrooms to make a delectable topping for the steak. Other "wild" or "exotic" mushrooms can be used. Sautéed potatoes are a fine accompaniment for this quick entrée, and so is Leek Compote (page 208).

MAKES 4 SERVINGS

Four 6-ounce rib-eye steaks, cut about ⅓ inch thick
¼ pound fresh wild mushrooms, such as chanterelles or shiitake mushrooms
About 2 tablespoons vegetable oil
4 tablespoons butter

1 large shallot, minced
Salt and freshly ground pepper
¼ pound white mushrooms, cut in half and sliced thin
⅓ cup Madeira
1 tablespoon minced fresh parsley

Pound steaks, 1 at a time, between 2 pieces of plastic wrap or wax paper to thickness of ¼ inch, using flat meat pounder or rolling pin. Gently rinse wild mushroom caps and dry on paper towels. If using shiitake mushrooms, remove stems and cut caps in half, then in thin slices; quarter chanterelles, if large.

Heat 1 tablespoon oil and 2 tablespoons butter in large heavy skillet over medium heat. Stir in shallot, then shiitake or chanterelle mushrooms, and salt and pepper to taste. Sauté, tossing often, until mushrooms are just tender, about 4 minutes. Remove from pan. Add remaining 2 tablespoons butter and melt over medium-high heat. Add white mushrooms and salt and pepper to taste and sauté until light brown, about 3 minutes. Return shiitake mushrooms or chanterelles to skillet and reheat mushroom mixture until sizzling. Add Madeira and simmer over medium heat, stirring, until it is absorbed by mushrooms, about 3 minutes. Taste and adjust seasoning.

Heat ridged stove-top grill over high heat until very hot; when one end of steak is touched to grill, it should make loud sizzling noise. Pat *paillardes* dry, season with salt and pepper, and brush lightly with oil. Put 1 or 2 *paillardes* on grill, depending on size. Cook 30 seconds per side for rare meat, brushing steaks lightly with oil before turning. If steak begins to curl up on grill, press it against ridges with wide spatula. Transfer steaks to ovenproof platter or plates, cover, and keep them warm in 275°F. oven while grilling remaining *paillardes.*

Reheat mushroom mixture, if necessary, and add parsley. Spoon mixture over *paillardes* and serve.

SAUTÉED STEAK WITH WHITE WINE AND FRESH THYME
Biftek sauté au vin blanc et au thym

When you have a high-quality cut of steak, such as rib-eye, a simple recipe like this highlights its great flavor. Chef Michel Marolleau, the first chef-instructor of La Varenne cooking school, advised setting cooked steaks on the edge of an upside-down plate after sautéing them, so they are not sitting in their juices while the sauce is being completed. Serve these steaks with any vegetable in season: asparagus in spring, fresh corn-on-the-cob in summer, or broccoli, cauliflower, or carrots at any time of the year.   MAKES 4 SERVINGS

1 1/2 to 2 pounds steak, such as top
    loin (New York), rib-eye,
    tenderloin, or top sirloin,
    about 3/4 to 1 inch thick
6 to 7 tablespoons butter
1 tablespoon vegetable oil
Salt and freshly ground pepper
2 tablespoons minced shallots

1/2 cup dry white wine
1/2 cup Beef Stock (see recipe) or
    unsalted packaged broth
1 tablespoon minced fresh parsley
1 tablespoon minced fresh thyme
    leaves
1 to 2 teaspoons hot water
    (optional)

Pat steaks dry, and trim fat from edges.

Cut 4 or 5 tablespoons butter (for finishing sauce) in 4 or 5 pieces and refrigerate. Heat oil and 1 tablespoon butter in large heavy skillet in which steaks can fit easily (or divide between 2 skillets) over medium-high heat until butter melts and foam begins to subside. Add steaks and sauté 2 to 3 minutes on first side, regulating heat so fat does not burn. Turn steaks, using tongs or slotted spatulas, and sauté second side 2 or 3 minutes. Check steaks: If meat does not resist when pressed, steak is rare; if it resists slightly, it is medium-rare.

Transfer steaks to ovenproof platter or plate, season lightly with salt and pepper, and keep warm in 180°F. oven.

Discard fat from skillet. Add 1 tablespoon butter to skillet and melt over low heat. Add shallots and cook, stirring, 1 minute. Add wine, dividing it between both skillets if using 2. Bring to a boil over high heat, stirring and scraping in browned bits. Combine both mixtures in 1 skillet and boil, stirring, until wine is reduced to approximately 2 tablespoons, about 2 minutes. Add stock and boil, stirring, until liquid is reduced to approximately ¼ cup and is thickened almost to syrupy consistency, about 2 minutes. Remove from heat and cool about 30 seconds.

Set skillet over low heat and add cold butter pieces, 2 at a time, shaking and rotating skillet continuously to blend butter into sauce. If sauce appears to be separating, remove from heat and add an additional tablespoon cold butter. Immediately pour sauce into small bowl and stir in parsley and thyme. If sauce is too thick, gradually stir in 1 or 2 teaspoons hot water. Taste and adjust seasoning. Transfer steak to plates, spoon sauce over steaks, and serve.

DIJON-STYLE STEAK WITH GREEN PEPPERCORNS
Entrecôte à la dijonnaise au poivre vert

Dijon mustard gives this dish character. You can experiment with a variety of flavored mustards and use mustard with green peppercorns or an herb mustard. Potatoes or steamed rice, as well as green beans or vegetables from the cabbage family, go well with this steak and its rich, zesty sauce.   MAKES 4 SERVINGS

1 ½ to 2 pounds steak, such as rib-eye, top loin (New York), tenderloin, or top sirloin, about ¾ to 1 inch thick
1 tablespoon vegetable oil

2 tablespoons butter
Salt and freshly ground pepper
2 tablespoons minced shallots
⅓ cup dry white wine
1 cup heavy cream

2 tablespoons Dijon mustard
3/4 teaspoon minced fresh thyme
　　leaves, or 1/4 teaspoon dried
　　leaf thyme, crumbled

1 tablespoon minced fresh parsley
2 teaspoons green peppercorns,
　　rinsed and drained

Pat steaks dry, and trim fat from edges.

Heat oil and 1 tablespoon butter in large heavy skillet in which steaks can fit easily (or divide between 2 skillets) over medium-high heat until butter melts and foam begins to subside. Add steaks and sauté 2 or 3 minutes on first side, regulating heat so fat does not burn. Turn steaks, using tongs or slotted spatulas, and sauté second side 2 or 3 minutes. Check steaks: If meat does not resist when pressed, steak is rare; if it resists slightly, it is medium-rare.

Transfer steaks to ovenproof platter, season lightly with salt and pepper, and keep warm in 180°F. oven.

Discard fat from skillet. Add remaining tablespoon butter to skillet and melt over low heat. Add shallots and cook, stirring, 1 minute. Add wine, dividing it between both skillets if using 2. Raise heat to high and bring to a boil, stirring and scraping in browned bits. Combine both mixtures in 1 skillet and boil, stirring, until wine is reduced to approximately 2 tablespoons, about 2 minutes. Add cream and boil, stirring, until sauce is thick enough to lightly coat a spoon, about 3 minutes. Reduce heat to low and whisk in mustard. Remove from heat and stir in thyme, parsley, and green peppercorns. Taste and adjust seasoning. Spoon sauce over center of steaks, leaving part of each steak showing.

TENDERLOIN STEAK WITH ROQUEFORT, GREEN ONIONS, AND WALNUTS
Tournedos au roquefort et aux noix

The robust taste of Roquefort cheese is a wonderful complement to steak. It melts easily into the sauce, and its flavor is slightly tamed by the cream.　　　　　　　　　　　　　MAKES 4 SERVINGS

*1 1/2 to 2 pounds tenderloin steaks,
about 3/4 to 1 inch thick*
1 tablespoon vegetable oil
2 tablespoons butter
Salt and freshly ground pepper
2 tablespoons minced shallots

1/3 cup dry white wine
1 cup heavy cream
1/2 cup crumbled Roquefort cheese
2 tablespoons minced green onions
*3 tablespoons chopped toasted
walnuts*

Pat steaks dry and trim fat from edges.

Heat oil and 1 tablespoon butter in large heavy skillet in which steaks can fit easily (or divide between 2 skillets) over medium-high heat until butter melts and foam begins to subside. Add steaks and sauté 2 or 3 minutes on first side, regulating heat so fat does not burn. Turn steaks, using tongs or slotted spatulas, and sauté second side 2 or 3 minutes. Check steaks: If meat does not resist when pressed, steak is rare; if it resists slightly, it is medium-rare.

Transfer steaks to ovenproof platter, season lightly with salt and pepper, and keep warm in 180°F. oven.

Discard fat from skillet. Add remaining tablespoon butter to skillet and melt over low heat. Add shallots and cook, stirring, 1 minute. Add wine, dividing it between both skillets if using 2. Raise heat to high and bring to a boil, stirring and scraping in browned bits. Combine both mixtures in 1 skillet and boil, stirring, until wine is reduced to approximately 2 tablespoons, about 2 minutes. Add cream and boil, stirring, until sauce is thick enough to lightly coat a spoon, about 3 minutes. Reduce heat to low and whisk in Roquefort cheese. Stir in green onions. Season to taste with pepper; salt may not be needed because cheese is salty. Spoon sauce over center of steaks, leaving part of each steak showing. Sprinkle steaks evenly with walnuts, and serve.

GRILLED STEAK WITH GARLIC AND SPINACH
Biftek grillé à l'ail et aux épinards

In this Provençal-style dish, sautéed garlic slices add a pleasant crunch and aroma to the steak. Here a large steak is grilled whole and then cut in slices, which are served on a bed of spinach. Instead of sirloin, a porterhouse, T-bone, or club steak can be used.

MAKES 3 TO 4 SERVINGS

9 garlic cloves
Freshly ground pepper
2 tablespoons Cognac or brandy
7 tablespoons olive oil
1 top sirloin steak (about 1 1/2
   pounds), about 1 inch thick

3 pounds fresh spinach, stems
   removed, leaves rinsed well, or
   two 10-ounce packages frozen
   leaf spinach
1 tablespoon butter
Salt

Finely chop 4 garlic cloves. In a shallow dish, combine chopped garlic with pepper, Cognac, and 3 tablespoons olive oil. Trim excess fat from steak. Add steak to dish and coat on all sides with Cognac mixture. Cover and marinate 2 hours at room temperature, or overnight in refrigerator.

Put fresh spinach in a large saucepan of enough boiling salted water to cover. Return to a boil and boil, uncovered, about 2 minutes, or until just tender and wilted. If using frozen spinach, cook according to package instructions until just separated. Drain spinach, rinse with cold running water until cool, and drain thoroughly. Squeeze spinach by handfuls to remove as much water as possible. Coarsely chop with a knife.

Cut remaining garlic in very thin slices lengthwise, cover, and reserve.

Prepare charcoal grill or heat ridged stove-top grill over high heat; or preheat broiler with rack about 3 inches from heat source.

Remove steak from marinade and pat dry. Grill or broil until browned on both sides and done to taste (about 5 minutes per side for medium-rare); rare meat does not resist when pressed, medium-rare meat resists slightly, medium-done meat resists slightly more, and meat that is well-done is springy to the touch. Transfer to carving board and keep warm.

Heat remaining 4 tablespoons olive oil in a medium skillet over low heat. Add garlic slices and cook until tender and lightly browned, turning occasionally, about 5 minutes. Remove with a slotted spoon.

Add spinach to oil from cooking garlic and heat, stirring. Add butter and stir until absorbed. Season to taste with salt and pepper.

To serve, cut steak in thin slices. Put spinach on hot plates, put slices of steak on top, and sprinkle with salt. Garnish with garlic slices and serve.

❧ RIB-EYE STEAKS WITH HORSERADISH CREAM AND BEETS
Entrecôte à la crème de raifort et aux betteraves

This Alsatian-inspired dish is perfect for a quick dinner. To save time, I like to grill these steaks on a ridged stove-top grill. You can also use an outdoor barbecue, but allow enough time to heat the coals. The fresh horseradish cream sauce has plenty of zip and may seem strong when tasted alone, but it is great with the grilled steak. In Alsace, horseradish sauce is often paired with fresh or smoked pork and smoked fish.   MAKES 4 SERVINGS

16 to 20 baby beets

HORSERADISH CREAM
½ cup Beef Stock (see recipe) or unsalted packaged broth

½ cup dry white wine

½ cup heavy cream

¾ cup finely grated peeled fresh horseradish (about 4½ ounces)

Salt and freshly ground pepper

2 rib-eye steaks (about 1½ pounds total), approximately 1 inch thick

Freshly ground pepper

Salt

Parsley sprigs for garnish

Steam beets in top of a covered steamer above boiling water about 15 to 20 minutes, or until tender. Rinse lightly, remove tops and root ends, and slip off skins. Return to steamer top with heat turned off, cover, and keep warm.

HORSERADISH CREAM
Boil stock and wine in a medium saucepan until reduced to about ⅓ cup. Add cream and simmer until thick enough to lightly coat a spoon. Remove from heat and stir in grated horseradish. Season to taste with salt and pepper.

Prepare charcoal grill or heat ridged stove-top grill over medium-high heat; or preheat broiler with rack about 3 inches from heat source. Season steaks with pepper. Grill or broil steaks until done to taste; for medium-rare, meat will resist only slightly when pressed, about 3 minutes per side. Transfer steaks to a plate, cover, and let stand 2 or 3 minutes, then sprinkle with salt.

Cut each steak in half. Spoon some sauce on each plate and set steak on top. Arrange beets around steaks, and garnish plate with parsley sprigs.

SAUTÉED STEAK WITH MUSHROOMS AND OREGANO
Biftek à l'origan et aux champignons

For this easy and tasty dish, the sautéed mushrooms simmer in a quick red wine sauce with a touch of oregano. I had a wonderful version of this entrée in a small restaurant in the Franche-Comté area of France near the Alps, where they used cèpes and local wild mushrooms called *mousserons*. The rib-eye steak was served with buttered green beans flavored with shallot and parsley, cauliflower florets, and French fries.   MAKES 4 SERVINGS

1 1/2 to 2 pounds steak, such as top loin (New York), rib-eye, tenderloin, or top sirloin, about 3/4 to 1 inch thick
7 tablespoons butter
4 to 6 ounces small mushrooms, quartered
Salt and freshly ground pepper
1 tablespoon vegetable oil
1 tablespoon minced shallots

1/2 cup dry red wine
1/2 cup Beef Stock (see recipe) or unsalted packaged broth
2 medium-size garlic cloves, minced
5 teaspoons minced fresh oregano
2 teaspoons minced fresh parsley
1 to 2 teaspoons hot water (optional)

Pat steaks dry, and trim fat from edges.

Cut 4 tablespoons butter in 4 pieces and refrigerate. Melt 1 tablespoon butter in medium, heavy skillet over medium heat. Add mushrooms, sprinkle with salt and pepper, and sauté, tossing often, until lightly browned, about 4 minutes.

Heat oil and 1 tablespoon butter in large heavy skillet in which steaks can fit easily (or divide between 2 skillets) over medium-high heat until butter melts and foam begins to subside. Add steaks and sauté 2 or 3 minutes on first side, regulating heat so fat does not burn. Turn steaks, using tongs or slotted spatulas, and sauté second side 2 or 3 minutes. Check steaks: If meat does not resist when pressed, steak is rare; if it resists slightly, it is medium-rare.

Transfer steaks to ovenproof platter, season lightly with salt and pepper, and keep warm in 180°F. oven.

Discard fat from skillet. Add 1 tablespoon butter to the skillet and melt over low heat. Add shallots and cook, stirring, 1 minute. Add wine, dividing it between both skillets if using 2. Bring to a boil over high heat, stirring and scraping in browned bits. Combine both mixtures in 1 skillet and boil, stirring, until wine is reduced to approximately 2 tablespoons, about 2 minutes. Add stock and garlic and boil, stirring, until liquid is reduced to approximately ¼ cup and is thickened almost to syrupy consistency, about 2 minutes. Reduce heat to low, add mushrooms with any liquid that has accumulated, and heat 1 minute, turning them over often.

Add cold butter, 2 pieces at a time, shaking and rotating skillet continuously to blend butter into sauce. Pour immediately into a small bowl and stir in oregano and parsley. If sauce is too thick, gradually stir in 1 or 2 teaspoons hot water. Taste and adjust seasoning. Transfer steaks to plates, and spoon sauce and mushrooms over them.

Roast Beef

Many cooks reserve roast beef for special occasions due to its high cost, realizing that roasts should be made from the best cuts of beef. In our markets, though, there are some cuts of beef that are not tender enough for roasting and yet are labeled "roast." "Shoulder roast," for example, is better made into stew.

The choice cuts for roasting are the rib roast, rib-eye roast, and tenderloin. In haute cuisine, roast beef is a grand affair, presented on an elegant platter and surrounded by mounds of assorted colorful vegetables. This style of serving still has enormous appeal.

The classic names of many roast beef dishes are determined by which vegetables accompany the meat. For example, *rôti de boeuf arlésienne,* named for the Provençal town of Arles, has a Mediterranean character—it is accompanied by sautéed eggplant slices, fried onions, and sautéed tomatoes. Beef Clamart, named for a suburb of Paris where peas were once grown, is surrounded by artichoke bottoms stuffed with peas. Today restaurants use these traditional names less often than before, but they still follow the time-honored principle of serving the beef with the best vegetables in season.

French cooks usually serve roast beef with a quick simple sauce made of the roasting juices. A favorite French technique is to put some diced onions and carrots in the roasting pan along with the beef, to give the juices additional flavor. After the beef is done, a little white or red wine and beef or veal stock are added to enhance the juices. The sauce may be thickened with a little arrowroot, but it is usually light-textured. Generally the sauce does not contain a large number of seasonings because its purpose is to moisten the meat and heighten its taste, not to disguise it.

Roasts make festive main courses because their size makes them easy to serve to a large gathering of people. Roasts should be fairly large so that they remain succulent. The largest roasts, such as rib roasts, are seared at a very high temperature, then roasting is finished at a lower temperature. A relatively small roast like the fillet, however, is roasted at a high temperature until it is done.

Hints

- A roast cooks more quickly and evenly if allowed to come to room temperature before being put in the oven.
- Check the temperature of roast beef either with a meat thermometer or an instant-read thermometer. A meat thermometer is inserted after about three-quarters of the cooking time has passed. An instant-read thermometer is inserted when the meat is nearly done, is left inside the meat for about 10 seconds, read, and removed. The thermometer should be inserted into the thickest part of the roast, at least 2 inches into the meat, and not in fat or bone.
- Roasts should be allowed to rest before being carved because the juices are driven to the interior of the meat during roasting, but as the meat stands, they slowly come back out and the color of the meat

becomes more uniform. The meat should be set to rest in a warm place.

BEEF TENDERLOIN ROAST WITH CÈPE SAUCE AND GARDEN VEGETABLES
Filet de boeuf jardinière, sauce aux cèpes

The tenderloin roast, the most luxurious cut, is also relatively lean. For this reason, use this easy roasting trick that I learned from a French chef: first sauté the beef briefly to seal in the juices, then roast at a high temperature. Because of its long thin shape, it cooks more quickly than other roasts. The deep-brown, rich-flavored cèpe sauce is a wonderful complement for the beef and vegetables.

MAKES 4 SERVINGS

1 beef tenderloin roast (2 1/4 to 2 1/2 pounds)
1/2 pound thin carrots, cut in 1 1/2-inch chunks
1/4 pound pearl onions
1 pound green beans, trimmed and broken in 2 pieces

1 small cauliflower, divided into medium florets
Salt and freshly ground pepper
2 tablespoons vegetable oil

CÈPE SAUCE
1 ounce dried cèpes or porcini, soaked 30 minutes in hot water to cover
1/2 teaspoon dried leaf thyme, crumbled
1 1/2 cups Beef Stock or Brown Veal Stock, (see recipes) or packaged broth

1/4 cup dry sherry
1 1/2 teaspoons potato starch or arrowroot dissolved in 1 tablespoon dry sherry

3 tablespoons butter

Trim beef of fat and connective tissue. Remove chain, a long thin sinewy piece along one side. Tie roast in even shape, and bring to room temperature. Pat dry. Preheat oven to 500°F.

Put carrots in a medium saucepan and add water to cover and a pinch of salt. Bring to a boil, cover, and cook over medium heat until just tender, about 20 minutes. Drain well and reserve at room temperature.

Add pearl onions to medium saucepan of boiling water and boil 1 minute. Drain, rinse with cold water, and peel with a paring knife. Return to saucepan and add water to cover and a pinch of salt. Bring to a boil, cover, and cook over medium heat until just tender, about 12 to 15 minutes. Drain well and reserve at room temperature.

In a large saucepan, boil enough water to generously cover beans and add a pinch of salt. Add beans and boil, uncovered, until just tender, about 8 minutes. Drain, rinse with cold water, and drain well. Reserve at room temperature. Cook cauliflower like beans, until just tender, about 7 minutes. Drain, rinse with cold water, and drain well. Reserve at room temperature.

Season beef evenly with salt and pepper. Heat oil in a small heavy roasting pan over high heat. Add beef and brown on all sides, about 4 minutes. Discard about half the oil.

Roast the beef in the oven, basting once or twice with juices in pan, about 20 minutes, or until a meat thermometer inserted in thickest part of beef registers 125°F. (for rare) or 130°F. (for medium-rare).

When roast is done, transfer it to a board and remove strings. Cover roast loosely with foil and let stand in a warm place for 10 to 15 minutes, while you prepare the sauce.

CÈPE SAUCE

Remove cèpes from soaking water, clean off any dirt, and cut in ½-inch pieces. Put in a medium saucepan with thyme and 1 cup stock. Bring to a boil. Simmer, uncovered, 10 minutes, or until mixture is reduced to about 1 cup. Reserve in pan.

Pour off fat from beef pan juices. Add sherry and ½ cup stock to roasting pan and bring to a boil, stirring and scraping to dissolve any browned bits in pan. Strain into cèpe mixture.

Bring sauce to a simmer over medium heat. Whisk potato starch or arrowroot mixture to blend, then gradually whisk half of it into simmering sauce. Return to a boil, whisking. If sauce is too thin, gradually whisk in remaining potato starch mixture and return to a boil. Remove from heat. Taste and adjust seasoning.

Melt 1½ tablespoons butter in each of 2 medium skillets over medium-low heat. Add carrots and onions to one, and cauliflower and green beans to the other. Sprinkle vegetables with salt and pepper and sauté, keeping each type separate, until hot. Keep warm over very low heat.

Carve roast in slices about ½ inch thick, and arrange them overlapping on a platter. Add carving juices to sauce. Surround meat with piles of each type of vegetable. Transfer sauce to a sauceboat and serve separately.

ROAST BEEF WITH PORT SAUCE
Filet de boeuf rôti, sauce au porto

Serve this festive roast surrounded by an assortment of seasonal vegetables. In summer, for example, try green beans, quartered artichoke hearts, yellow summer squash, and cherry tomatoes.

MAKES 4 SERVINGS

1 beef tenderloin roast (2¼ to 2½ pounds)
Salt and freshly ground pepper
2 tablespoons vegetable oil
¼ cup port

¼ cup Beef Stock (see recipe) or packaged broth
1 cup Quick Brown Sauce (see recipe)
1 tablespoon butter

Trim beef of fat and connective tissue. Remove chain, a long thin sinewy piece along one side. Tie roast in even shape and bring to room temperature. Pat dry. Preheat oven to 500°F.

Season beef evenly with salt and pepper. Heat oil in a small heavy roasting pan over high heat. Add beef and brown on all sides, about 4 minutes. Discard about half the oil.

Roast the beef in the oven, basting once or twice with pan juices, about 20 minutes, or until a meat thermometer inserted in thickest part of beef registers 125°F. (for rare) or 130°F. (for medium-rare).

When roast is done, transfer to a board and remove strings. Cover roast loosely with foil and let stand in a warm place for 10 to 15 minutes.

Pour off fat from beef pan juices. Add port and stock and bring to a boil, stirring and scraping to dissolve any browned bits in pan. Strain into a small saucepan. Add brown sauce and bring to a boil, whisking. Simmer, if necessary, until thick enough to lightly coat a spoon. Whisk in butter in small pieces. Taste and adjust seasoning.

Carve roast in slices about 1/2 inch thick. Add carving juices to sauce, transfer sauce to a sauceboat, and serve separately.

BEEF RIB ROAST WITH STUFFED PEPPERS AND SAUTÉED EGGPLANT
Côte de boeuf rôtie aux poivrons farcis et à l'aubergine

This is a grand recipe for a lavish feast. The impressive rib roast has rich juicy meat and is one of the most delicious cuts for making roast beef. Around it on the platter are peppers stuffed with a colorful rice pilaf, and slices of sautéed eggplant topped with tomato "fondue," or tomatoes that are lightly cooked until meltingly tender. The vegetables are prepared while the beef is roasting.

MAKES 8 SERVINGS

1 beef standing rib roast (5 1/2 to 6 pounds), tied
Salt and freshly ground pepper

1 large onion, quartered
1 large carrot, cut in 4 chunks

PEPPERS STUFFED WITH RICE PILAF

3 tablespoons olive oil
1 onion, finely chopped
1 small red bell pepper, cut in small dice
1 1/2 cups long-grain rice
2 3/4 cups boiling water or White Veal Stock or Chicken Stock (see recipes) or packaged broth
1/2 teaspoon dried leaf thyme
1 bay leaf

Salt and freshly ground pepper
1 cup fresh shelled or frozen peas, cooked
8 small or 4 medium-sized red bell peppers
1 cup Brown or White Veal Stock, Beef Stock, or Chicken Stock (see recipes), or packaged broth or water

SAUTÉED EGGPLANT WITH TOMATOES

7 tablespoons olive oil

1 medium-size garlic clove, minced

1 pound ripe tomatoes, peeled,
   seeded, and chopped, or one
   28-ounce can whole plum
   tomatoes, drained and chopped

1/2 teaspoon dried leaf thyme

Salt and freshly ground pepper

1 large fairly thin eggplant (1 1/4
   to 1 1/3 pounds)

BEEF PAN SAUCE

1/3 cup dry white wine

2 cups Beef Stock or Brown Veal
   Stock (see recipes) or packaged
   broth

2 teaspoons tomato paste

1 tablespoon cornstarch, potato
   starch, or arrowroot dissolved
   in 2 tablespoons water

2 tablespoons chopped fresh parsley

Preheat oven to 500°F. Season beef evenly with salt and pepper. Set beef, bone side down, on a rack in a medium roasting pan and roast 15 minutes.

Add quartered onion and carrot to pan carefully to avoid splatters. Reduce oven temperature to 350°F. and roast, stirring onion and carrot occasionally, until a meat thermometer inserted in thickest part of beef registers 125°F. (for rare) or 130°F. (for medium-rare), about 1 3/4 hours.

While beef is roasting, prepare stuffed peppers, eggplant, and tomatoes.

PEPPERS STUFFED WITH RICE PILAF

Heat oil in a sauté pan or large deep skillet over low heat. Add chopped onion and pepper and cook, stirring, about 10 minutes, or until soft but not brown. Add rice and sauté, stirring, about 2 minutes. Add water or stock, thyme, bay leaf, 1/2 teaspoon salt, and a pinch of pepper. Stir once and return to a boil. Cover and cook over low heat, without stirring, 15 minutes, or until rice is just tender and liquid is absorbed. Discard bay leaf. Using fork, lightly fluff rice and stir in cooked peas. Taste and adjust seasoning. (Rice can be kept, covered, 2 days in refrigerator; before continuing, reheat in 1 to 2 tablespoons olive oil in a skillet over medium-low heat.)

If using small peppers, cut a slice from top, with stem, and remove seeds. If using medium-size peppers, cut them in half and carefully remove core and seeds. Set peppers in an oiled baking dish. Fill each whole or half pepper with rice. Add stock or water to pan. Cover tightly with foil. Bake at 350°F. for 50 minutes or until peppers are very tender.

SAUTÉED EGGPLANT WITH TOMATOES
Heat 1 tablespoon oil in a medium skillet over medium-high heat. Add garlic, tomatoes, thyme, and salt and pepper. Cook, stirring often, about 7 minutes, or until tomatoes are tender and mixture is dry. Taste and adjust seasoning.
Cut eggplant in ½-inch slices crosswise. Heat 3 tablespoons oil in a large heavy skillet over medium-high heat. Add half the eggplant slices and sauté about 3 minutes per side, or until tender. Remove with a slotted spatula to a paper towel–lined tray. Heat 3 tablespoons oil in skillet and sauté remaining eggplant slices. Transfer them to tray. Season eggplant with salt and pepper, and put in a large baking dish in one layer, for reheating.

When roast is done, transfer it to a cutting board, leaving oven on. Remove strings from roast, cover loosely with foil, and let stand in a warm place for 20 minutes. Cover peppers and eggplant and reheat in oven. Reheat tomatoes and keep warm over low heat.

BEEF PAN SAUCE
Pour off fat from pan juices but leave in onion and carrot. Add wine and ½ cup stock and bring to a boil, stirring and scraping to dissolve any browned bits in pan. Boil mixture until reduced by about half. Strain into a medium saucepan, skim fat again, and add remaining 1½ cups stock. Boil 2 to 3 minutes to reduce until well flavored. Whisk in tomato paste.
Bring sauce to a simmer over medium heat. Whisk cornstarch or potato starch or arrowroot mixture to blend, then gradually whisk half of it into simmering sauce. Return to a boil, whisking. If sauce is too thin, gradually whisk in remaining starch mixture and return to a boil. Remove from heat. Taste and adjust seasoning.

Carve about two-thirds of roast in slices about ½ inch thick, and arrange them overlapping on a platter. Add piece of uncarved roast to platter. Surround meat with stuffed peppers and eggplant slices.

Spoon some tomato onto center of each eggplant slice, and sprinkle
with parsley. Serve sauce separately.

Beef Ragoûts

Something delicious happens when chunks of beef, a generous portion of colorful vegetables, and a luscious sauce come together in a
ragoût, or stew. During the gentle cooking, a flavor exchange takes
place among all the ingredients, creating a wonderful harmony of
tastes. The result is a heartwarming dish guaranteed to take the chill
off a winter's eve.

What distinguishes a great stew from a good one is fork-tender
meat. Slow simmering is the key. Although the cooking time of beef
stews is long, they demand minimal attention and can be more or less
left alone while they simmer. These economical "meals in one pot"
are convenient to prepare because they can be kept warm over very
low heat and require little, if any, last-minute work. Such entrées can
also be reheated easily; in fact, they are often better when prepared
a day or two ahead, since the tastes of the components meld over time.

French cooks have developed time-honored procedures for high-
lighting the best qualities of the beef and producing an aromatic,
delectable sauce. The beef is cut in cubes so it will brown nicely and
absorb the seasonings. After being browned, the beef is often sprinkled lightly with flour. When combined with the oil used for sautéing,
the flour acts as a roux and thickens the cooking liquid of the stew.
This technique yields a rich, smooth sauce of a warm brown color. The
cooking liquid of beef stews also thickens naturally by reduction during the long simmering. The sauce is not thick and clinging, however,
but just lightly coats a spoon.

The beef is well complemented by a wide range of seasonings,
from delicate herbs such as chives, tarragon, parsley, and thyme; to
the more assertive rosemary, basil, oregano, fresh coriander, and
mint; to pungent spices, including saffron and curry. Onions are the

most frequently used aromatic vegetable in France and appear in beef stews wherever they are made; garlic is a close second.

The best cooking liquid is a rich homemade stock. It adds depth to the flavor of the sauce and an appealing color. The refreshing acidity of dry white and red wine and tomatoes makes them favorite additions, too. When they are used, or when liberal amounts of spices or herbs are added, stock may not be needed and water can be substituted, as the sauce will gain enough character from these flavorings and from the beef.

Fresh seasonal vegetables are important not only for their visual and nutritional contributions, but also for their taste; and they enable us to create a variety of beef stews. In addition to the vegetables used in the following recipes, fine choices are asparagus, eggplant, leeks, artichoke hearts, corn, and all sorts of beans. Depending on their cooking times, vegetables are added when the meat is partially or completely cooked, so they will retain good texture and color.

A stew is practically a meal in itself. Since rice, potatoes, and pasta are marvelous when moistened with the sauce, they are the most popular accompaniments. Or—simpler still—you could provide some crusty French or Italian bread and leave it at that.

Hints

• Beef stews make use of relatively inexpensive cuts of meat. Chuck (shoulder), especially boneless chuck pot roast, is the best choice because it is juicy and flavorful. Bottom round roast is leaner but also yields good results. Lean fresh brisket (the flat half of the brisket) is delicious and gives natural body to the sauce; its cooking time, however, is relatively long (about 4 hours). Any of these, as well as meat labeled "beef for stew," which comes from an assortment of cuts, can be used in these recipes.

• For even heating during browning and simmering, a heavy pan is essential. An enameled cast-iron casserole is best and is often attractive enough to bring to the table, but a stainless-steel casserole or a Dutch oven is also suitable. The pan should have a tight-fitting lid so that the liquid does not evaporate too quickly.

• Pat the beef cubes dry before browning. Avoid crowding the pan, or the meat will steam instead of browning.

- When browning the beef, do not stir it continuously, because this inhibits browning. If using butter as part of the browning fat, however, stir often because butter burns more easily than oil.
- Stews can be cooked over low heat on top of the stove instead of in the oven. After sprinkling the flour over the beef, cook 5 minutes over low heat, stirring constantly. After adding the liquid, simmer the stew over low heat. Cooking times will be approximately the same as in the oven.
- Regulate the heat so the cooking liquid bubbles gently. Do not let it boil or the meat may become tough and dry.
- If a stew is too thick, add a little stock or water. Since stews thicken on standing, it is often necessary to add a little water when reheating them.
- Before serving a beef stew, skim fat from the sauce, if necessary.
- Beef stews can be refrigerated up to 3 days or frozen 1 month. Undercook vegetables if making stew ahead. Reheat stews in a covered casserole over medium-low heat, occasionally stirring very gently.

BEEF RAGOÛT WITH GARBANZO BEANS, GARLIC, AND ZUCCHINI
Ragoût de boeuf à l'occitane

This stew, redolent of garlic and rosemary, exemplifies the hearty cuisine of southwest France, which boasts the creation of cassoulet—in essence a glorified meat ragoût with beans.   MAKES 4 SERVINGS

3/4 cup dried garbanzo beans, rinsed and sorted, or 1 1/2 cups canned garbanzo beans

2 pounds boneless beef chuck, excess fat trimmed, cut in 1 1/4- to 1 1/2-inch pieces

3 tablespoons vegetable oil

1 large onion, chopped

1 tablespoon plus 1 teaspoon all-purpose flour

2 1/4 pounds ripe tomatoes, peeled, seeded, and chopped, or two 28-ounce cans whole plum tomatoes, drained and chopped

1 3/4 to 2 1/4 cups Beef Stock (see recipe) or packaged broth or water

Pinch of cayenne pepper, or 1 serrano pepper, seeds and ribs discarded, minced

1 tablespoon minced fresh rosemary,   1 tablespoon tomato paste
    or 1 teaspoon dried   1 pound zucchini, cut in ½-inch
Salt   cubes
8 medium-size garlic cloves, minced

Soak dried garbanzo beans in bowl of 3 cups cold water in cool place
for 8 hours or overnight. Drain beans and rinse. Put them in medium
saucepan and add 3 cups fresh water. Bring to a boil, reduce heat to
low, cover, and simmer until tender, about 1 hour and 15 minutes.

Position rack in lower third of oven and preheat to 450°F. Pat
beef dry. Heat oil in 4- to 5-quart heavy flameproof casserole
over medium-high heat. Add one-third to one-half the beef, keeping the pieces from touching. Brown on all sides, taking 6 or 7 minutes. Using a slotted spatula, transfer to a plate and continue with remaining beef.

Add onion to casserole and cook over low heat, stirring often,
until softened, about 7 minutes. Return meat to pan, reserving any
juices on plate, and sprinkle with flour, tossing lightly to coat. Bake,
uncovered, stirring once, 5 minutes. Remove casserole and reduce
oven temperature to 325°F.

Pour juices from plate over beef. Stir in tomatoes and 1¾ cups
stock or water, or enough to barely cover beef. Add cayenne or hot
pepper, rosemary, salt to taste, and 1 tablespoon garlic and bring to
a boil, stirring often and scraping any browned bits from sides and
bottom of pan. Cover and bake 1 hour, stirring and turning beef cubes
over occasionally.

If pan appears dry or sauce is too thick, stir in an additional ½
cup stock. Stir tomato paste into stew. Drain garbanzo beans and add
them to stew. Continue baking, stirring occasionally, until beef is just
tender when pierced with thin-bladed knife, about 30 to 45 minutes.

Transfer stew to top of stove and uncover. Sauce should be thick
enough to lightly coat a spoon. If it is too thick, stir in a few tablespoons stock to thin it out. If it is too thin, carefully remove beef and
vegetables with a slotted spoon; boil sauce, uncovered, stirring often,
until lightly thickened, and then return beef and vegetables to casserole. (Stew can be kept, covered, 3 days in refrigerator or 1 month
in freezer. Reheat in covered casserole before continuing.)

Add zucchini, cover, and simmer until tender, about 5 minutes.
Stir in remaining garlic and simmer, uncovered, 30 seconds. Taste

and adjust seasoning. Serve stew from enameled casserole or deep
serving dish.

🌿 BEEF STEW WITH MUSHROOMS, BABY ONIONS, AND TOMATO-HERB SAUCE
Ragoût de boeuf chasseur

Make this stew on days when you are looking for the comfort of
tastes that are familiar, delicious, and sure to appeal to everyone. A
great accompaniment is creamy mashed potatoes or steamed new
potatoes.   MAKES 4 SERVINGS

*2 pounds boneless beef chuck, excess
    fat trimmed, cut in 1 1/4- to
    1 1/2-inch pieces*

3 tablespoons vegetable oil

TOMATO-HERB SAUCE
1 large onion, chopped
1 medium-size garlic clove, crushed
*1 sprig fresh thyme, or 1/2 teaspoon
    dried leaf thyme, crumbled*
1 bay leaf
6 parsley stems
*1 tablespoon plus 1 teaspoon
    all-purpose flour*

*2 1/4 pounds ripe tomatoes, peeled,
    seeded, and chopped, or two
    28-ounce cans whole plum
    tomatoes, drained and chopped*
*1 3/4 to 2 1/4 cups Beef Stock (see
    recipe) or packaged broth or
    water*
Salt and freshly ground pepper

8 ounces pearl onions
1 tablespoon butter
2 tablespoons vegetable oil
*8 ounces medium-size mushrooms,
    quartered*

1 tablespoon snipped fresh chives
*1 tablespoon minced fresh tarragon
    or basil, or 1 teaspoon dried
    leaf tarragon*
1 tablespoon minced fresh parsley

Position rack in lower third of oven and preheat to 450°F. Pat beef
dry. Heat oil in 4- to 5-quart heavy flameproof casserole over medium-high heat. Add one-third to one-half the beef, or enough so
pieces do not touch. Brown on all sides, taking 6 to 7 minutes. Using
a slotted spatula, transfer to a plate and continue with remaining beef.

TOMATO-HERB SAUCE

Add chopped onion to casserole and cook over low heat, stirring often, until softened, about 7 minutes. Meanwhile, put garlic, thyme, bay leaf, and parsley stems on piece of cheesecloth and tie in a bundle. Return meat to pan, reserving any juices on plate, and sprinkle with flour, tossing lightly to coat. Bake, uncovered, stirring once, 5 minutes. Remove casserole and reduce oven temperature to 325°F.

Pour juices from plate over beef. Stir in tomatoes and 1¾ cups stock, or enough to barely cover beef. Add cheesecloth bag and salt and pepper and bring to boil, stirring often and scraping any browned bits from sides and bottom of pan. Cover and bake, stirring and turning beef cubes over occasionally, 1 hour and 15 minutes. If pan appears dry or sauce is too thick, stir in an additional ½ cup stock. Continue baking, stirring occasionally, until beef is just tender when pierced with tip of knife, about 15 to 30 minutes. Discard cheesecloth bag.

Meanwhile, add pearl onions to medium saucepan of boiling water and boil 1 minute. Drain, rinse with cold water, and peel with a paring knife. Heat butter and 1 tablespoon oil in medium, heavy skillet over medium-high heat. Add pearl onions and sauté, shaking pan occasionally, until lightly browned, about 4 minutes. Remove with a slotted spoon. Heat remaining tablespoon oil in skillet. Add mushrooms and salt and pepper and sauté until lightly browned, about 3 minutes.

Transfer stew to top of stove and uncover. Add onions and mushrooms and simmer until onions are tender, about 25 minutes. Sauce should be thick enough to lightly coat a spoon. If it is too thick, stir in a few tablespoons stock or water to thin it out. If it is too thin, carefully remove beef and vegetables with a slotted spoon; boil sauce, uncovered, stirring often, until lightly thickened, and then return beef and vegetables to casserole. (Stew can be kept, covered, 3 days in refrigerator or 1 month in freezer. Reheat in covered casserole before continuing.)

Stir in chives, tarragon or basil, and parsley. Taste and adjust seasoning. Serve stew from enameled casserole or deep serving dish.

NOTE: For other possible cuts of beef to use, see page 163.

⚜ LIGHT BEEF BOURGUIGNON WITH COLORFUL VEGETABLES
Boeuf bourguignon léger aux légumes variés

Although beef bourguignon traditionally contains salt pork or bacon, today many cooks prefer using plenty of fresh vegetables instead, as in this version. Burgundian chefs also prepare veal shoulder the same way, but its cooking time is only about 40 to 50 minutes.

MAKES 4 SERVINGS

2 pounds boneless beef chuck, excess
    fat trimmed, cut in 1 1/4- to
    1 1/2-inch pieces

2 tablespoons vegetable oil
1 tablespoon butter

RED WINE SAUCE
1 large onion, chopped
1 medium-size garlic clove, crushed
1 sprig fresh thyme, or 1/2 teaspoon
    dried leaf thyme, crumbled
1 bay leaf
6 parsley stems

1 tablespoon plus 1 teaspoon
    all-purpose flour
1 1/4 cups dry red wine
1 3/4 to 2 1/4 cups Beef Stock (see
    recipe) or packaged broth
Salt and freshly ground pepper

8 ounces thin carrots, peeled and
    cut in 1-inch chunks
6 ounces pearl onions
1 tablespoon butter
1 small fennel bulb (about 5
    ounces), stalks discarded, diced
    (optional)

1 pound fresh peas (about 1 cup
    shelled), or 1 cup frozen
2 tablespoons minced fresh parsley

Position rack in lower third of oven and preheat to 450°F. Pat beef dry. Heat oil and butter in 4- to 5-quart heavy flameproof casserole over medium-high heat. Add one-third to one-half the beef, keeping the pieces from touching, and brown beef on all sides, taking 6 to 7 minutes. Using a slotted spatula, transfer to a plate and continue with remaining beef.

RED WINE SAUCE

Add chopped onion to casserole and cook over low heat, stirring often, until softened, about 7 minutes. Meanwhile, put garlic, thyme, bay leaf, and parsley stems on piece of cheesecloth and tie in bundle. Return meat to pan, reserving any juices on plate, and sprinkle with flour, tossing lightly to coat. Bake, uncovered, stirring once, 5 minutes. Remove casserole and reduce oven temperature to 325°F.

Pour juices from plate over beef. Stir in wine and 1¾ cups stock, or enough to barely cover beef. Add cheesecloth bag and salt and pepper and bring to a boil on top of the stove, stirring often and scraping any browned bits from sides and bottom of pan. Cover and bake, stirring and turning beef cubes over occasionally, 45 minutes.

Add carrots to stew and push down into liquid. Cover and continue baking, stirring occasionally, until beef and carrots are just tender when pierced with tip of knife, about 45 minutes to 1 hour. Discard cheesecloth bag.

Add pearl onions to medium saucepan of boiling water and boil 1 minute. Drain, rinse with cold water, and peel with a paring knife. Melt 1 tablespoon butter in medium, heavy skillet over medium-high heat. Add onions and sauté until lightly browned, about 4 minutes. Remove with a slotted spoon and add to stew. Add fennel, if using, and continue baking 20 minutes.

Sauce should be thick enough to lightly coat a spoon. If it is too thick, stir in a few tablespoons stock or water to thin it out. If it is too thin, carefully remove beef and vegetables with a slotted spoon; boil sauce, uncovered, stirring often, until lightly thickened, and then return beef and vegetables to casserole. (Stew can be kept, covered, 3 days in refrigerator or 1 month in freezer. Reheat in covered casserole before continuing.)

Add peas, cover, and simmer until all vegetables are tender, about 10 minutes if using fresh peas, or 5 minutes for frozen peas. Stir in parsley. Taste and adjust seasoning. Serve stew from enameled casserole or deep serving dish.

❧ AROMATIC BEEF STEW WITH GREEN BEANS AND CILANTRO
Ragoût de boeuf aux haricots verts et à la coriandre fraîche

Ginger, curry, and cilantro give this stew a delightful spicy accent. You can also add 1 or 2 chopped jalapeño or serrano peppers at the same time as the ginger, if you like hot food. Basmati rice is the perfect accompaniment.   MAKES 4 SERVINGS

2 pounds boneless beef chuck, excess
    fat trimmed, cut in 1 1/4- to
    1 1/2-inch pieces
3 tablespoons vegetable oil
1 large onion, chopped
1 tablespoon plus 1 teaspoon
    all-purpose flour
2 1/4 pounds ripe tomatoes, peeled,
    seeded, and chopped, or two
    28-ounce cans whole plum
    tomatoes, drained and chopped

1 3/4 to 2 1/4 cups water
1 tablespoon curry powder
2 large garlic cloves, minced
1 tablespoon minced peeled fresh
    ginger
Salt and freshly ground pepper
3 tablespoons minced cilantro (fresh
    coriander)
3/4 pound green beans, trimmed
    and broken in 2 pieces

Position rack in lower third of oven and preheat to 450°F. Pat beef dry. Heat oil in 4- to 5-quart heavy flameproof casserole over medium-high heat. Add one-third to one-half the beef, keeping the pieces from touching, and brown on all sides, about 6 or 7 minutes. Using a slotted spatula, transfer it to a plate. Continue with remaining beef.

Add onion to casserole and cook over low heat, stirring often, until softened, about 7 minutes. Return meat to pan, reserving any juices on plate, and sprinkle meat with flour, tossing lightly to coat. Bake, uncovered, stirring once, 5 minutes. Remove casserole and reduce oven temperature to 325°F.

Pour juices from plate over beef, and stir in tomatoes and 1 3/4 cups water, or enough to barely cover beef. Add curry powder, garlic, ginger, salt, pepper, and 2 tablespoons cilantro and bring to a boil, stirring often. Cover and bake, stirring and turning beef cubes over occasionally, 1 hour and 15 minutes. If pan appears dry or sauce is too thick, stir in an additional ½ cup water. Continue baking, stirring occasionally, until beef is just tender when pierced with tip of knife, about 15 to 30 minutes.

Put green beans in enough boiling salted water to generously cover and boil until nearly tender, about 3 minutes. Drain and rinse with cold water. Transfer stew to top of stove. Stir beans into stew and push them down into sauce. Simmer, uncovered, until tender, about 7 minutes.

Sauce should be thick enough to lightly coat a spoon. If it is too thick, stir in a few additional tablespoons water to thin it out. If it is too thin, carefully remove beef and vegetables with a slotted spoon; boil sauce, uncovered, stirring often, until lightly thickened, and then return beef and vegetables to casserole. (Stew can be kept, covered, 3 days in refrigerator or 1 month in freezer. Reheat in covered casserole before continuing.)

Stir in remaining tablespoon cilantro, and taste and adjust seasoning. Serve stew from enameled casserole or deep serving dish.

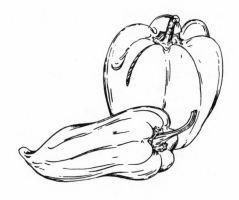

BEEF RAGOÛT WITH PEPPERS AND POTATOES
Ragoût de boeuf aux poivrons et aux pommes de terre

This colorful French ragoût is enhanced by the Moroccan spice combination of cumin, paprika, and hot pepper. It is a meal in one pot; all that is needed to complete it is a simple salad or a green vegetable.

MAKES 4 SERVINGS

2 pounds boneless beef chuck, excess fat trimmed, cut in 1 1/4- to 1 1/2-inch pieces

4 tablespoons vegetable oil

1 large onion, chopped

1 tablespoon plus 1 teaspoon all-purpose flour

3 to 3 1/2 cups Beef Stock (see recipe) or unsalted, packaged broth

3 large garlic cloves, minced

Pinch of cayenne pepper, or 1 fresh jalapeño pepper, seeds and ribs discarded, minced

2 teaspoons ground cumin

1 teaspoon paprika

Salt

1 1/2 pounds small red-skinned potatoes, peeled and put in cold water

1 medium-size red bell pepper, seeds and ribs discarded, cut in lengthwise strips 1 1/4 inches wide

1 medium-size green bell pepper, seeds and ribs discarded, cut in lengthwise strips 1 1/4 inches wide

Position rack in lower third of oven and preheat to 450°F. Pat beef dry. Heat 3 tablespoons oil in 4- to 5-quart heavy flameproof casserole over medium-high heat. Add one-third to one-half the beef, keeping the pieces from touching, and brown on all sides, about 7 minutes. Using a slotted spatula, transfer it to a plate. Continue with remaining beef.

Add onion to casserole and cook over low heat, stirring often, until softened, about 7 minutes. Return meat to pan, reserving any juices on plate, and sprinkle meat with flour, tossing lightly to coat. Bake, uncovered, stirring once, 5 minutes. Remove casserole and reduce oven temperature to 325°F.

Pour juices from plate over beef, and stir in 3 cups stock, or enough to barely cover beef. Add garlic, cayenne or jalapeño pepper, cumin, paprika, and salt and bring to a boil, stirring often. Cover and bake, stirring and turning beef cubes over occasionally, 1 hour and 15 minutes.

If pan appears dry or sauce is too thick, stir in an additional 1/2 cup stock. Quarter potatoes, add to stew, and push down into liquid. Continue baking, stirring occasionally, until beef and potatoes are just tender when pierced with tip of knife, about 30 to 40 minutes.

Sauce should be thick enough to lightly coat a spoon. If it is too thick, stir in a few tablespoons water to thin it out. If it is too thin, carefully remove beef and vegetables with a slotted spoon; boil sauce,

GRILLED CHICKEN AND AVOCADO SALAD
WITH OLIVES, TOMATOES, AND MINT

*Salade de poulet grillé aux avocats, aux olives,
aux tomates, et à la menthe*

BRAISED VEAL SHANKS
WITH ORANGES, PRUNES,
AND RED WINE

*Jarrets de veau braisés
à l'orange
et aux pruneaux*

GOOSE WITH GRAPES, ORANGES, AND KIWIS
Oie aux raisins, à l'orange, et aux kiwis

SAUTÉED VENISON
WITH RED WINE GAME SAUCE

Sauté de chevreuil grand veneur

SALMON WITH
AVOCADO SAUCE
Saumon aux avocats

SCALLOPS WITH SAFFRON, TOMATOES,
AND VERMOUTH

Coquilles Saint-Jacques au safran, aux tomates,
et au vermouth

SAUTÉED TURKEY WITH BASIL
AND SUMMER VEGETABLES
*Escalopes de dinde au basilic
et aux légumes d'été*

CRAB WITH SHRIMP BUTTER SAUCE
ON A BED OF FRESH PASTA

Crabe au beurre de crevettes sur lit de pâtes fraîches

uncovered, stirring often, until lightly thickened, and then return beef and vegetables to casserole. (Stew can be kept, covered, 3 days in refrigerator. Reheat in covered casserole before continuing.)

Heat remaining tablespoon oil in large skillet over medium heat, add bell pepper strips, and sauté, stirring often, 3 minutes. Stir pepper into stew and simmer until tender, about 5 minutes. Taste and adjust seasoning. Serve stew from enameled casserole or deep serving dish.

PROVENÇAL MARINATED BEEF STEW WITH RED WINE
Daube de boeuf à la provençale

Daube is a red wine meat stew that varies from place to place in southern France and is often flavored, as in this recipe, with olive oil, tomatoes, and a hint of orange and lemon peel. Some versions add olives, cèpes, or celery. In Avignon, *daube* is made with lamb instead of beef. The classic accompaniment is pasta, usually fettuccine and occasionally ravioli, which is moistened with the rich beef cooking juices. Now that fresh stuffed pasta is widely available, it is easy to follow this delightful custom. Use ravioli or tortellini filled with meat, ricotta, or spinach.   MAKES 5 OR 6 SERVINGS

3 pounds beef chuck, excess fat
    trimmed, cut in 1 1/2-inch
    pieces
2 cups dry red wine
1 large onion, thinly sliced
2 sprigs fresh thyme, or 1/2
    teaspoon dried leaf thyme,
    crumbled
2 bay leaves
3 tablespoons olive oil
6 parsley stems
One 3-inch strip orange rind
One 2-inch strip lemon rind
2 whole cloves

5 large garlic cloves, chopped
1/2 pound ripe tomatoes, peeled,
    seeded, and chopped, or one
    14-ounce can whole plum
    tomatoes, drained and chopped
1/2 cup water
Salt and freshly ground pepper
1/2 pound pearl onions, peeled
1 pound carrots, cut in 3/4-inch
    slices
Pinch of sugar (optional)
Buttered ravioli, fettuccine, or other
    stuffed or flat pasta

In a large ceramic or glass bowl, combine beef with wine, sliced onion, thyme, bay leaves, and 1 tablespoon olive oil and marinate, covered and chilled, turning occasionally, for at least 4 hours or overnight.

Drain beef and onions, reserving marinade, thyme sprigs (dried thyme will remain in marinade), and bay leaves, and pat beef dry. Tie thyme sprigs, bay leaves, parsley stems, orange rind, lemon rind, and cloves in a cheesecloth bag.

In a large heavy flameproof casserole, heat remaining 2 tablespoons oil over medium-high heat until hot and brown beef in batches, transferring it with a slotted spoon to a plate as it is browned.

Add sliced onion to casserole and cook over low heat, stirring, for 10 minutes. Add garlic and cook 1 minute, stirring, then add tomatoes and cook 1 minute more. Return beef to casserole with any juices that have accumulated on plate, add marinade and the ½ cup water, and season with salt and pepper to taste. Bring to a boil, stirring. Reduce heat to low and simmer, covered, 1 hour, stirring occasionally.

Meanwhile, place pearl onions in medium saucepan of boiling water and boil 1 minute. Drain, rinse with cold water, and peel with a paring knife; set aside.

After beef has cooked 1 hour, add carrots and cheesecloth bag and simmer, covered, 2 hours. Add pearl onions and simmer, covered, 1½ hours. Remove cover and simmer 1 hour more, or until ingredients are tender and sauce is well flavored. Discard cheesecloth bag. Taste and adjust seasoning, and add a pinch of sugar, if necessary. (Stew can be kept, covered, 3 days in refrigerator or 1 month in freezer. Reheat in covered casserole before continuing.)

Serve the *daube* from an enameled casserole or from a heated deep serving dish, accompanied by buttered pasta. Spoon pasta onto each heated plate and spoon stew over or alongside it.

BEEF RAGOÛT WITH MINT, CELERY, AND SAFFRON
Ragoût de boeuf à la menthe, aux céleris, et au safran

Mint is not used in the cooking of much of France, yet it is popular in the stews of Languedoc in the southwest. It gives this stew a refreshing taste and balances its richness. I like to serve couscous as an accompaniment. MAKES 4 SERVINGS

2 pounds boneless beef chuck, excess fat trimmed, cut in 1 1/4- to 1 1/2-inch pieces
4 tablespoons vegetable oil
1 large onion, chopped
1 tablespoon plus 1 teaspoon all-purpose flour
3 to 3 1/2 cups water
1/4 teaspoon firmly packed crushed saffron threads (2 large pinches)

Salt and freshly ground pepper
1 tablespoon tomato paste
1 pound celery (5 large stalks), peeled, halved lengthwise, and cut in 2-inch pieces
2 tablespoons minced fresh mint
1 teaspoon strained fresh lemon juice

Position rack in lower third of oven and preheat to 450°F. Pat beef dry. Heat 3 tablespoons oil in 4- to 5-quart heavy flameproof casserole over medium-high heat. Add one-third to one-half the beef, or enough so pieces do not touch, and brown on all sides, about 7 minutes. Using a slotted spatula, transfer it to a plate and continue with remaining beef.

Add onion to casserole and cook over low heat, stirring often, until softened, about 7 minutes. Return meat to pan, reserving any juices on plate, and sprinkle meat with flour, tossing lightly to coat. Bake, uncovered, stirring once, 5 minutes. Remove casserole and reduce oven temperature to 325°F.

Pour juices from plate over beef and stir in 3 cups water, or enough to barely cover beef. Bring to a boil, stirring often. Add saffron and salt and pepper to taste. Cover and bake, stirring and turning beef cubes over occasionally, 1 hour and 15 minutes. If pan appears dry or sauce is too thick, stir in an additional 1/2 cup water. Continue baking, stirring occasionally, until beef is just tender when pierced with a thin-bladed knife, about 15 to 30 minutes. Stir in tomato paste.

Heat remaining tablespoon oil in large skillet over medium-high heat, add celery, and sauté until beginning to soften (but do not brown) about 3 minutes. Add celery pieces to stew and push them down into sauce. Bake until celery is just tender, about 15 minutes.

Sauce should be thick enough to lightly coat a spoon. If it is too thick, stir in a few additional tablespoons water to thin it out. If it is too thin, carefully remove beef and vegetables with a slotted spoon; boil sauce, uncovered, stirring often, until lightly thickened, and then return beef and vegetables to casserole. (Stew can be kept, covered, 3 days in refrigerator. Reheat in covered casserole before continuing.)

Remove from heat and stir in mint and lemon juice. Taste and adjust seasoning. Serve stew from enameled casserole or deep serving dish.

Grilled and Sautéed Lamb

We often associate lamb with Mediterranean cooking, and it is indeed a meat of choice in southern France, where it is often served with eggplant, peppers, and tomatoes, or with ratatouille.

Yet lamb is also a specialty of Normandy and Brittany in northwestern France. Certain highly prized lambs feed on the salt marshes on the border between these two provinces, near the impressive monastery of Mont-Saint-Michel, and gain a delicately salted taste. In Normandy, a popular accompaniment is asparagus, and a touch of Calvados may be added to the pan juices; whereas in neighboring Brittany, artichoke hearts are often served with lamb. White beans and new peas with lamb are loved in all the regions of France.

It was perhaps in Paris, though, that I sampled the most delicious lamb dishes I can remember. One was lamb noisettes with tarragon sauce, a classic entrée taught by Chef Claude Vauguet at La Varenne cooking school. It is a prime example of a wonderful recipe: the tender meat was perfectly sautéed so it was beautifully browned but pink inside and was topped with a marvelous brown sauce with a lively touch of fresh tarragon. It was the inspiration for Lamb Paillardes with Tarragon Vinegar.

Grilling and broiling are the favorite techniques for cooking lamb chops, especially thick ones, and for good reason—lamb is rich so it remains succulent when grilled or broiled, and these techniques give the lamb a pleasant brown crust as well. When cooked this way, the lamb is moist and flavorful enough to be served without sauce, or with just a simple sauce or seasoned butter.

Sautéing is ideal for thin lamb chops, because it is easier to cook them accurately and prevent them from overcooking. In addition, the pan juices can be the base for a quick and tasty pan sauce made by deglazing the skillet with wine or stock.

Hints

• Young lamb is best because its flavor is delicate. To ensure lamb of good quality, buy it from a good butcher, and choose lamb chops that are relatively small.

• When grilling lamb, use tongs to turn it; if the meat is pricked with a fork, it loses some of its juices and may become dry.

• See also hints on beef *paillardes* and steaks (pages 143–44) and on grilled chicken (page 52).

GRILLED LAMB CHOPS WITH PEAS À L'ORIENTALE
Côtes d'agneau grillées aux petits pois à l'orientale

The familiar pairing of grilled lamb with buttered peas gains an Oriental twist in this new fast and easy recipe, with the addition of water chestnuts, straw mushrooms, and a hint of fresh ginger.

MAKES 4 SERVINGS

2 1/2 pounds fresh peas (about 2 1/2 cups shelled), 2 1/2 cups frozen, or 1 pound sugar snap peas, trimmed
8 loin or rib lamb chops, about 1 1/2 inches thick, excess fat trimmed
1 tablespoon vegetable oil
Salt and freshly ground pepper

3 tablespoons butter
1 teaspoon finely grated peeled fresh ginger
1/4 cup canned water chestnuts, rinsed and drained, cut in half crosswise
1/2 cup canned straw mushrooms, rinsed and drained
1/4 teaspoon sugar

Preheat broiler with rack about 3 inches from heat source; or prepare charcoal grill or stove-top ridged grill.

Cook peas in a large pan of boiling salted water until just tender, about 4 minutes for fresh green peas, about 1 minute for frozen, or about 3 minutes for sugar snap peas. Drain well.

Lightly rub chops with oil on both sides and season with salt and pepper. Grill or broil until done to taste, about 5 or 6 minutes per side for medium-rare. To check for doneness, slit meat in thickest part near bone; if it is reddish-pink, it is rare; if it is pink, it is medium-rare; if it is brown with a tinge of pink, it is medium.

Melt 2 tablespoons butter in a medium saucepan, and add ginger, water chestnuts, and mushrooms. Cook about 1 minute over low heat, then add peas, sugar, and salt to taste and cook until heated through, about 30 seconds. Add remaining tablespoon butter and toss until just blended. Taste and adjust seasoning. Serve lamb chops alongside or on a bed of the vegetables.

SEE JACKET PHOTOGRAPH.

LAMB PAILLARDES WITH TARRAGON VINEGAR
Paillardes d'agneau au vinaigre d'estragon

The zesty sauce flavored with tarragon and tarragon vinegar is the ideal complement for these lamb *paillardes,* which are made from lamb steaks. The size of lamb steaks varies, depending on the point of the leg of lamb from which they are cut. Pounding not only makes them thin, but also helps to give them a more attractive shape.

MAKES 3 OR 4 SERVINGS

1 1/2 pounds lamb steaks from boned leg of lamb, cut about 1/2 inch thick

Salt and freshly ground pepper
1 tablespoon vegetable oil
1 tablespoon butter

TARRAGON-GARLIC SAUCE
7 tablespoons butter
2 tablespoons minced garlic
1/3 cup tarragon wine vinegar (5% acidity)

1 cup Beef Stock (see recipe) or unsalted, packaged broth
2 teaspoons tomato paste
1 tablespoon minced fresh tarragon

Using the point of a sharp knife, remove skin and excess fat from lamb. Cut large lamb steaks in half crosswise, dividing them through hole left when bone was removed. Set a lamb steak on plastic wrap or wax paper and push it together into an oval shape. Cover with plastic wrap or wax paper and pound with flat meat pounder or rolling pin until flattened to about ¼ inch. Carefully peel off plastic. Repeat with remaining steaks.

Season lamb with salt and pepper. Heat oil and butter in large heavy skillet over medium-high heat until butter melts. Add half of lamb *paillardes* carefully so they keep their shape and sauté until browned on both sides but still pink, about 1½ minutes per side. Turn carefully using 2 wide spatulas. (Some lamb *paillardes* might not keep an oval form after sautéing, but they will be delicious anyway.) Transfer lamb to ovenproof platter, arrange pieces side by side, cover, and keep them warm in 275°F. oven while sautéing remaining lamb. Pour off fat from skillet.

TARRAGON-GARLIC SAUCE

Cut 6 tablespoons butter in 6 pieces and refrigerate. Add 1 other tablespoon butter to skillet and melt over low heat. Add garlic and cook, stirring, 30 seconds. Add vinegar and bring to a boil over medium heat, stirring and scraping browned bits from pan. Simmer vinegar over medium-high heat until reduced to about 3 tablespoons. Add stock and any juices that escaped from meat and bring to a boil. Boil over high heat, stirring often, until mixture is reduced to about ½ cup, about 3 minutes. Transfer sauce to small heavy saucepan and whisk in tomato paste.

Bring sauce to a simmer, reduce heat to low, and gradually whisk in cold butter pieces, 1 at a time. Remove sauce from heat and stir in tarragon. Taste and adjust seasoning, then pour sauce over lamb and serve.

LAMB CHOPS WITH CARROT PURÉE AND LEMON-MINT BUTTER
Côtes d'agneau à la purée de carottes, beurre de citron à la menthe

In this elegant main course designed for a meal in minutes, the mint butter adds a fresh touch to both the grilled lamb and the carrot purée.   MAKES 4 SERVINGS

LEMON-MINT BUTTER

1/4 cup chopped fresh mint
1/2 cup butter, softened
1 1/2 teaspoons finely grated lemon
*   peel*

1 1/2 teaspoons strained fresh lemon
*   juice*
Salt and freshly ground pepper

1 3/4 to 2 pounds carrots, cut in
*   1/2-inch slices*
Salt
12 small rib lamb chops, about 1
*   inch thick (2 to 2 1/4 pounds*
*   total)*

About 1 tablespoon vegetable oil
Freshly ground pepper

LEMON-MINT BUTTER

Thoroughly mix mint with butter, then stir in lemon peel. Gradually stir in lemon juice, and season to taste with salt and pepper. (Seasoned butter can be kept, covered, 2 days in refrigerator.)

Put carrots in a medium saucepan with enough water to cover and a pinch of salt. Bring to a boil, reduce heat to low, cover, and simmer about 30 minutes, or until carrots are very tender when pierced with a sharp knife. Using a slotted spoon, drain carrots and transfer to a food processor or blender. Purée until smooth. If using a blender, purée in small amounts and use a little liquid with each batch. (Carrot purée can be kept, covered, 2 days in refrigerator.) Return purée to saucepan.

Heat broiler with rack about 3 inches from heat source; or prepare charcoal grill or stove-top ridged grill. Trim excess fat from chops, rub lightly with oil, and season with salt and pepper on both sides. Grill or broil until done to taste, about 3 minutes per side for medium-rare; meat resists slightly when pressed, or if cut near bone, meat is pink.

Meanwhile, heat carrot purée until hot. Remove from heat and stir in 6 tablespoons lemon-mint butter. Taste and adjust seasoning.

Spoon carrot purée onto plates next to chops. Put about 1/2 teaspoon lemon-mint butter on each chop, and serve immediately.

LAMB CHOPS WITH ASPARAGUS AND MADEIRA
Côtes d'agneau aux asperges et au madère

A favorite meat for springtime, lamb is often served with spring vegetables, as in this quick, festive entrée. In addition to asparagus, artichoke hearts filled with buttered peas are a well-loved partner for lamb in France. Instead of the lamb chops, you can use beef tenderloin steaks for this dish.   MAKES 4 SERVINGS

½ to ¾ pound thin asparagus	1 to 2 tablespoons vegetable oil
2 tablespoons butter	½ cup Brown Veal Stock or Beef
12 small rib lamb chops, about ¾	Stock (see recipes) or unsalted,
inch thick	packaged broth
Salt and freshly ground pepper	¼ cup plus 2 teaspoons Madeira

Cut off asparagus tips and cut stalks in 3-inch pieces, discarding any thick white bases. Boil asparagus in a saucepan of boiling salted water for 2 minutes. Drain, rinse with cold water, and drain thoroughly. Cut 1 tablespoon butter in 2 pieces and refrigerate.

Trim excess fat from chops, and season lightly with salt and pepper on both sides. Heat oil in a heavy skillet over high heat. Add chops and sauté 2 minutes on each side. To check for doneness, press quickly on chops with your finger: if meat resists slightly, it is medium-rare. Transfer to a platter and keep warm.

Melt 1 tablespoon butter in a skillet over medium-low heat. Add asparagus and salt and pepper and sauté 2 minutes, or until tender. Keep warm.

Discard fat from pan. Add stock and ¼ cup Madeira and bring to a boil, stirring to scrape up browned bits in pan. Boil until reduced to about ⅓ cup. With pan over low heat, add cold butter pieces, shaking pan to incorporate them. Remove from heat and stir in remaining 2 teaspoons Madeira. Taste and adjust seasoning.

To serve, discard juices from platter of lamb, spoon a little sauce over each chop, and serve asparagus on side.

LAMB CHOPS WITH LENTILS
Côtes d'agneau aux lentilles

Lamb with lentil purée is a classic combination. Here is an easier, fresher rendition of the pair—the lentils gain zip from chopped green onions and diced fresh tomatoes that are added at the last moment. A long-time staple of regional cooking, especially in central France, lentils have recently become "chic" and are served in stylish restaurants. The fastest-cooking of all the legumes, requiring only about 30 minutes, lentils do not need to be soaked. Serve this with steamed white rice and sautéed or grilled yellow and green patty pan squash or zucchini.   MAKES 4 SERVINGS

1 1/2 cups lentils (about 10 ounces)
1 whole clove
1 small onion
1/2 small carrot
1 bay leaf
1/2 teaspoon dried leaf thyme
Salt and freshly ground pepper
8 to 12 rib lamb chops, about 1 inch thick (2 to 2 1/4 pounds total)

About 1 tablespoon vegetable oil
3 small ripe tomatoes (about 3/4 pound total), diced
3 tablespoons chopped fresh parsley
1/2 cup chopped green onions
2 tablespoons extra-virgin olive oil

Sort lentils, discarding any broken ones and any stones. Rinse lentils and drain, then put in heavy saucepan. Stick clove into onion and add to pan. Add carrot, bay leaf, thyme, and 5 cups water and bring to a boil. Reduce heat to low, cover, and cook about 30 to 35 minutes, or until tender but not falling apart. Discard onion, carrot, and bay leaf. Season with salt and pepper. (Lentils can be kept in their liquid, covered, 1 day in refrigerator. Reheat lentils in their liquid.) Keep warm over low heat.

Heat broiler with rack about 3 inches from heat source; or prepare charcoal grill or ridged stove-top grill. Trim excess fat from chops, rub lightly with vegetable oil, and season with salt and pepper on both sides. Grill or broil until done to your taste, about 3 minutes per side for medium-rare; meat resists slightly when pressed, or if cut near bone, meat is pink.

Reserve ¼ cup diced tomatoes and 1 tablespoon parsley for garnish. Drain lentils and transfer to a bowl. Add green onions, 2 tablespoons parsley, remaining tomatoes, and olive oil and toss gently to combine. Taste and adjust seasoning.

Serve lamb with lentils, garnishing lentils with reserved tomato dice and parsley.

Lamb Roasts and Ragoûts

In France, lamb roasts are the feasts of spring. Family celebrations may feature a roast leg of lamb, or even an elegant rack of lamb. The roasts are often served surrounded by a beautiful assortment of the first spring vegetables, making an impressive entrée.

Roasting lamb is much like roasting beef. The meat is naturally moist and does not need extra fat. Like beef, lamb is best loved when it is fairly rare or medium-rare, so it remains juicy and tender. A simple pan sauce can accompany the roast, but cream or butter sauces are not usually served with lamb because the meat is rich.

Lamb ragoûts, or stews, are hearty dishes made most often with shoulder of lamb. They are prepared like beef ragoûts (see page 162) but their cooking time is shorter because lamb is more tender. Seasonal vegetables are often added toward the end of the cooking to lend freshness and color. In Provence, lamb is made into a special red wine stew called a *daube,* and is prepared like beef *daube* (see page 171). Lamb stew is also the basis for many versions of cassoulet (page 92).

The classic seasoning for lamb, whether cooked as a roast or a ragoût, is garlic. For roasts, garlic slivers may be inserted directly into the meat, where they flavor it as it cooks. Rosemary is also popular with lamb, especially in southern France.

Hints

- It is best to use a heavy roasting pan that can also be used on top of the stove for deglazing.
- See also hints for roasting beef (page 154).

LEG OF LAMB WITH GARLIC SAUCE AND BEAN MEDLEY
Gigot d'agneau à l'ail et aux haricots panachés

Garlic and beans are traditional accompaniments for leg of lamb. The garlic can flavor both the lamb and the sauce, as in this recipe where garlic slivers are inserted in the lamb and roasted garlic cloves appear in the rosemary-scented sauce. French cooks pair a variety of beans with roast lamb. Some prefer large white beans, which are so associated with leg of lamb that they are called *pois a gigot* (peas for leg of lamb). Many like to serve more than one type of bean, for example green beans and dried beans such as flageolets. We are using lima beans, which are much more available here, together with green beans and yellow beans. A semi-boneless leg of lamb is a convenient cut to choose because it is easy to carve.

MAKES 8 TO 10 SERVINGS

1 semi-boneless leg of lamb (5 1/2 pounds), or 1 bone-in leg of lamb (6 pounds)
20 medium-size garlic cloves, peeled
2 tablespoons olive oil
Salt and freshly ground pepper
2 sprigs fresh rosemary, or 1/2 teaspoon dried
One 10-ounce package frozen lima beans, or 1 3/4 pounds fresh (weight with pods)

1/2 teaspoon dried leaf thyme, crumbled
1 pound green beans, ends trimmed
1 pound wax beans, ends trimmed
1/2 cup Brown Veal Stock or Chicken Stock (see recipe) or packaged broth
2 tablespoons butter

Preheat oven to 450°F. Trim off skin from lamb and as much excess fat as possible. Tie with string so it will stay in a neat shape.

Peel 2 garlic cloves and cut in thin slices, then in thin lengthwise slivers. Make slits in lamb about 1 inch deep with a small sharp knife, spacing them fairly evenly. Insert garlic slivers in slits.

Set lamb on a rack in a large heavy roasting pan. Spoon oil over lamb, season with salt and pepper, and roast 15 minutes.

Meanwhile, put remaining garlic cloves in pan of water, bring to boil, and simmer 5 minutes. Drain well.

Reduce oven temperature to 350°F. and roast the lamb for 1 hour, basting occasionally with juices. Add garlic cloves and rosemary sprigs to roasting pan. Continue roasting, basting occasionally, 15 to 30 minutes, or until lamb is done to taste. Check with a meat thermometer or instant-read thermometer inserted into thickest part of lamb; leg of lamb is medium-rare at 135°F., and medium at 145°F.

If using fresh lima beans, shell them. Cook beans in 2 cups boiling water with thyme, covered, about 7 minutes for frozen beans or about 15 to 20 minutes for fresh, or until tender; taste a bean to check. Drain, reserving cooking liquid.

Cook green and wax beans in 2 medium saucepans of boiling salted water until just tender: green beans about 5 minutes, wax beans about 7 minutes. Drain, rinse with cold water, and drain well.

Transfer lamb to a carving board, cover loosely with foil, and let stand 10 to 15 minutes.

If garlic cloves are not very tender, roast 5 more minutes, stirring occasionally. Remove garlic and chop finely with a knife, not a food processor. Add 1 cup lima bean cooking liquid and stock to roasting pan and bring to a simmer, stirring. Strain into a small saucepan, skim off excess fat, stir in chopped garlic, bring sauce to a simmer, and keep warm.

Melt butter in a large skillet or sauté pan, add all of beans, and toss over low heat until coated. Cover and heat over low heat until just hot. Season with salt and pepper and toss.

To carve lamb, hold shank bone with a towel and carve meat from rounded side of leg in several thin slices, cutting away from you. There is no need to carve all the way to the bone. Turn lamb over, carved side down, and cut meat from opposite side of leg. Last, carve slices from shank portion of meat, closest to bone. Drain carving juices into sauce and heat gently.

To serve, arrange lamb slices on plates with vegetables next to them. Serve sauce separately; stir before serving.

❧ ROAST RACK OF LAMB WITH AÏOLI-GLAZED CAULIFLOWER
Carré d'agneau rôti, chou-fleur glacé à l'aïoli

Rack of lamb is one of the most elegant of roasts, but its cooking time is brief. It has the additional advantage of being very simple to carve—you just cut between the chops. The aïoli-glazed cauliflower is a new twist on the classic custom of coating cauliflower with hollandaise sauce and browning it in the oven. The lamb can instead be served with spring vegetables (as in Chicken with Spring Vegetables), with stuffed peppers and eggplant (as in Beef Rib Roast with Stuffed Peppers and Sautéed Eggplant), or with celery root purée.

MAKES 4 TO 6 SERVINGS

AÏOLI
4 medium-size garlic cloves, peeled
2 extra-large egg yolks, room temperature
1 tablespoon strained fresh lemon juice

1 cup extra-virgin olive oil, room temperature
1 tablespoon warm water
Salt and freshly ground pepper

2 medium-size cauliflower heads, divided into medium florets
2 trimmed racks of lamb (also called lamb rib roasts) (about 1 1/4 pounds each)
Salt and freshly ground pepper

1 cup Brown or White Veal Stock (see recipe) or packaged broth
8 to 12 cherry tomatoes, cut in half
Parsley or watercress sprigs for garnish

AÏOLI

Cut off brown end and any brown spots from garlic. Cut garlic cloves in half lengthwise and remove any green sprouts from centers. Drop garlic cloves through feed tube of food processor fitted with metal blade, with motor running, and process until finely chopped. Add egg yolks, lemon juice, 1 tablespoon oil, and a pinch of salt and pepper and process until thoroughly blended, scraping bottom and sides of container several times. With motor running, gradually pour in oil in a thin trickle. After adding 1/4 cup oil, remaining oil can be poured in a little faster, in a fine stream. With motor still running, gradually pour in the 1 tablespoon warm water in 3 additions. Taste and adjust seasoning, and transfer to a bowl.

Cook cauliflower, uncovered, in a large saucepan of boiling salted water about 5 minutes, or until barely tender. Drain, rinse with cold water, and drain well. Arrange in lightly oiled baking dish. Dip each floret in aïoli to coat; wipe off excess with your finger. Reserve at room temperature while roasting lamb.

Preheat oven to 450°F. Trim excess fat from lamb, and season with salt and pepper. Put in roasting pan, bone side down. Roast about 25 minutes, turning over after 15 minutes, or until meat thermometer registers 135°F. for medium-rare. Remove and let rest 10 minutes in warm place. Leave oven on.

Meanwhile, bake cauliflower about 5 minutes, or until lightly dotted with brown.

To make a pan sauce, pour off fat from roasting pan. Add stock and bring to a boil, stirring to dissolve any browned bits. Strain into a small saucepan, and taste and adjust seasoning.

Carve lamb into chops. Reheat sauce gently. Serve lamb with cauliflower, tomatoes, and parsley or watercress, and spoon a little sauce over lamb.

❧ HERBED LAMB RAGOÛT WITH ARTICHOKES
Ragoût d'agneau aux artichauts et aux herbes

In this ragoût—which features favorite Provençal flavors of olives, tomatoes, thyme, marjoram, and garlic—artichokes add a fresh taste and lightness to balance the rich lamb. Serve it with potatoes or rice.   MAKES 4 SERVINGS

2½ pounds lamb shoulder with
   bone, or 2 pounds boneless
   lamb shoulder or lamb stew
   meat
2 tablespoons olive oil
1 onion, finely chopped
4 large garlic cloves, minced
Salt and freshly ground pepper
2 pounds ripe tomatoes, peeled,
   seeded, and chopped, or two
   28-ounce cans whole plum
   tomatoes, drained and chopped
2 tablespoons minced fresh
   marjoram, or 2 teaspoons
   dried, crumbled

2 teaspoons fresh thyme leaves or
   ¾ teaspoon dried leaf thyme,
   crumbled
1 cup water
1 bay leaf
4 fresh artichokes, or 16 frozen
   artichoke heart pieces
1 lemon (if using fresh artichokes),
   or 1 teaspoon lemon juice (if
   using frozen)
½ cup pitted black olives, drained
2 tablespoons minced fresh parsley

Trim excess fat from lamb, cut in 1- to 1¼-inch pieces, and pat dry.

In a heavy flameproof casserole, heat oil over medium-high heat. Add lamb in batches, taking care not to crowd it, and brown on all sides, about 4 minutes per batch. With a slotted spoon, transfer lamb pieces as they brown to a plate. Add onion to casserole and cook over low heat, stirring often, about 5 minutes, or until softened; do not brown.

Return lamb to casserole, reserving any juices that have accumulated on plate. Add garlic and a pinch of salt and pepper, and cook over low heat, stirring, for 30 seconds. Stir in tomatoes, marjoram, and thyme, and bring to a boil. Add juices from plate, 1 cup water, and bay leaf and bring mixture to a boil, stirring. Cover and cook, stirring occasionally, about 1 hour, or until lamb is just tender when pierced with a knife.

If using fresh artichokes, squeeze juice of ½ lemon into a medium bowl of cold water. Trim leaves to shape artichoke in hearts (see page 311). Put each artichoke heart in bowl of lemon water.

Prepare a medium saucepan of boiling salted water and squeeze in any juice remaining in lemon (if using fresh artichokes), or add 1 teaspoon lemon juice (if using frozen). Add fresh or frozen artichoke hearts to saucepan, cover, and simmer over low heat until tender when pierced with knife, 15 to 20 minutes for fresh or about 7 minutes for frozen. Cool to lukewarm in liquid. Using a teaspoon, scoop out hairlike choke from center of each fresh artichoke heart. Return artichokes to liquid until ready to use. Cut each fresh artichoke in 4 pieces.

Remove lamb from casserole with a slotted spoon. Boil cooking liquid, stirring, until it is reduced to 2 cups. Drain liquid from meat a few times and add to casserole as liquid reduces. Discard bay leaf.

Return meat to sauce, add artichokes and olives, and heat over low heat 1 to 2 minutes. (Stew can be kept, covered, 2 days in refrigerator or 1 month in freezer. Reheat over low heat, covered.) Taste and adjust seasoning; flavor generously with freshly ground pepper. Sprinkle with parsley. Serve stew from enameled casserole or from a heated deep serving dish.

LAMB SHOULDER WITH FLAGEOLETS, TOMATOES, AND CORN
Épaule d'agneau aux flageolets, aux tomatoes, et au maïs

Lamb stew with beans is a frequently prepared family supper in France. Pale green flageolets are the most delicate beans and look pretty in this ragoût, but if they are not available, dried white beans can be substituted. The corn is not traditional, but it adds good taste, texture, and color. MAKES 4 SERVINGS

COOKED BEANS

1 cup dried flageolets (about 7
     ounces) or Great Northern
     white beans
1 bay leaf

¼ teaspoon dried leaf thyme,
     crumbled, or 1 sprig fresh
Pinch of salt

2 tablespoons vegetable oil
2 pounds boned lamb shoulder,
     excess fat trimmed, cut in
     1-inch cubes, or cubed lamb
     for stew
1 large onion, chopped
3 large garlic cloves, chopped
1 pound ripe tomatoes, peeled,
     seeded, and chopped, or one
     28-ounce can whole plum
     tomatoes, drained and chopped
1 cup water

1 small carrot, cut in half
     lengthwise
1 bouquet garni (1 sprig thyme, 1
     bay leaf, 5 parsley stems tied
     together)
Salt and freshly ground pepper
2 cups corn kernels, cut from cob,
     or one 10-ounce package
     frozen
Cayenne pepper to taste
2 tablespoons chopped fresh parsley

COOKED BEANS

Sort beans, discarding any broken ones and any stones. Soak beans in 3 cups cold water in a large bowl in a cool place for 8 hours or overnight. Or, for a quicker method, combine beans and 3 cups water in a large saucepan, bring to a boil, and boil 2 minutes; cover and let stand off heat 1 hour.

Rinse beans and drain. In a medium saucepan, combine beans with bay leaf, thyme, and 1 quart water. Bring to a boil, reduce heat to low, cover, and cook 1 hour. Add a pinch of salt and cook about 30 minutes longer, or until just tender. (Beans can be kept in their cooking liquid for 1 day in refrigerator. Reheat before continuing.) Discard bay leaf.

Heat oil in heavy wide casserole. Add lamb cubes to pan in batches, taking care not to crowd, and brown on all sides over medium-high heat. Remove, add onion, and cook over low heat until softened; do not brown. Add garlic and cook 30 seconds, then stir in tomatoes and cook 2 minutes more.

Return lamb to pan. Add 1 cup water, carrot, bouquet garni, and a little salt and pepper. Bring to a boil, reduce heat, cover, and simmer

45 minutes, or until lamb is tender. Discard carrot and bouquet garni, and skim off excess fat. Add corn and cook until just tender, about 7 minutes for fresh or 2 minutes for frozen.

Drain beans, reserving a few tablespoons of their cooking liquid, and add beans to lamb stew. If stew is too thick, add some reserved bean cooking liquid. Bring to a boil, reduce heat to very low, and cook 5 minutes to blend flavors. (Stew can be kept, covered, 2 days in refrigerator or 1 month in freezer.) If stew is too soupy, cook, uncovered, 5 minutes more. Add cayenne, and taste and adjust seasoning. Sprinkle with parsley and serve.

Pork Roasts and Chops

Pork chops and roasts are staples of French home cooking. Cooks have developed many delicious ways to use these cuts, most often by pairing them with assertive seasonings—favorites are sage, mustard, garlic, rosemary, capers, and cornichons. The flavorful meat is complemented by the sharpness of vinegar (as in Pork Chops with Glazed Radishes) or by the sweetness of fruit (as in Roast Pork with Sautéed Apples and Ginger Cream). Pork chops are marvelous with zesty sauces, such as Roquefort Sauce (see page 149) or Horseradish Cream (see page 152).

Unlike beef and lamb chops and steaks, pork chops are best when cooked partially by moist heat, so that the meat does not dry out. Roasts cook at a lower temperature than those of red meats and for a longer time so they will be well done. Although the accepted internal temperature for roasting pork used to be 170°F. to 185°F., today 160°F. to 165°F. is considered perfectly safe and yields meat that is more moist.

Potatoes of all types, especially roasted, sautéed, or made into a creamy purée, are the most popular accompaniment for pork. Other vegetables that are often served with pork are the hearty ones—endive, red and green cabbage, Brussels sprouts, and Jerusalem artichokes; as well as legumes—lentils, chick-peas, and dried beans.

ROAST PORK WITH SAUTÉED APPLES AND GINGER CREAM
Rôti de porc aux pommes sautées et à la crème de gingembre

In this new twist on the ever-popular pair of pork and apples, the roast is accompanied by a fresh ginger sauce lightly thickened with bread crumbs. Some chefs today favor this old-fashioned technique of thickening sauces because there is no problem of the flour not cooking properly—after all, it has already been baked as bread. The pork is roasted on the bone, which makes for more flavorful meat.

MAKES 4 SERVINGS

One 3-pound pork loin or rib roast, bone in
1 teaspoon vegetable oil

Salt and freshly ground pepper
1/2 teaspoon ground ginger

GINGER CREAM

1 1/2 cups White Veal Stock or Chicken Stock (see recipes) or packaged broth, plus 2 or 3 tablespoons more, if needed
3/4 cup dry white wine

3 tablespoons bread crumbs
3/4 cup heavy cream
2 tablespoons finely grated peeled fresh ginger
Salt and freshly ground pepper

3 tart apples, such as Granny Smith

2 tablespoons butter
Parsley sprigs for garnish

Preheat oven to 400°F. Trim most of fat from meat, and set on a rack in a medium roasting pan. Rub pork with oil, sprinkle with salt, pepper, and ginger, and rub spices into meat.

Roast meat 15 minutes. Reduce oven temperature to 325°F. and roast meat, basting every 30 minutes with pan juices, for about 1 hour and 45 to 55 minutes, or until a thermometer inserted in thickest part of meat registers 165°F.; juices that run from meat when it is pricked should be clear, not pink.

Transfer pork to a cutting board. Remove strings, cover pork, and keep warm. Let rest 15 to 20 minutes.

GINGER CREAM

Discard excess fat from roasting pan. Add ¾ cup stock to pan and bring to a boil, stirring in juices. Strain into a medium saucepan.

Add wine and remaining ¾ cup stock and boil until reduced to about 1 cup. Add bread crumbs and simmer 2 minutes, then add cream and simmer until thick enough to very lightly coat a spoon. Remove from heat. Add juices that have accumulated from pork roast and stir in grated ginger. Season to taste with salt and pepper. Bring just to a simmer. Sauce thickens on standing; add a few additional tablespoons stock if it becomes too thick.

Peel apples and cut in eighths. Melt butter in a large skillet over medium heat. Add apples and sauté 3 to 4 minutes on each side, or until lightly browned and tender.

Carve thicker part of roast in slices, cutting to detach ends of each slice from bone. Spoon a little sauce on each plate and top with pork. Surround with apple slices and garnish with parsley sprigs.

SAGE-SCENTED ROAST PORK WITH STUFFED VEGETABLES
Rôti de porc à la sauge et aux légumes farcis

Sage is a widely used partner for roast pork. Here the roast is served as a French feast, surrounded by baked stuffed vegetables. The vegetables are often filled with a pork stuffing, but I prefer the lighter mushroom stuffing used here.　　　　　　MAKES 4 SERVINGS

18 fresh sage leaves, or ½
　　teaspoon dried sage
1 boneless pork loin roast (3
　　pounds), tied

3 tablespoons olive oil
Salt and freshly ground pepper
12 large mushrooms
4 small tomatoes

MUSHROOM STUFFING

8 ounces medium-size mushrooms,
    quartered
1 tablespoon butter
2 medium-size shallots, minced
1 medium-size garlic clove, minced
1/4 teaspoon dried leaf thyme

Salt and freshly ground pepper
2 tablespoons dry white wine
3 tablespoons stock or broth (veal,
    chicken, or beef)
1 tablespoon dried unseasoned bread
    crumbs, or more if needed

Preheat oven to 400°F. If using fresh sage, make about 6 slits about 1 inch deep in top of pork with a small sharp knife, spacing them fairly evenly. Tightly roll up 6 sage leaves and insert in slits. Slip remaining sage leaves under strings used to tie pork. If using dried sage, stir it into the olive oil.

Set pork in a small roasting pan. Spoon 2 tablespoons oil over pork and season with salt and pepper. Roast 10 minutes, then reduce oven temperature to 325°F. Roast meat for 1 hour, basting every 15 minutes with pan juices.

Meanwhile, separate mushroom caps from stems with a twisting motion. Reserve stems for stuffing. Carefully cut off green stem end of tomatoes without making a hole. Turn over and cut a slice off tops. Remove tomato pulp with a small spoon, leaving shells for stuffing and reserving the pulp. Season tomatoes lightly with salt, turn over, and set on a rack to drain for 30 minutes. Chop tomato pulp.

MUSHROOM STUFFING

Combine reserved mushroom stems with quartered mushrooms and chop very finely with on/off turns of food processor, or with a knife. Melt butter in a medium skillet, add shallots, and cook over low heat about 1 minute. Add chopped mushrooms, garlic, thyme, and salt and pepper and cook over medium-high heat, stirring often, about 7 minutes, or until liquid that escapes from mushrooms evaporates. Add wine and cook until dry, then add stock and cook, stirring, until absorbed. Stir in bread crumbs. If mixture seems a bit wet, stir in a little more. Taste and adjust seasoning.

Season tomato shells with pepper and mushroom caps with salt and pepper. Spoon stuffing into tomato shells and mushroom caps. Lightly oil a shallow heavy baking dish, transfer stuffed vegetables to oiled dish, and sprinkle with remaining tablespoon olive oil.

After pork has roasted for a total of 1 hour and 10 minutes, add chopped tomato pulp to roasting pan. Continue roasting pork until a thermometer inserted in thickest part of meat registers 165°F. (about 45 minutes); juices that run from meat when it is pricked should be clear, not pink. Meanwhile, bake vegetables at 325°F. until tender, about 20 minutes. Remove and keep warm.

Transfer pork to a cutting board. Remove strings, cover, and keep warm. Strain roasting juices into a small saucepan and skim off excess fat, if desired. Taste and adjust seasoning.

Cut pork in thin slices and arrange on a platter, surrounded by stuffed vegetables. Reheat juices, if necessary, pour into a sauceboat, and serve separately.

PORK CHOPS WITH WHITE WINE, TARRAGON, AND THYME
Côtes de porc au vin blanc et aux herbes

The sauce in this Alsatian dish tastes quite sharp on its own because of the generous amount of white wine, but it is just right with the pork chops. Serve them with glazed or steamed carrots and buttered potatoes, or with spaetzle. MAKES 4 SERVINGS

4 pork rib chops, about 1 to 1 1/2 inches thick
3 tablespoons butter
2 tablespoons vegetable oil
5 medium-size shallots, finely chopped
2 tablespoons all-purpose flour
1 1/2 cups dry white wine, preferably Riesling
3/4 cup Chicken Stock or White Veal Stock (see recipe) or packaged broth

1 sprig fresh thyme, or 1/2 teaspoon dried leaf thyme, crumbled
1 sprig fresh tarragon
Salt and freshly ground pepper
1 1/2 teaspoons chopped fresh thyme, or 1/2 teaspoon dried leaf thyme, crumbled
1 tablespoon chopped fresh tarragon
1 tablespoon chopped fresh parsley

Pat chops dry. Refrigerate 1 tablespoon butter.

Heat oil and remaining 2 tablespoons butter in a medium, deep skillet or sauté pan over medium-high heat. Add chops and brown on both sides, about 3 minutes per side. Transfer to a plate.

Add shallots to pan and cook over low heat, stirring often, until softened. Remove from heat and stir in flour. Cook 1 or 2 minutes over low heat, stirring. Whisk in wine and stock and bring to a boil, whisking. Add thyme sprig or dried thyme, tarragon sprig, and salt and pepper. Cook over low heat, stirring occasionally, 10 minutes.

Return chops to sauce, cover, and simmer 20 to 25 minutes, or until tender. To check, make a small slit near bone—meat should be white, with no pink. (Chops can be kept, covered, overnight in refrigerator. Reheat before continuing.) Remove chops from sauce, cover, and keep warm. If sauce is too thin, simmer it, uncovered, stirring often, until thick enough to lightly coat a spoon. Remove thyme and tarragon sprigs.

Add chopped thyme and chopped tarragon to sauce. Over low heat, swirl in reserved cold butter. Taste and adjust seasoning. Serve chops on hot plates, spoon sauce over, and sprinkle with parsley.

PORK CHOPS WITH GLAZED RADISHES
Côtes de porc aux radis glacés

It might seem unusual to cook radishes, but they are good with pork chops. They become light pink when cooked and resemble turnips in taste. After the chops are sautéed, the juices are deglazed with red wine vinegar, which provides a pleasant counterpoint to the rich meat. Serve these chops with baked or mashed potatoes.

MAKES 4 SERVINGS

3 tablespoons butter
28 to 32 small red radishes, rinsed
*   and scraped if necessary (1 1/2*
*   pounds total)*
Pinch of sugar
Salt and freshly ground pepper

4 pork chops, about 1 inch thick
*   (about 2 pounds total)*
1 tablespoon vegetable oil
3 tablespoons mild red wine vinegar
*   (5% acidity)*
1 tablespoon chopped fresh parsley

Melt 2 tablespoons butter in a medium saucepan, add radishes, sugar, salt and pepper to taste, and 1/2 cup water. Cook, uncovered, over low heat about 15 minutes, or until tender when pierced with a knife. Remove radishes. Boil liquid until it coats bottom of pan. Return radishes to pan and cook over low heat, shaking pan often, until they are coated and shiny. Be careful not to brown. Cover and keep warm.

Pat meat dry, and season on both sides with salt and pepper. Heat oil and remaining tablespoon butter in a large skillet or sauté pan. Add pork chops and sauté over medium-high heat to brown lightly, about 3 minutes per side. Cover and cook over low heat 6 minutes, turning once; to test if done, cut meat near bone—juices should be clear and meat should be white, not pink.

Remove pork chops, put on platter, and keep warm. Discard most of fat. Reheat juices in skillet, then add vinegar and bring to a boil, stirring; it evaporates rapidly. Quickly add chopped parsley and pour into small bowl.

Serve pork with radishes, and pour vinegar-flavored juices over meat.

Braised and Poached Pork

Long the most common meat in provincial France, pork is the meat of choice in several of France's most famous regional specialties—notably the world-renowned Alsatian *choucroute* and many versions of cassoulet, the superb stew of Languedoc.

There are other, lesser-known but wonderful pork dishes created by cooks in all the provinces of France. In Burgundy, pork is gently stewed with white wine, onions, and garlic, then the sauce is finished with grapes and crème fraîche. Cooks in Limousin in central France prepare pork in a similar way, but braise chestnuts along with it. Apples, onions, and cream flavor the braised pork of Normandy. In southern France, it is cooked as a zesty fricassee with accents of sage, rosemary, and garlic. Of all these savory preparations, my favorite is perhaps pork braised in the Basque style, with tomatoes and a variety of peppers.

🦎 ALSATIAN SAUERKRAUT WITH FRESH AND SMOKED PORK
Choucroute à l'alsacienne

Plenty of cabbage grows in Alsace. Much of it is pickled and turned into the region's most famous specialty—*choucroute,* the French version of sauerkraut. As in Germany, it is a hearty dish, crowned by sausages and smoked meats and served with potatoes and mustard. The French version, however, is surprisingly delicate in comparison— for several reasons. First, the French rinse their sauerkraut thoroughly so it will not be aggressively acidic. Instead of adding apples and sugar to obtain a strong sweet-and-sour taste, they simmer the sauerkraut gently in dry Riesling wine. Alsatians often begin by cooking the meat separately, so that the sauerkraut remains light and does not become greasy. The meat finishes cooking with the sauerkraut to promote an exchange of flavors. Smoked and fresh pork, bacon, and sausages are most frequently served with it.

Alsatian-style restaurants called *brasseries,* featuring *choucroute* and beer, are popular in many French cities. Often a variety of meats are set atop the sauerkraut for a version called *choucroute royale.* For festive occasions, the pork is sometimes replaced by roast duck, goose, or game birds, such as pheasant or partridge. In "modern" restaurants, sauerkraut may even be served with a selection of fresh and smoked fish.

This version of sauerkraut uses less lard or oil than traditional ones, because today many people prefer a lighter sauerkraut. Besides, French bacon is leaner than ours.   MAKES 4 TO 6 SERVINGS

4 pounds uncooked sauerkraut
3 tablespoons lard or vegetable oil
2 onions, sliced
1 bay leaf
3 whole cloves
6 juniper berries (optional)
6 coriander seeds
6 peppercorns
6 garlic cloves, peeled
2 cups Riesling wine

1 piece fresh pork loin (1 1/2 pounds)
Pinch of salt
1 pound smoked pork loin chops or slices
3/4 pound lean bacon slices
4 to 6 smoked sausages
4 to 6 hot boiled potatoes
Dijon mustard

Rinse sauerkraut thoroughly under cold running water. Drain and squeeze out excess liquid.

Heat lard or oil in a large casserole, add onions, and cook over low heat, stirring, until soft but not brown. Tie bay leaf, cloves, optional juniper berries, coriander seeds, peppercorns, and garlic in cheesecloth. Add sauerkraut, cheesecloth bag, and wine to casserole. Cover and simmer 45 minutes.

Meanwhile, put fresh pork in a medium saucepan, add a small pinch of salt, and 5 cups water. Bring to a boil, reduce heat to low, cover, and cook 15 minutes. Add smoked pork and simmer 30 minutes more.

Put bacon in a saucepan, cover with water, and bring to a simmer. Simmer 1 minute, and drain thoroughly.

Add fresh and smoked pork to sauerkraut, reserving their cooking liquid. Taste the cooking liquid; if it is not too salty, add ½ cup liquid to sauerkraut. Add bacon. Spoon some of sauerkraut over pork. Cover and continue simmering another hour, or until sauerkraut and meats are tender, adding water if pan becomes dry and turning meats over occasionally. (Sauerkraut can be kept, covered, 1 day in refrigerator. Reheat, covered, before continuing.)

Cook sausages in pork cooking liquid, covered, over low heat for about 2 minutes. Remove from heat and let stand, covered, 7 minutes. Drain well, cover, and keep warm.

Discard cheesecloth. Taste sauerkraut and adjust seasoning. If mixture is very soupy, simmer uncovered a few minutes to evaporate excess liquid. Slice fresh pork. Spoon sauerkraut onto a large platter and arrange pork slices, smoked pork, sausages, and potatoes over it. Serve mustard separately.

PORK TENDERLOIN WITH PEPPER SAUCE
Filet de porc à la basquaise

One of my favorite pork recipes, this entrée is delicious, easy to prepare, and colorful. The tenderloin is a tasty, tender cut, and the Basque combination of sweet and hot peppers and tomatoes makes a sensational braising sauce. At a restaurant at Saint-Jean-Pied-de-Port in the French Basque region bordering on Spain, we enjoyed a similar

dish, but instead of being served with fresh pork, the sauce was topped
with sautéed country ham.   MAKES 4 SERVINGS

6 tablespoons vegetable oil
1 large onion, chopped
1 large green bell pepper, cored,
    seeded, finely diced
1 large red bell pepper, cored,
    seeded, finely diced
1 or 2 fresh jalapeño peppers,
    cored, seeded, and finely
    chopped
2 medium-size garlic cloves, chopped
2¼ pounds ripe tomatoes, peeled,
    seeded, and chopped, or two
    28-ounce cans whole plum
    tomatoes, drained and chopped

Salt
2 pork tenderloins (about 1½
    pounds total), trimmed and
    patted dry
Freshly ground pepper
¾ cup Brown or White Veal Stock
    or Chicken Stock (see recipes)
    or packaged broth

Heat 4 tablespoons oil in a large deep sauté pan or casserole. Add
onion and cook over low heat, stirring often, about 7 minutes, or until
soft but not brown. Add bell peppers and cook 5 minutes. Stir in hot
pepper and garlic, then tomatoes and salt and cook, uncovered, over
medium heat, stirring often, about 20 minutes, or until mixture is
thick. (Tomato-pepper mixture can be kept, covered, 2 days in refrigerator; reheat before continuing.)

Season pork with salt and pepper. Heat remaining 2 tablespoons
oil in a sauté pan or deep skillet. Add pork and sauté over medium-
high heat until browned on all sides, about 8 minutes. Transfer pork
to tomato mixture.

Add stock, bring to a simmer, cover, and cook over low heat
about 30 minutes, or until pork is tender; a meat thermometer or
instant-read thermometer should register 165°F. Taste sauce and adjust seasoning. If sauce is thin, remove pork and boil sauce, stirring
often, until thickened. Slice pork, and serve slices overlapping on a
bed of sauce.

~ PORK RAGOÛT WITH ONIONS AND ARMAGNAC
Ragoût de porc aux oignons et à l'armagnac

Armagnac is made in southwest France and is used often in cooking, as in this aromatic winter stew that is flavored with a generous amount of onions and garlic. Serve it with a green vegetable and potatoes, corn, or Parmesan-topped pasta.   MAKES 4 SERVINGS

2 pounds pork stew meat (in 1-inch cubes) or 1 piece pork loin with bone (3 pounds)

3 large onions (1½ to 2 pounds total)

10 medium-size peeled garlic cloves

3 tablespoons lard or vegetable oil

1 tablespoon all-purpose flour

1 cup dry white wine

¼ cup Armagnac, Cognac, or brandy, or more to taste

1 cup Chicken Stock (see recipe) or packaged broth

½ cup canned tomato purée

1 bay leaf

½ teaspoon dried leaf thyme

Salt and freshly ground pepper

Freshly grated nutmeg

2 tablespoons chopped fresh parsley

If using a cut of meat with bone, remove meat from bone, trim excess fat, cut meat in 1-inch cubes, and pat dry; reserve bone. Chop onions and garlic together. (If using a food processor, first chop garlic, then add onions and chop together).

Heat 2 tablespoons lard or oil in a large enameled casserole. Add pork in batches, taking care to keep pieces separate, and brown lightly on all sides over medium-high heat. Remove with a slotted spoon.

Add remaining tablespoon lard or oil and heat over medium heat. Add onion-garlic mixture and cook, stirring often, until softened but not brown, about 5 minutes. Add flour and cook over low heat about 1 minute. Stir in wine and ¼ cup Armagnac and bring to a boil, then stir in stock and tomato purée and return to a boil. Add meat and reserved bone and stir. Add bay leaf, thyme, and salt and pepper, bring to a simmer, cover, and cook over low heat 40 to 45 minutes, or until meat is very tender.

Remove meat cubes with tongs. Discard bone and bay leaf. Cook sauce, uncovered, over medium heat until thick. Add nutmeg, and taste and adjust seasoning. Return meat to sauce. (Stew can be kept, covered, 2 days in refrigerator. Reheat before continuing.)

If desired, add an additional 1 or 2 teaspoons Armagnac. Stir in parsley and serve hot.

FRICASSEE OF PORK WITH ROSEMARY AND GARLIC
Fricassée de porc au romarin et à l'ail

Provence is known for its coastal towns with their seafood dishes, but in its mountainous northern section, hearty meat stews are enjoyed. In this one, rosemary, sage, and garlic impart a wonderful aroma to the meat. The touch of hot pepper, however, is more in the style of France's Basque region, where I tasted a similar dish at a *routier,* or truck-stop restaurant. There it was served with buttered rice garnished with green olives and strips of sautéed peppers. In this modern modification, broccoli and cauliflower add color and lightness and turn the fricassee into a complete main course.

MAKES 4 SERVINGS

2 pounds boneless pork, either loin country-style ribs or blade shoulder country-style butt
3 tablespoons olive oil, vegetable oil, or lard
Salt and freshly ground pepper
2 medium-size garlic cloves, minced

1 tablespoon chopped fresh rosemary
2 tablespoons chopped fresh sage
1/2 cup water
1 dried hot red pepper (optional)
2 cups small cauliflower florets
2 cups small broccoli florets

Trim excess fat from pork but leave a little on. Cut in 1-inch cubes, and pat dry.

Heat oil or lard in a large heavy skillet or casserole over medium-high heat. Add pork in batches, taking care to keep pieces separate, and brown on all sides, about 4 minutes; remove each batch with a slotted spoon as it browns. After pork is browned, reduce heat to low, return meat to skillet, and season with salt and pepper. Stir in garlic, rosemary, and half the sage. Add water and hot pepper, if desired, and bring to a simmer. Cover and cook over low heat about 20 to 25 minutes, or until meat is tender; cut a piece to check—juices should be clear and meat should be white, not pink. (Meat can be kept, covered, 1 day in refrigerator. Reheat in covered pan before continuing.)

Meanwhile, cook cauliflower in a medium saucepan of boiling water over high heat, uncovered, 1 minute. Add broccoli and boil 2 minutes, or until both are crisp-tender. Drain, rinse with cold water, and drain thoroughly.

Remove meat with slotted spoon, leaving hot pepper in pan. Boil cooking liquid over high heat, stirring occasionally, until it reduces by about half and just coats the base of pan. Remove hot pepper. Add meat, broccoli, and cauliflower and heat gently, tossing. Taste and adjust seasoning. Add remaining sage, and serve hot.

Game Meats

French markets are exciting for game lovers, especially in the fall. In addition to a variety of game birds, there is a choice of venison, hare, and wild boar. The cuts of meat for roasting are barded and neatly tied in a way only French butchers seem to know how to do—they look almost like they're gift-wrapped!

For most of us who are not hunters, the game meats available are cultivated rather than wild, but they are tasty and lean and a pleasant way to vary main courses.

Rabbit is similar to chicken in flavor and cooking properties, and is cooked by many of the same methods, especially as sautés and braised dishes. In France, rabbit is often sold alongside poultry. It can be roasted, but dries out more easily than chicken and, therefore, must be protected with bacon and sauce, for example, as in Roasted Rabbit with Tomatoes and Thyme.

Venison is cooked like beef and resembles beef somewhat in taste, but extra care must be taken not to overcook it because it is leaner than beef. Since venison steaks and chops are the forms most available to us, we have concentrated on them in this chapter. Like beef, venison is good with brown sauces, especially those made with fortified wines like Madeira. French cooks also prepare venison with fruit, as in Venison with Leek Compote and Sautéed Pears. A traditional accompaniment is sautéed wild mushrooms, which, like game, are in season in autumn.

🌿 RABBIT WITH MUSTARD AND SHALLOT SAUCE
Lapin à la moutarde et à l'échalote

Mustard is the favorite condiment for rabbit in France. Of the many versions of the entrée, I love this one best—the zesty creamy sauce is excellent with the tender rabbit meat. Chef Claude Vauguet of La Varenne sometimes finishes cooking steamed potatoes along with the rabbit and enriches the sauce with herb butter. I also enjoyed the way this dish was presented at a small Parisian restaurant—the rabbit was set on a bed of spinach and accompanied by fresh noodles, which were also moistened with the mustardy sauce. Chicken pieces can be substituted for the rabbit.   MAKES 4 SERVINGS

1 rabbit (about 2 1/2 pounds), cut
    in 6 pieces
Salt and freshly ground pepper
1 tablespoon vegetable oil
1 tablespoon butter
4 medium-size shallots, minced
2/3 cup dry white wine

1/2 cup Chicken Stock (see recipe)
    or packaged broth
2 sprigs fresh thyme, or 1/2
    teaspoon dried leaf thyme,
    crumbled
1 cup heavy cream
2 tablespoons Dijon mustard

Pull off excess fat from rabbit. Pat rabbit pieces dry, and season with salt and pepper. If kidneys are attached to saddle pieces, leave them on.

Heat oil and butter in a large heavy skillet over medium-high heat. Add enough rabbit pieces to make one layer in pan and brown them lightly on both sides, then transfer to a plate. Repeat with other pieces, removing them when brown.

Add shallots to skillet and cook 1 minute over low heat. Add wine, stock, and thyme and bring to a boil. Return rabbit pieces to pan and add any juices from plate. Cover and cook over low heat 15 minutes; turn pieces over and cook about 15 minutes, or until tender when pierced with a knife. (Rabbit can be kept, covered, 1 day in refrigerator. Reheat in covered pan over low heat before continuing.) Transfer rabbit to a platter with a slotted spoon, cover, and keep warm. Discard thyme sprig.

Boil cooking liquid until reduced to about ½ cup. Add cream and boil until thick enough to lightly coat a spoon. Whisk mustard into sauce and heat gently over low heat. Taste and adjust seasoning.

Return rabbit to sauce and heat briefly, uncovered, over low heat, turning pieces over to coat them with sauce. Serve hot.

NOTE: Although a rabbit is generally cut in 6 pieces, it makes 4 servings because some are less meaty than others.

ROASTED RABBIT WITH TOMATOES AND THYME
Lapin rôti aux tomates et au thym

For this aromatic Provençal specialty, small pieces of bacon hold fresh thyme sprigs and garlic cloves in place on each rabbit piece, so they add their flavor during the roasting. A vivid tomato sauce enhanced by a generous amount of shallots keeps the rabbit moist. In keeping with its country style, serve the rabbit directly from the baking dish.   MAKES 4 SERVINGS

3 tablespoons olive oil
8 ounces shallots, sliced
2 pounds ripe tomatoes, peeled, seeded, and coarsely chopped, or two 28-ounce cans whole plum tomatoes, drained and chopped
Salt and freshly ground pepper

1 rabbit (about 2½ pounds), cut in 6 pieces
3 garlic cloves, peeled and cut in half lengthwise
6 large sprigs thyme
3 bacon slices, cut in half crosswise
1 tablespoon fresh thyme leaves

In a medium saucepan over low heat, heat oil, add shallots, and cook about 7 to 8 minutes, or until soft and just beginning to brown lightly at edges. Add tomatoes and salt and pepper, and bring to a boil. Reduce heat to low and simmer 20 minutes. (Tomato sauce can be kept, covered, 1 day in refrigerator. Reheat before continuing.)

Preheat oven to 375°F. Pull off excess fat from rabbit. Pat pieces dry and season all over with salt and pepper, rubbing seasonings into rabbit. Place rabbit pieces hollow side up. Put a garlic piece and a sprig of thyme on each rabbit piece and cover with a slice of bacon.

Add thyme leaves to tomato sauce. Spread sauce in a large gratin dish or other heavy flameproof baking dish, and put rabbit pieces on top. Bake 15 minutes. Spoon some sauce over rabbit and continue baking, basting once more with sauce, about 30 to 35 minutes, or until tender.

Remove rabbit, cover, and keep warm. Cook sauce in gratin dish over medium heat on top of stove until thickened to taste. Discard thyme sprigs and garlic from rabbit pieces. Replace bacon slices on rabbit and set in sauce. Serve from dish.

MARINATED RABBIT WITH COGNAC, BEETS, AND ASPARAGUS
Lapin mariné au cognac, avec betteraves, et avec asperges

Cognac is the base for a zesty marinade that permeates the rabbit meat, and for the simple but richly flavored accompanying sauce. Pearl onions, steamed beets, and asparagus turn the rabbit into a festive entrée.   MAKES 4 SERVINGS

1 rabbit (2½ pounds), cut in 6 pieces	7 tablespoons butter
⅓ cup dry white wine	½ cup Chicken Stock (see recipe) or packaged broth
⅔ cup plus 1 to 1½ teaspoons Cognac or brandy	12 baby beets
20 pearl onions (5 to 6 ounces)	12 asparagus tips
Salt and freshly ground pepper	2 teaspoons snipped chives

Pull off any pieces of fat on rabbit. Put rabbit in a shallow dish and pour wine and ⅔ cup Cognac over it. Cover and marinate 2 or 3 hours, turning pieces once or twice.

Put onions in a medium saucepan, cover with water, bring to a boil, and boil 1 minute. Drain, rinse under cold water, and drain well. Peel with a paring knife.

Remove rabbit pieces from marinade, reserving marinade, and pat them dry. Season with salt and pepper.

Cut 3 tablespoons butter in 6 pieces and refrigerate. Heat 2 tablespoons butter in a large deep skillet or sauté pan over medium-high heat and brown rabbit pieces in batches, about 5 minutes for each; if rabbit kidneys are detached, add them for the last 2 minutes. Remove rabbit to a plate. Discard fat from skillet.

Melt remaining 2 tablespoons butter in pan over low heat. Add onions and roll them in butter. Return rabbit pieces to pan and add juices from plate, reserved marinade, and stock, and bring to a simmer. Cover and cook over low heat 15 minutes; turn pieces over and continue cooking, 10 to 15 minutes more, or until tender.

Meanwhile, steam baby beets about 15 to 20 minutes, or until tender. Rinse, slip off skins, cover, and keep warm in steamer top with heat turned off.

Cook asparagus in a medium saucepan of boiling salted water over high heat, uncovered, about 2 minutes, or until just tender. Drain, rinse with cold water, and drain well.

Transfer rabbit and onions to a platter, cover, and keep warm. (If onions are not yet tender, transfer only rabbit to platter and continue simmering onions until they are tender; then transfer them to platter.)

Strain rabbit juices, bring them to a boil, and heat asparagus in sauce. Remove asparagus and keep warm.

Boil juices until reduced to about ½ cup. With pan over low heat, add cold butter, 1 piece at a time, shaking pan to blend butter into sauce. Taste and add 1 or 1½ teaspoons Cognac or brandy, and salt and pepper. Pour sauce over rabbit and sprinkle with chives. Serve surrounded by onions, beets, and asparagus.

VENISON WITH LEEK COMPOTE AND SAUTÉED PEARS
Côtes de chevreuil à la compote de poireaux et aux poires

Here the traditional pairing of venison and fruit appears in an easy modern dish—the venison is garnished with sautéed pears spiked with pear brandy. Leek compote, a popular side dish, is made of sliced leeks that cook gently and become slightly sweet. Since venison is new at our markets, the cuts are not as standardized as with beef. Try to buy boneless venison chops or steaks from a young animal so that they will be tender.   MAKES 4 SERVINGS

LEEK COMPOTE

2 pounds leeks, white and light
    green parts only, split and
    rinsed
3 tablespoons butter

1 cup Brown Veal or Beef Stock
    (see recipe), or packaged broth
1 teaspoon cornstarch, potato
    starch, or arrowroot dissolved
    in 2 teaspoons water
2 firm pears, preferably Anjou
    (about 1 pound total)
3 tablespoons butter
4 tablespoons dry white wine

Salt and freshly ground pepper
1/4 cup Chicken or White Veal
    Stock (see recipes) or packaged
    broth

4 chops or steaks of young venison,
    3/4 to 1 inch thick (about
    1 1/2 pounds total)
Salt and freshly ground pepper
1 tablespoon vegetable oil
1 tablespoon plus 1 teaspoon pear
    brandy or Cognac
3 tablespoons pear brandy
    (optional)

LEEK COMPOTE

Cut leeks in thin slices. Melt butter in a large sauté pan. Add leeks and salt and pepper to taste, and toss over low heat until coated. Add stock and bring to a boil. Reduce heat to low, cover, and simmer, stirring often, about 20 minutes, or until very tender. If any liquid remains, uncover and simmer until it evaporates. Taste and adjust seasoning. (Compote can be kept, covered, 2 days in refrigerator; reheat before using and keep warm over low heat.)

Bring stock to a simmer over medium heat. Whisk cornstarch or potato starch or arrowroot mixture to blend, then gradually whisk half of it into simmering stock. Return to a boil, whisking. Remove from heat and reserve.

Peel pears, core them from the bottom, and cut crosswise in round slices about 3/8 inch thick. Cover with plastic wrap.

Melt 2 tablespoons butter in a large skillet over medium-high heat. Add half the pears and sauté about 2 minutes per side, or until just beginning to brown at edges and barely tender; do not let them get too soft. Remove with a slotted spoon. Repeat with remaining pears. Transfer pears to a baking dish or plate in one layer and keep hot, covered, in a 300°F. oven. Add 2 tablespoons wine to skillet in which pears were cooked, bring to a boil, and pour into brown sauce.

Pat venison dry, and season with salt and pepper. Heat oil and remaining tablespoon butter in large skillet over medium-high heat. Add meat and sauté about 4 minutes per side for medium-rare; meat should still be pink inside—cut in thickest part to check. Remove to plate, cover, and keep warm.

Add remaining 2 tablespoons wine to skillet and bring to a boil, stirring to dissolve browned bits. Add reserved sauce and bring to a boil. Reduce heat to low and simmer until thick enough to lightly coat a spoon. Off heat, add 1 tablespoon plus 1 teaspoon pear brandy or Cognac.

Sprinkle 3 tablespoons pear brandy (but not Cognac) over pear slices and turn them over to coat. To serve, spoon some leek compote onto each plate next to the venison, top with sauce, and garnish plate with pear slices.

VENISON CHOPS WITH RED WINE GAME SAUCE
Côtes de chevreuil grand veneur

This recipe is inspired by an entrée I enjoyed at the Auberge de l'Ill, the most celebrated restaurant in Alsace and one of the best in France. The venison was served with a marvelous red wine sauce, accompanied by apples poached in white wine, *airelles* (a tiny relative of the cranberry), fresh noodles, and sautéed fresh chanterelles.

In this version, the venison is sautéed and served with a deep brown sauce, a rich but easier-to-prepare cousin of the classic *sauce poivrade* for game. It is based on meat stock, with red wine and red currant jelly adding a slight sweet-and-sour note. Serve the venison with the same side dishes as the Auberge de l'Ill, or with sugar snap peas or *haricots verts* (French green beans).   MAKES 4 SERVINGS

RED WINE GAME SAUCE

1 tablespoon butter
½ onion, diced
1 small carrot, diced
2 cups dry red wine
1 tablespoon red wine vinegar
1 large sprig fresh thyme
1 sprig fresh rosemary, or pinch of dried rosemary
1 bay leaf

1 clove
¾ cup Brown Veal Stock or Beef Stock (see recipes) or packaged broth
2 teaspoons tomato paste
Salt and freshly ground pepper
⅓ cup heavy cream or crème fraîche
1 teaspoon red currant jelly

4 chops or steaks of young venison,   1 tablespoon vegetable oil
    ¾ to 1 inch thick (about   2 tablespoons butter
    1½ pounds total)   3 tablespoons Cognac or brandy
Salt and freshly ground pepper

RED WINE GAME SAUCE

Melt butter in a large heavy saucepan. Add onion and carrot and cook over medium heat, stirring often, until beginning to brown, about 10 minutes. Add wine, vinegar, thyme, rosemary, bay leaf, and clove, and bring to a boil. Simmer, uncovered, over medium heat, skimming occasionally, for 30 minutes. Add stock, tomato paste, and a small pinch of salt and pepper, and bring to a boil; simmer 10 minutes. Strain sauce, pressing on vegetables, then bring to a boil. Whisk in cream and return to a boil. If sauce is too thin, boil it, whisking often, until it is thick enough to lightly coat a spoon. Whisk in jelly. (Sauce can be kept, covered, 1 day in refrigerator; reheat over low heat.)

Pat venison thoroughly dry, and season with salt and pepper. Heat oil and butter in large heavy skillet over medium-high heat. Add meat and sauté about 4 minutes per side for medium-rare; meat should still be pink inside—cut in thickest part to check. Remove to a plate, set aside, and keep warm for 5 minutes.

Pour off most of fat from skillet. Off heat, add Cognac and stir quickly to dissolve juices; it quickly evaporates from heat of pan. Stir meat juices in pan into sauce, and add juices from plate of venison. Taste and adjust seasoning, adding plenty of pepper. Serve immediately; if chops are boneless, they can be carved in slices. Serve sauce separately.

SEE PHOTOGRAPH (STEAK VERSION).

Fish and Shellfish

I love shopping for fish in Paris. There is a vast array of glistening fresh fish in many colors. Although Paris is not on the sea, there is such a demand for fresh fish that the greatest effort is made to provide it. And for good reason—fresh fish and shellfish are essential for delectable seafood dishes; if it is not fresh, even the best recipe will prove disappointing.

At the markets in France most of the fish is displayed whole. When you buy a fish, usually the fishmonger asks whether you would like it filleted, and whether you would like the bones for stock—what a treat! In America you can ask for bones for stock, but you will get them only at well-stocked fish markets. If they are not available, however, you can substitute the inexpensive fish pieces sold for chowder.

Seafood seems to have been designed for quick cooking. Since fish and most shellfish are naturally tender, they require brief cooking so they remain moist and keep in their natural flavor.

Although properly cooked seafood is delicious on its own, it becomes festive when enhanced by an appropriate sauce. Many of the best sauces for fish require only a few minutes of simmering, and some need no cooking at all. Try the quick, easy sauce from Shark with Herbed Sour Cream Sauce or the zesty butter from Baked Trout with Spiced Butter and Sautéed Vegetables also with salmon, swordfish, or any of your favorite seafood. Experiment with marinating, using a quick marinade of lemon juice and oil, as in Sea Bass with Pistou Sauce, with any other fish before cooking it.

In classic cuisine, seafood was once often served without a vegetable accompaniment or with potatoes only. Although fish and potatoes make a fine match, many other vegetables add color, texture, and excitement to contemporary seafood entrées. You can pair the colorful vegetables of any season, from leeks and carrots to tomatoes, peppers, eggplant, fresh corn, and zucchini, with the variety of fish and shellfish to add exuberance and beauty to every dish. Pasta and rice also are ideal complements for seafood, especially when served with a sauce, as in Crab with Shrimp Butter Sauce on a Bed of Pasta.

Many of the recipes in this chapter have a Mediterranean inspiration. This is natural because the vibrant flavorings of that sunny area—olive oil, garlic, fresh thyme, and basil, for example—are ideal in fish cookery and are very popular today. They can help to quickly turn a simple fish into an exciting dish with a minimum of fuss.

Most fish and many shellfish are good both hot and cold. Some of the following recipes—such as Monkfish with Leeks, Tomatoes, and Olives and Baked Cod with Pipérade Sauce—can be served either way. Others, such as Sea Bass with Pistou Sauce and Mussels in Provençal Tomato Sauce, can be prepared at leisure well in advance and served cold or at cool room temperature.

Sometimes we want to shake loose from usual cooking routines and take it easy. For entertaining, there is no need to always follow a rigid plan and design menus of many courses. Prepare a light seafood entrée, present it with a glass of chilled white wine and some crusty French or Italian bread, add a salad, follow it with ice cream and fruit, and you will have a meal that everyone loves.

Sautéed Fish

It is not surprising that sautéing is the preferred technique of the French for preparing their exquisite sole. This method, which is sometimes called pan-frying, calls for briefly cooking the fish in a small amount of butter or oil over fairly high heat, thus sealing in its delicate natural taste. Ideal for cooking for a small number of people, sautéing is one of the fastest and simplest ways to cook fish and it enables the cook to have a delicious main course ready in just five minutes. This classic technique remains popular both among home cooks and in restaurants of every degree of elegance.

Purists serve sautéed fish alone or embellished only with a wedge of lemon. However, the technique lends itself to improvisation. A French chef might garnish the fish with lemony parsley butter or, if he is from the south, he might crown it with a zesty topping of tomatoes, garlic, and chopped anchovies. Other flavoring possibilities might include a luscious cream sauce, a simple oil-and-vinegar sauce made right in the skillet, or a colorful mix of seasonal vegetables and nuts sautéed in butter and sprinkled over the fish. Even the culinarily sophisticated French rarely develop elaborate garnishes for fish sautés, because they like to preserve the straightforward, simple character of these dishes.

All varieties of freshwater and saltwater fish can be sautéed, from the lean, such as trout, to the rich, such as mackerel. Sautéing is best for relatively thin pieces of fish because the heat can penetrate them easily—fillets, steaks up to 1 inch thick, and small whole fish. Use whole fillets that are relatively firm; if they are beginning to fall apart before they reach the pan, they will probably disintegrate during cooking.

The French term for sautéing fish, *à la meunière,* comes from the word for flour miller, and flour plays a central role in the technique. Before being sautéed, the fish is protected with a light coating, usually of flour and sometimes of bread crumbs. The coating prevents the fish from sticking to the pan, helps hold it together, and also forms a thin, crisp crust, which is appealing in contrast to the moist fish.

Although the coating has a protective function, it, too, must be treated with care. Coated fish should not sit for more than a few minutes, because moisture from the fish will make the coating gummy. For the same reason, it is best not to stack any coated fish, before or after cooking.

Butter imparts a lovely flavor to sautéed fish, but it can burn at the high temperature required for sautéing. To prevent this, it can be clarified or combined with oil. Either vegetable oil or olive oil can be used alone. Thin fish fillets are sautéed over medium-high heat. If the heat is too low, the fish absorbs too much fat and begins to stick. Because a longer cooking time is needed for thicker fillets and whole fish, it is often necessary to reduce the heat during sautéing so that the oil or butter will not burn.

The choice of pans is also important. A heavy skillet large enough to hold the fish in one layer will produce a crisp, perfectly cooked result. It should be large enough so the fish has plenty of room. If they are spaced too closely together in the pan, they will steam, releasing liquid that causes the fish to fall apart; if spaced too far apart, the fat in the pan can burn. It is better to cook the fish in batches than to crowd the pan. Many chefs like to use an oval skillet, which will accommodate a whole fish or long fillets; however, a round skillet can be substituted.

Sautéed thin fillets (½ inch or less) are the easiest to check for doneness; when their coating is browned, they are cooked. A convenient and accurate test for thicker fillets, steaks, and whole fish, is to insert a metal skewer into the thickest part of the fish. If it comes out hot, the fish is cooked.

A simple rice pilaf and steamed vegetables are good partners for fish sautés. Any accompaniments, though, should be prepared before the fish is cooked. Like any last-minute entrée, a fish sauté should be served as soon as possible. The rule used for soufflés can also be applied here: It is better to have guests wait for the fish than to have the fish wait for the guests.

Hints

- Allow about 6 ounces of fillet per person. If serving fish steaks, which have a bone in the center, use slightly more. Serve 1 small whole fish per person (10 to 12 ounces).
- Short fillets are easiest to sauté because they are less likely to break when turned or transferred to the serving platter.
- Remove tiny bones in a fish fillet by pulling them out with tweezers, a pastry crimper, small pliers, or with your fingers aided by a small knife, being careful not to make holes.
- Always prepare all utensils, ingredients, and platters ahead. Once the fish begins to cook, it should wait as little as possible.
- To coat fish with flour: Spread flour on a large plate. Pat fish dry, then dip both sides in flour to coat thoroughly. Hold fish lightly in one hand and pat it a few times to remove any excess flour. Arrange fish in a single layer on a dry plate, handling as little as possible to prevent coating from rubbing off.
- To prevent sticking and to crisp the coating, the fat in the skillet should be hot before the fish is added. Oil is hot enough when its surface begins to ripple. If the fish browns too quickly, reduce the heat. Increase the heat when turning fish, to crisp second side.
- Sauté the attractive side of a fish first; side that touches hot fat first browns best.
- A frying screen can be used to cover the skillet so that the fat won't splatter.
- If all the fat is absorbed after cooking several batches of fish, add more fat to keep the bottom of the skillet coated. Scrape off any coating that sticks to skillet before sautéing next batch.
- To avoid having to keep the fish warm in the oven, the fish can be sautéed in 2 skillets; the amount of fat should be increased so that both skillets are coated.
- To turn fish easily, use 2 very large slotted pancake turners or large shovel-shaped slotted spoons.
- Fish with a flaky texture, such as scrod, cook more rapidly than those with dense flesh, such as halibut.
- If a fish sauté must wait, it's best to keep it warm, uncovered, in a low oven and to add any sauce at the last minute, just before serving.

SALMON FILLETS WITH LEEK CREAM
Filets de saumon à la crème de poireaux

Feasting on a turbot with leek sauce at the renowned Parisian restaurant Taillevent gave me the idea for this entrée. The leek cream is easy to make, and is also delicious with grilled or broiled salmon steaks.   MAKES 4 SERVINGS

3 large leeks (1½ pounds), white
  and light green parts, split
  and rinsed thoroughly
2 tablespoons butter
Salt and freshly ground pepper
⅓ cup dry white wine
1 cup Fish Stock (see recipe), if
  possible made with salmon
  heads, tails, and bones, or ¾
  cup bottled clam juice

1 cup heavy cream
1½ pounds salmon fillet with
  skin, preferably from tail end
2 tablespoons vegetable oil

Cut leeks in thin slices. Melt 2 tablespoons butter in a large deep skillet and add leeks and a little salt and pepper. Cover and cook over low heat, stirring occasionally, 10 minutes, or until tender but not brown. Add wine and bring to a boil, then add fish stock or clam juice and return to a boil. Add cream and boil until thick enough to coat a spoon. Taste and adjust seasoning. (Sauce can be kept, covered, 1 day in refrigerator. Reheat, uncovered, over low heat.)

Run your fingers over salmon to check for bones and remove any you find with tweezers, a pastry crimper, or small sharp knife. Pat salmon dry, and place fillet, skin side down, on cutting board. Using a long, sharp, flexible knife, cut salmon in thin diagonal slices, cutting against skin to remove each slice from skin. If any are too thick, place them between 2 sheets of wax paper or lightly oiled parchment paper and flatten them by pounding lightly until about ¼ inch thick.

Heat 1 tablespoon oil in large heavy skillet until very hot. Season salmon with salt and pepper, and add enough salmon pieces to skillet to make one layer. Cook over medium-high heat about 45 seconds per side, or until it becomes lighter in color around edges; salmon should be barely cooked. Remove to a platter and keep warm in 250°F. oven. Heat remaining tablespoon oil in skillet and sauté remaining salmon. To serve, spoon leek sauce on plates and set salmon on top.

SAUTÉED HADDOCK WITH RED PEPPERS AND WALNUTS
Aiglefin sauté aux poivrons et aux noix

This colorful dish of fish topped with sautéed vegetables and crunchy walnuts is made very quickly. I like to serve it with steamed rice or pilaf.   MAKES 4 SERVINGS

2 celery stalks, peeled
1 small red bell pepper, cored and
  seeded
4 tablespoons plus 2 teaspoons
  butter
1/2 cup walnut halves, cut in half
  lengthwise

Salt
1/4 cup all-purpose flour
Freshly ground pepper
4 haddock or halibut steaks, about
  1 inch thick (1 3/4 pounds
  total)
3 tablespoons vegetable oil

Cut celery in half horizontally, then cut celery and pepper in 1 1/2-by-1/4-inch strips.

Melt 2 teaspoons butter in small heavy skillet over medium-low heat. Add walnuts and a pinch of salt, and sauté until lightly toasted, about 3 minutes. Transfer to plate and reserve at room temperature.

Spread flour in large plate. Season fish with salt and pepper on both sides, then lightly coat it with flour on both sides. Tap and shake to remove excess flour. Transfer fish to large plate and arrange side by side.

Heat oil and 2 tablespoons butter in large heavy skillet over medium-high heat until butter melts. Add 2 haddock or halibut steaks and sauté over medium-high heat about 2 minutes, then over medium heat 2 minutes. Turn carefully with 2 wide slotted metal spatulas. Sauté second side over medium-high heat 2 minutes, then over medium heat until a thin skewer inserted in thickest part of fish for 10 seconds comes out hot when touched to inside of wrist, about 2 minutes more. If fat in skillet begins to brown, reduce heat to medium-low. Transfer fish steaks to ovenproof platter or plates, arrange them side by side, and keep warm in 275°F. oven. Sauté remaining fish.

Melt remaining 2 tablespoons butter in medium skillet. Add celery and pepper and cook over low heat, stirring often, until tender but not brown, about 6 minutes. Spoon vegetables with their butter over fish, sprinkle with sautéed walnuts, and serve immediately.

SAUTÉED HALIBUT FILLETS WITH SHRIMP
Flétan sauté aux crevettes

For a light version of this tasty dish, you can omit the creamy sauce; simply sauté or steam the shrimp and scatter them over the top of the sautéed fish fillets. If you would like to include the sauce, there are numerous ways to vary it. You can stir fresh herbs, such as tarragon or even cilantro, into the sauce at the last moment. Just before serving, you can add sautéed quartered mushrooms, cooked vegetable julienne, or diced uncooked tomato. Or you can replace the shrimp with steamed mussels. Pasta lovers will enjoy the fish on a bed of fresh egg noodles or spinach fettuccine.   MAKES 4 SERVINGS

1 1/2 pounds halibut fillets	1 tablespoon white wine vinegar
Salt and freshly ground pepper	3 tablespoons dry white wine
1/3 cup all-purpose flour	3/4 cup heavy cream
2 tablespoons vegetable oil	1/4 pound small uncooked shrimp
3 tablespoons butter	2 tablespoons chopped chives or
2 shallots, finely chopped	fresh parsley

Check fillets to be sure they don't have any bones. If you find any, remove them with tweezers, a pastry crimper, or small sharp knife. Season fillets with salt and pepper on both sides. Dredge them lightly with flour and tap to remove excess.

Heat oil and 1 tablespoon butter in a large skillet over medium-high heat. Add fillets and sauté about 2 minutes on each side, or until they can be pierced easily with a skewer. Transfer to a platter and keep warm.

Add shallots to skillet and cook over low heat for a few minutes until softened. Pour in vinegar and wine and bring to a boil. Stir in cream and a little salt and pepper, and simmer over medium heat, stirring, until sauce is reduced to about ½ cup and is thick enough to coat a spoon.

Add shrimp to sauce and heat about 1 minute over low heat. Taste and adjust seasoning. Remove from heat and add remaining 2 tablespoons butter in 3 or 4 pieces, gently stirring it into sauce.

Pour sauce and shrimp over fillets, sprinkle with chives or parsley, and serve immediately.

SAUTÉED SOLE WITH FRESH BREAD CRUMBS AND PARSLEY-LEMON BUTTER
Sole au beurre maître d'hôtel

A classic entrée, this has always remained popular because the gentle seasoning highlights the natural taste of the fish. Accompany it with its time-honored partner of steamed potatoes, or with seasonal vegetables.   MAKES 4 SERVINGS

PARSLEY-LEMON BUTTER
6 tablespoons butter
1 ½ teaspoons strained fresh lemon juice

Salt and freshly ground pepper
1 ½ tablespoons chopped fresh parsley

½ cup butter
¾ cup fine fresh bread crumbs (see note)
1 ½ pounds sole or flounder fillets, about ¼ inch thick

Salt and freshly ground pepper
½ cup milk

PARSLEY-LEMON BUTTER

Beat butter in medium bowl until very smooth. Gradually beat in lemon juice, and season to taste with salt and pepper. Stir in parsley. (Seasoned butter can be kept, covered, 2 days in refrigerator. Bring to room temperature before serving.) Spoon into piping bag fitted with small star tip, if desired.

Clarify ½ cup butter for sautéing by melting it in small heavy saucepan over low heat. Skim off white foam from surface, and pour remaining clear butter carefully into large heavy skillet, without adding white sediment at bottom of saucepan.

Spread bread crumbs on large plate. Season fish with salt and pepper on both sides. Dip each fillet in milk; then dip on both sides in bread crumbs and press so they adhere. As each fillet is dipped, transfer it to tray or large plate and arrange side by side.

Heat clarified butter in skillet over medium-high heat. Using tongs, add enough fillets to make one layer in skillet. Sauté until golden brown on both sides, about 1 minute per side; turn fish carefully with 2 wide slotted metal spatulas. If butter begins to brown, reduce heat to medium. Carefully transfer fillets to ovenproof platter, arrange side by side, and keep warm in 275°F. oven, while sautéing remaining fillets.

To serve, pipe parsley-lemon butter in decorative line down center of each fillet; or spoon a few dabs of the flavored butter onto each. Serve remaining parsley-lemon butter separately.

NOTE: To prepare fresh bread crumbs, slice French bread and let dry, uncovered, 1 to 2 days. Remove crust and cut bread in pieces. Pulverize bread pieces in food processor until very fine.

SAUTÉED SNAPPER WITH LIGHT MUSTARD SAUCE
Perche de mer sautée, sauce moutarde

Mustard sauce is fine with fish as well as with meat. Serve this fish sauté with potatoes or rice and with vegetables that are good with mustard, such as crisp-tender cauliflower or broccoli florets or fresh spinach. MAKES 4 SERVINGS

1 1/2 pounds thin fillets of snapper,
cod, haddock, or halibut
Salt and freshly ground pepper
1/3 cup all-purpose flour
2 tablespoons vegetable oil
2 tablespoons butter
2 shallots, finely chopped

1/2 cup dry white wine
1 cup heavy cream
1 1/2 to 2 tablespoons Dijon
mustard
2 tablespoons chopped fresh parsley
(optional)

Check fillets to be sure they don't have any bones. If you find any, remove them with tweezers, a pastry crimper, or small sharp knife.

Season fillets with salt and pepper. Dredge them lightly with flour and tap to remove excess.

Heat oil and butter in a large skillet. When very hot, add fillets in batches. Sauté over medium-high heat about 2 minutes on each side, or until they can be pierced easily with a skewer. Transfer to a platter and keep warm.

Add shallots to skillet and cook over low heat for a few minutes until softened. Pour in wine and bring to a boil, then simmer, stirring, until reduced to about 2 tablespoons. Stir in cream and cook over medium heat, stirring often, until sauce is thick enough to coat a spoon.

Transfer sauce to a saucepan and heat over low heat. Whisk in mustard and taste and adjust seasoning. Pour sauce over fillets, sprinkle with parsley, if desired, and serve immediately.

SALMON WITH SPINACH AND ROASTED PEPPER BUTTER
Saumon aux épinards au beurre de poivrons grillés

This is one of my favorite dishes—the lightly cooked salmon with its grilled red pepper sauce is irresistible! Prepare it in the summer, when fresh salmon is in season. It is inspired by a recipe I learned from Michel Lorain, chef/owner of the celebrated La Côte Saint-Jacques restaurant in Burgundy and a great teacher. Incidentally, this is one of the easiest butter sauces to make. Rice, preferably Basmati, is a wonderful complement for the salmon and its sauce.

MAKES 4 SERVINGS

ROASTED PEPPER BUTTER SAUCE

2 medium-size red bell peppers	4 sprigs fresh thyme
1/2 cup dry white wine	Salt and freshly ground pepper
6 tablespoons white wine vinegar (5% acidity)	1 cup well-chilled unsalted butter, cut in 1/2-inch pieces

1 1/2 pounds salmon fillet, preferably from tail end	2 tablespoons butter
2 bunches spinach (about 12 ounces each), stems removed, leaves rinsed well	Salt and freshly ground pepper
	2 tablespoons vegetable oil

ROASTED PEPPER BUTTER SAUCE

Preheat broiler. Broil peppers about 2 inches from heat source until they are blistered and charred, turning often. Transfer to plastic bag, close bag, and let stand 10 minutes. Peel with a paring knife. Cut peppers in half and remove cores and seeds. Drain well in colander, pat dry, and purée in food processor until very fine.

Combine wine, vinegar, and thyme in medium saucepan and bring to a boil. Boil over medium-high heat until liquid is reduced to 3 tablespoons. Strain into small heavy saucepan, and add pepper purée and salt and pepper and return to a boil. (Sauce can be prepared up to 1 day ahead to this point and kept, covered, in the refrigerator.) Keep butter pieces in refrigerator.

Run your fingers over salmon to check for bones. Remove any bones with tweezers, a pastry crimper, or small sharp knife. Pat salmon dry, and place fillet, skin side down, on cutting board. Using a long, sharp, flexible knife, cut salmon in fairly thin diagonal slices, cutting against skin to remove each slice from skin. Place slices between 2 sheets of wax paper or lightly oiled parchment paper and flatten them by pounding lightly until about 1/4 inch thick.

Cook spinach, uncovered, in large saucepan of boiling salted water over high heat until just tender, about 2 minutes. Drain, rinse under cold water, drain well, and squeeze gently to remove excess liquid. Melt 2 tablespoons butter in medium skillet over low heat. Add spinach and salt and pepper and cook, stirring, 2 minutes. Taste and adjust seasoning.

To finish sauce: Set pan of pepper mixture over low heat and bring to simmer, whisking. Add 1 piece of cold butter, whisking constantly. When butter piece is nearly blended into liquid, add another piece, still whisking. Continue adding butter pieces, 1 at a time, whisking constantly. Sauce should be pleasantly warm to the touch. (If at any time sauce becomes too hot and drops of melted butter appear, remove pan immediately from heat and whisk well; add next butter pieces off heat, whisking constantly. When temperature of sauce drops again to warm, return to low heat and continue adding remaining butter pieces.) Remove from heat as soon as last butter piece is incorporated. Taste and adjust seasoning. Keep sauce warm in its uncovered saucepan on a rack above hot but not boiling water, in a double boiler, or in a thermos.

Heat 1 tablespoon oil in large heavy skillet until very hot. Season salmon with salt and pepper. Add enough salmon pieces to skillet to make one layer. Cook over high heat about 30 seconds per side; salmon should be barely cooked. Remove to a platter and keep warm. Heat remaining tablespoon oil in skillet and sauté remaining salmon.

Quickly reheat spinach, if necessary. Coat bottom of platter or plates with sauce, set salmon on top, and arrange spinach around edge of salmon. Serve immediately with any remaining sauce alongside.

Grilled Fish

Mediterranean southern France is where grilled fish are most popular. Even large whole fish, especially sea bass, are grilled. In the rest of the country, cooks prefer to grill smaller fish, fish steaks, and thick fillets, particularly of rich fish such as salmon and swordfish. They often marinate the fish in lemon juice, oil, and sometimes herbs before grilling it to add flavor and prevent it from becoming dry.

Grilled fish, like baked fish, are good with a simple seasoned butter. They are also wonderful with a rich sauce, which is a perfect complement to their lean texture. The sauces of choice for grilled fish are those with a zesty flavor: Garlicky aïoli, béarnaise redolent of fresh tarragon, tomato béarnaise, and mustard hollandaise stand up to the slightly smoky taste of grilled fish and are its traditional partners. Recent rivals are sauces in the beurre blanc family and cream-reduction sauces, and they can now be found accompanying grilled fish on France's best menus. At Taillevent, for instance, one of Paris's finest restaurants, I feasted on an exquisite grilled turbot with a sauce of leek cream.

Grilled fish are classically served with decoratively shaped lemon halves and a small bouquet of parsley. Sauces are generally served on the side, so the attractive grilled fish shows.

🥬 GRILLED RED SNAPPER FILLETS SAINT-MALO
Perche de mer grillée Saint-Malo

Saint-Malo is a pretty coastal town in Brittany, a French province well known for its fish and its cauliflower, which are paired in this dish. The zesty sauce, a type of hollandaise, is flavored with white wine, mustard, and a hint of anchovy.   MAKES 4 SERVINGS

*1/2 pound ripe tomatoes, peeled,
    seeded, and coarsely chopped
1 tablespoon plus 1 1/2 teaspoons
    vegetable oil
1/2 teaspoon white wine vinegar
Salt and freshly ground pepper
4 teaspoons thinly sliced chives*

*1 1/2 pounds red snapper, sea bass,
    halibut, or haddock fillets, in
    4 pieces
1 large cauliflower (about 2
    pounds), divided into medium
    florets*

MUSTARD AND ANCHOVY HOLLANDAISE
*2 shallots, minced
1/2 cup dry white wine
Freshly ground pepper
3/4 cup unsalted butter*

*3 egg yolks
2 1/2 teaspoons Dijon mustard
1 3/4 teaspoons anchovy paste*

Drain chopped tomato in colander 15 minutes, tossing occasionally. Gently mix tomatoes with 1 1/2 teaspoons oil, vinegar, salt, pepper, and 1 teaspoon chives. Taste and adjust seasoning. Let stand at room temperature until ready to use, or up to 2 hours.

Run your fingers over fish and carefully pull out any bones with tweezers, a pastry crimper, or sharp paring knife. Pat fish dry. Prepare pan of warm water or thermos for keeping sauce warm.

Cook cauliflower, uncovered, in large saucepan of boiling salted water over high heat until just tender, about 7 minutes. Drain well, cover, and keep warm.

MUSTARD AND ANCHOVY HOLLANDAISE

Combine shallots, white wine, and pinch of pepper in small heavy saucepan. Bring to a boil, then lower heat to medium, and simmer until liquid is reduced to about 3 tablespoons. Cool slightly. Melt butter in another small heavy saucepan over very low heat. Skim off white foam from surface and cool to lukewarm.

Whisk yolks into shallot mixture. Set pan over low heat and cook, whisking vigorously and constantly, until mixture is creamy and thick enough so that the trail of the whisk can be seen on base of pan, about 4 minutes. Remove pan occasionally from heat; sides of pan should not become too hot to touch. If pan does become too hot, mixture will curdle. Remove pan immediately from heat and whisk mixture about 30 seconds.

Gradually whisk in melted butter, drop by drop, until sauce has absorbed 2 or 3 tablespoons. Whisk in remaining butter in a very thin stream. Whisk in mustard, anchovy paste, and a pinch of pepper. Taste and adjust seasoning. Set pan of sauce uncovered in pan of warm water off heat, in a double boiler, or pour into thermos or vacuum bottle while cooking fish.

Preheat broiler or grill. Brush fillets with remaining tablespoon oil and season lightly with salt and pepper. Arrange on broiler pan or grill, in batches if necessary to avoid crowding. Broil or grill about 2 inches from heat source until just opaque and tender, about 2 minutes per side.

Arrange fish on 4 plates and surround with cauliflower. Spoon some of sauce over fish and sprinkle with remaining 3 teaspoons chives. Spoon a little tomato mixture on both sides of fish with a slotted spoon. Serve remaining sauce separately.

🌿 GRILLED SHARK WITH HERBED SOUR CREAM SAUCE
Filet de requin grillé, crème aigre aux herbes

Swordfish or sea bass are used in France more often than shark, and they can be substituted here. In this refreshing entrée, ideal for summer, the fish and its assertively seasoned sauce are served at room temperature and garnished with shrimp. Present the fish with crisp strips of red peppers, carrots, and celery, which provide a pleasant contrasting texture to the smooth sauce.   MAKES 4 SERVINGS

HERBED SOUR CREAM SAUCE

2 large garlic cloves, peeled
1/2 jalapeño pepper, seeded and quartered, or a pinch of cayenne pepper
1/4 cup loosely packed cilantro (fresh coriander) leaves, patted dry

1/4 cup packed small parsley sprigs, patted dry
Salt
2 large egg yolks, room temperature
3/4 cup vegetable oil
1/2 cup sour cream

1 1/2 pounds shark or swordfish fillet, about 1 inch thick, rinsed and patted dry
2 teaspoons strained fresh lemon juice
3 tablespoons vegetable oil

8 large shrimp (about 5 ounces), unshelled, rinsed
Salt and freshly ground pepper
2 teaspoons white wine vinegar
8 leaves green leaf lettuce, cut in half

HERBED SOUR CREAM SAUCE

With the blade of food processor turning, drop garlic and hot pepper pieces through feed tube and chop finely. Scrape down mixture and process until well blended. Add cilantro, parsley, and pinch of salt and chop finely.

Add egg yolks and 1 tablespoon oil and process until blended. With machine running, add remaining oil through feed tube in thin stream and blend until sauce is smooth and thick, stopping to scrape down sides of bowl. Transfer to mixing bowl and stir in sour cream.

Add cayenne, if using; taste and adjust seasoning. Refrigerate until ready to use. (Sauce can be kept, covered, 1 day in refrigerator.)

Trim shark of any dark red spots and cut in 4 pieces. Put shark pieces in shallow bowl and sprinkle with lemon juice and 1 tablespoon oil. Let stand 30 minutes, turning twice.

Preheat broiler or grill. Broil or grill shrimp in shells about 2 inches from heat about 1½ minutes per side, or until shells turn bright pink. Transfer to plate. Season shark with salt and pepper. Grill or broil about 3 minutes per side, or until a skewer inserted into center of shark comes out hot to touch and meat loses its raw pink color. Transfer to plate and let cool to room temperature. Shell shrimp.

Whisk remaining 2 tablespoons oil with vinegar and salt and pepper. Toss lettuce with dressing in bowl, and taste and adjust seasoning. Arrange lettuce on platter or on plates, set fish on top, discarding any liquid that escaped onto plate, and coat fish with sauce. Set 2 shrimp on each piece of fish, and serve remaining sauce separately.

᨞ BROILED SWORDFISH WITH AÏOLI
Espadon grillé à l'aïoli

Garlicky aïoli, the most famous sauce of Provence, makes a superb topping for broiled fish. Here the sauce is spread on the fish and browned lightly in the broiler, then it is garnished with grilled pepper strips. MAKES 8 SERVINGS

AÏOLI

6 *medium-size garlic cloves, peeled*
2 *egg yolks, room temperature*
About 2 tablespoons strained fresh
  lemon juice

1½ *cups extra-virgin olive oil,*
  room temperature
Salt and freshly ground pepper
1 *tablespoon water*

2 *medium-size green bell peppers*
2 *medium-size red bell peppers*
3 *pounds swordfish or shark fillet,*
  about 1 inch thick, cut in 8
  pieces, rinsed, and patted dry

Salt and freshly ground pepper
4 *teaspoons olive oil*

AÏOLI

Cut off brown ends and any brown spots from garlic and cut cloves in half lengthwise, removing any green sprouts from center.

Make aïoli in food processor (see following note if food processor is not available). Drop garlic cloves through feed tube of food processor fitted with metal blade, with motor running, and process until finely chopped. Add egg yolks, 1 tablespoon lemon juice, 1 tablespoon oil, and a pinch of salt and pepper and process until thoroughly blended, scraping bottom and sides of processor container several times. With motor running, gradually pour in oil in a thin trickle. After adding ¼ cup oil, remaining oil can be poured in a little faster, in a fine stream. With motor still running, gradually pour in remaining tablespoon lemon juice, 1 teaspoon at a time. Gradually add 1 tablespoon lukewarm water, 1 teaspoon at a time, to make sauce slightly thinner. Taste and adjust seasoning. (Aïoli can be kept, covered, 1 day in refrigerator, but garlic flavor becomes stronger.)

Preheat broiler. Broil peppers about 2 inches from heat source until they are blistered and charred, turning often, about 15 minutes. Transfer to plastic bag, close bag, and let stand 10 minutes. Peel with a paring knife, then cut peppers in half and remove cores. Pat peppers dry. Cut halves in lengthwise strips about ⅜ inch wide.

Position broiler rack 4 inches from heat source. Season fish with salt and pepper on both sides, brush one side with oil, and put on broiler rack, oiled side down. Broil about 3 minutes per side, or until a skewer inserted into center of fish comes out hot to touch and fish is just opaque.

Reserve 16 red and 8 green pepper strips for garnish. Arrange remaining pepper strips on fish in single layer. Spoon aïoli over pepper strips, using a total of about 1 cup, and gently spread nearly to edge of fish. Broil just until aïoli browns, watching carefully, about 30 seconds. Garnish fish with reserved pepper strips and serve.

NOTE: If food processor is not available, prepare aïoli using mixer or whisk. Chop garlic as finely as possible so that it becomes almost a purée. Combine garlic, egg yolks, 1 tablespoon lemon juice, and a pinch of salt and pepper in mixer bowl or a medium, heavy bowl set on a towel. Beat at high speed or whisk until thoroughly blended. Begin beating in oil, drop by drop. When 2 or 3 tablespoons oil have

been added, continue beating in oil in very fine stream until 1 cup
has been added. Beat in 1 teaspoon of remaining lemon juice to thin
sauce and make beating easier. Gradually beat in remaining oil in
fine stream. Gradually beat in remaining lemon juice, 1 teaspoon at
a time, then 1 tablespoon water, 1 teaspoon at a time. Taste and adjust
seasoning.

GRILLED SALMON WITH RED WINE BUTTER SAUCE
Saumon grillé au beurre rouge

Serving fish with red wine sauce became fashionable in the hey-
day of nouvelle cuisine in the seventies. But it has its roots in regional
cuisine, in provinces famous for their red wine—Bordeaux, Burgundy, and the Loire Valley. The red wine butter sauce is a version
of beurre blanc and is a perfect match for the grilled salmon steaks.
Good accompaniments are glazed pearl onions, Leek Compote (page
208), or steamed potatoes.   MAKES 4 SERVINGS

4 salmon steaks, 1 inch thick | *1 cup cold unsalted butter, cut in*
(about 2 1/2 pounds total) | *1/2-inch pieces*
2 cups dry medium- or full-bodied | *About 1 teaspoon sugar*
red wine | *About 1/2 teaspoon strained fresh*
3 tablespoons finely minced shallots | *lemon juice*
Salt and white pepper |

Remove any scales from salmon steaks, rinse, and pat dry.

Combine wine and shallots in small heavy saucepan and boil over
medium-high heat until reduced to 1/2 cup. Lower heat to medium
and simmer until reduced to 2 to 3 tablespoons. Season with salt and
pepper. (Mixture can be kept, covered, 2 or 3 hours at room temperature.)

Preheat broiler or grill with rack about 4 inches from heat source,
or heat stove-top ridged grill over medium-high heat. Lightly oil grill
or broiler rack. Season salmon with salt and pepper on both sides and

set on broiler rack or grill. Broil or grill about 4 minutes per side, or until skewer inserted into thickest part is hot when touched to underside of your wrist. Transfer to a platter, cover, and keep warm.

To finish sauce, set pan of shallot mixture over low heat and season lightly with salt and white pepper. Add 1 piece of cold butter, whisking constantly. When butter piece is nearly blended into liquid, add another piece, still whisking. Continue adding butter pieces, 1 at a time, whisking constantly. The sauce should be pleasantly warm to touch. (If at any time sauce becomes too hot and drops of melted butter appear, remove pan immediately from heat and whisk well; add next butter pieces off heat, whisking constantly. When temperature of sauce drops again to warm, return to low heat to continue adding remaining butter pieces.) Remove from heat as soon as last butter piece is incorporated. Taste sauce and adjust seasoning. Gradually whisk in sugar and fresh lemon juice to taste. If smoother sauce is desired, strain through fine sieve, pressing on shallots with spoon. Serve as soon as possible. Sauce can be kept warm briefly on a rack above a pan of hot water or in a double boiler.

Remove salmon skin and center bone. Put salmon on heated plates and serve with sauce alongside.

Baked Fish

Baking fish, sometimes referred to as roasting fish, is an easy technique for cooking whole fish, thick fillets, and steaks. Like roast meat and poultry, fish are baked at relatively high heat so they are in the oven for as short a time as possible and don't have time to dry out. In contrast to braised fish, which is covered, baked fish are baked uncovered.

Fish can be baked with a sauce, as in Baked Cod with Pipérade Sauce, so they absorb flavor from the sauce, in this case of bell peppers, as they bake. They are then served directly from the baking dish. Thick tomato sauces can be used in the same way, in the Provençal style, and the baked fish can be topped with black olives just before being served. Many French cooks like to spread a seasoned butter on the fish prior to baking, as in Baked Trout with Spiced Butter and Sautéed Vegetables, so it bastes the fish as it melts.

Whole fish can also be stuffed and baked. Vegetable stuffings, such as Spinach and Shallot Stuffing (see following recipe), are popular in France, as are stuffings made of a mousseline of fish or shellfish.

SPINACH-STUFFED TROUT
Truite farcie aux épinards

Burgundy's seafood specialties are made with freshwater fish and, in keeping with the region's great vinicultural tradition, are often cooked with wine. Yet for this light Burgundian dish, you do not have to use an expensive wine, only one that is pleasant to drink. To make the preparation easy, ask the fishmonger to butterfly the trout (remove the center bone and open the fish so it lies flat) for you. Instead of trout, you can also use the pretty pink-fleshed salmon trout, sometimes called baby salmon. During the short period that I trained in the kitchen at Maxim's, the chefs prepared a spinach stuffing similar to this one and used it to fill a flat fish called *dorade* (porgy).

MAKES 4 SERVINGS

SPINACH AND SHALLOT STUFFING

2 pounds spinach, stems discarded, leaves rinsed thoroughly
1 tablespoon butter
2 shallots, finely chopped
1 egg

1 tablespoon heavy cream
2 tablespoons unseasoned bread crumbs
Freshly grated nutmeg
Salt and freshly ground pepper

4 small trout (about 1/2 pound each), butterflied
Salt and freshly ground pepper
1 small shallot, chopped
1/4 cup dry white wine
1/4 cup heavy cream (optional)

A few drops of lemon juice (optional)
Zigzag-cut lemon half with parsley sprig in center for garnish (optional)

SPINACH AND SHALLOT STUFFING

Put spinach leaves in a large pan of boiling salted water and boil 1 minute until just tender. Rinse under cold running water, drain thoroughly, and squeeze out as much liquid as possible. Coarsely chop spinach.

Melt butter in a skillet or sauté pan, add shallots, and cook over low heat, stirring often, about 3 minutes, or until soft but not browned. Add spinach and stir over low heat 1 minute. Transfer to a bowl and let cool slightly. Add the egg, cream, bread crumbs, nutmeg, and salt and pepper to taste.

Run your finger along flesh of trout about ¾ inch from the backbone line, on both sides of it; you will find a row of small bones running parallel to the backbone. Run the point of a boning knife along both sides of each row of bones, and pull out bones, if possible, with a pastry crimpers or tweezers. Cut off fins and shorten tail. Season with salt and pepper inside and outside before stuffing.

Preheat oven to 425°F. Lightly butter a shallow baking dish and add the chopped shallot. Set stuffed trout in dish on their sides. Add wine and bake about 15 minutes, or until trout is just tender and filling is hot when pierced with a skewer.

Transfer trout to a platter, cover, and keep warm. If you'd like to serve them with a sauce, pour cooking liquid, along with chopped shallot, into a small saucepan. Boil until reduced to about 3 tablespoons. Add cream and boil, stirring, until sauce is thick enough to lightly coat a spoon. Add lemon juice, and taste and adjust seasoning.

If desired, use a sharp knife to remove skin from side of trout facing up. Serve trout on its platter and pass sauce, if prepared, separately. Garnish, if desired, with zigzag lemon with parsley sprig in center.

BAKED SEA BASS WITH MINT BUTTER
Bar au four au beurre de menthe

Quick, easy, and fresh-tasting, the fish is simply baked with fresh bread crumbs and served with a mint butter. It makes a fine entrée at any season, accompanied by vegetables, steamed or baked potatoes, or a salad.   MAKES 4 SERVINGS

MINT BUTTER

6 tablespoons butter, softened	Salt and freshly ground pepper
1 tablespoon chopped fresh mint leaves	

½ cup bread crumbs	Salt and freshly ground pepper
¼ cup butter, melted	1 lemon, quartered
1½ pounds sea bass or halibut fillets	

MINT BUTTER

Thoroughly mix softened butter with mint. Season to taste with salt and pepper. (Seasoned butter can be kept, covered, 1 day in refrigerator.)

Preheat oven to 425°F. Spread bread crumbs on a plate and pour melted butter into a shallow bowl. Season fish fillets with salt and pepper, and dip on both sides into the melted butter, then into bread crumbs. Arrange in one layer in a buttered baking dish.

Bake fish in preheated oven for about 15 minutes, or until it is tender, can be pierced easily with a skewer, and skewer comes out hot to the touch.

Using a pastry bag fitted with a star tip, or a spoon, put a little mint butter on each piece of fish. Garnish with lemon quarters. Serve any remaining mint butter separately.

BAKED COD WITH PIPÉRADE SAUCE
Cabillaud en pipérade

Good hot or cold, this fish in its zesty pepper-tomato sauce from the Basque region of France, which borders on Spain, is light and simple to prepare. Steamed rice and crisp-tender green beans go well with the fish.   MAKES 6 SERVINGS

1 fresh hot pepper, such as jalapeño
   or serrano (see note)
¼ cup vegetable oil
2 onions, chopped
3 medium-size red bell peppers,
   chopped
3 medium-size garlic cloves, chopped
2½ pounds ripe tomatoes, peeled,
   seeded and chopped, or two
   28-ounce cans whole plum
   tomatoes, drained and chopped

Salt
2 pounds cod, halibut, or snapper
   fillets
Freshly ground pepper

Discard seeds and ribs from hot pepper and finely chop. Wash your hands, cutting board and knife immediately. (Wear gloves when handling hot pepper, if you are sensitive.)

Heat oil in a sauté pan or deep skillet. Add onions and cook over low heat until soft but not brown. Add bell peppers, garlic, and hot pepper and cook, stirring often, about 5 minutes, or until peppers soften.

Add tomatoes and a pinch of salt and cook, uncovered, over medium heat, stirring often, about 30 minutes, or until mixture is thick. Reduce heat to low and continue simmering, stirring often, 15 to 20 minutes more, or until the mixture is very thick and dry. Taste and add more salt, if desired. (Sauce can kept, covered, 5 days in refrigerator; or it can be frozen.)

Preheat oven to 425°F. Lightly oil a large shallow baking dish. Reheat sauce, if necessary, then spread half the sauce in dish. Arrange halibut fillets on top in one layer. Season them lightly with salt and pepper. Spread remaining sauce over fish.

Bake about 15 minutes, or until thickest part of fillets is tender when pierced with a sharp knife. Serve hot or at room temperature.

NOTE: A dried hot pepper can be substituted for fresh. Soak it in cold water for 20 minutes before removing seeds and chopping.

BAKED TROUT WITH SPICED BUTTER AND SAUTÉED VEGETABLES
Truite au four au beurre épicé

Cumin and garlic flavor the seasoned butter, which is spread on the trout before baking so its taste is absorbed. A little more spiced butter is served with the fish, which is accompanied by sautéed zucchini and potatoes. MAKES 4 SERVINGS

4 trout (about 10 ounces each), rinsed inside and out and patted dry
2 teaspoons ground cumin
1 teaspoon minced garlic

2 tablespoons strained fresh lemon juice
2 tablespoons vegetable oil
Salt and freshly ground pepper

SPICED BUTTER

3/4 cup butter, softened
2 teaspoons ground cumin
1 tablespoon finely minced garlic
1 1/2 teaspoons paprika

1 teaspoon strained fresh lemon juice
Pinch of cayenne pepper
Salt and freshly ground pepper

3 medium-size white potatoes (about 1 pound)
2 tablespoons vegetable oil
2 tablespoons butter

Salt and freshly ground pepper
2 small zucchini (about 1/2 pound), cut in 1/4-inch slices

Snip trout fins and trim tails straight with sturdy scissors. Put trout in shallow oval baking dish.

Combine cumin, garlic, lemon juice, oil, and salt and pepper thoroughly in small bowl, and pour over trout. Rub seasonings inside and out, and let stand 1 hour.

SPICED BUTTER

Beat butter in medium bowl until smooth. Stir in cumin, garlic, paprika, lemon juice, and cayenne. Season to taste with salt and pepper. Let stand at least 1 hour to blend flavors. (Seasoned butter can be kept, covered, 1 day in refrigerator; bring to room temperature before using.) Spoon into pastry bag fitted with small star tip.

Preheat oven to 400°F. Put potatoes in medium saucepan, cover with water, bring to a boil, and add salt. Reduce heat to low, cover, and simmer 10 minutes. Drain thoroughly. Let stand until cool enough to handle, then peel by scraping gently with a paring knife. Cut potatoes in ⅜-inch-thick slices.

Spoon 2 teaspoons cumin-garlic butter inside each trout and spread with your fingers. Bake trout with its marinade, basting twice, until skewer inserted into thickest part of trout comes out hot to the touch, about 12 minutes.

Heat 1 tablespoon oil and 1 tablespoon butter in large heavy skillet over medium heat. Add enough potato slices to make one layer and sprinkle with salt and pepper. Sauté, shaking pan occasionally, 4 minutes. Turn potatoes over, season with salt and pepper, and sauté on second side until golden brown, about 4 minutes. Turn over once again, raise heat to medium-high, and sauté potatoes until tender and golden brown, about 2 minutes more. Remove with a slotted spatula. Add remaining tablespoon oil to skillet and heat. Repeat sautéing with remaining slices.

In another skillet, heat remaining 1 tablespoon butter. Add zucchini slices and season with salt and pepper. Sauté over medium heat until just tender, about 2 minutes on each side. Remove with a slotted spatula.

Remove upper trout skin by scraping gently with a paring knife. Put trout on heated plates. Spoon zucchini slices on one side of fish and potato slices on the other.

To serve, pipe cumin-garlic butter in decorative line down center of each trout, from head to tail. Serve immediately; flavored butter melts quickly from contact with hot fish. Serve remaining butter separately.

Poached and Braised Fish

Fish is fabulous when paired with a delicate sauce. And the most widely used techniques to prepare a fish to be accompanied by a tomato sauce, a smooth cream sauce, or a rich butter sauce, are poaching and braising.

Poaching and braising work magic on fish. The results are sweet, tender, perfectly cooked fish every time—without fail. These techniques are versatile, lending themselves to whole fish, fish steaks, and fillets. The essence of both methods is the aromatic cooking liquid, which keeps the fish moist during cooking and subtly enhances its taste. And this flavorful cooking liquid will impart a special something to the sauce of your choice.

Both cooking methods are essentially fat-free and are simple to master. For poaching, the fish is cooked gently in enough liquid, usually wine or fish stock, to just cover it. This is one of the most popular ways to cook a whole fish, but it also works well for thick fillets.

For braising, the fish is placed in a buttered baking dish with minced shallots. Garlic can also be used, or the white part of green onions, or briefly sautéed yellow onion. As in poaching, it is usually wine or fish stock that moistens the fish, but for braising, only a small amount of liquid is used. The fish is seasoned lightly with salt and pepper or a pinch of herbs or spices, covered, and simply baked a few minutes. Unlike braised meat, fish does not require preliminary browning. During braising, a parchment covering traps some of the liquid and also allows some to escape as steam, which means that the stock or wine in the dish reduces slightly and makes a delicious addition to sauces.

Besides white wine and fish stock, other liquids can be used for poaching and braising. Red wine or alcoholic cider can replace the white wine, and clam juice can be substituted for the fish stock. Another possibility is using Court Bouillon (page 289).

The most expedient way to sauce a poached or braised fish is to start the sauce first so that the fish will not need to wait long before being served. Once the fish has finished cooking, the braising liquid can be added to the sauce, marrying the two components—fish and sauce—beautifully. Braised Scrod with Fresh Tomato Sauce and Lemon Grass is a good example of this technique. Sometimes the liquid is quickly boiled down a bit further for an even more concentrated taste and then added to a sauce, as in Braised Halibut with Mussels, Ginger, and Cream.

For the following recipes, choose whichever fish is freshest in your market. Fish are interchangeable to a large degree in recipes, and almost any fish can be poached or braised. Round out the menu with colorful vegetables, rice, potatoes, or a loaf of French bread. A bottle of white wine or even a light red wine would also be nice with the meal.

Hints

- Fold thin fillets in half and cut very long fillets in half crosswise so that they are easy to remove when cooked. Cooked fish is fragile; be careful when transferring to a platter.
- For braising, an oval or rectangular baking dish best suits the shape of the fish. Choose a dish that allows the pieces to fit comfortably without overlapping but does not leave wide spaces, which cause the liquid to evaporate too quickly, and even burn. There should be enough liquid to cover the base of the dish easily. If in doubt, add a little extra.
- Time is only a guide for cooking fish; also be sure to check to see if the fish is done.
- Do not leave cooked fish in the hot liquid after it is done; it can overcook.
- Before coating a fish with sauce, discard any liquid that escaped from the fish onto the platter to avoid diluting the sauce. The easiest way is to put your hand on the paper covering the fish, hold the fish, and tilt the platter so that the liquid runs off. If the platter is too heavy to do this, blot it dry with paper towels.
- When serving a whole fish, spoon only a little sauce over it. Serve the remaining sauce separately so that it can be spooned over the fish after the bones are removed.
- To minimize standing time, you can freeze the braising liquid from one fish recipe and use it to make sauce the next time you braise a fish.
- The liquid from braising or poaching fish can be frozen and used as fish stock.
- Brief cooking is most important for keeping fish moist. If in doubt, undercook the fish slightly rather than overcooking it. It is easy to tell if a fish is cooked sufficiently by inserting a thin skewer or cake tester into the thickest part of its flesh; if the skewer comes out hot to the touch, the fish is done.

ALSATIAN SALMON STEAKS WITH RIESLING WINE AND CHIVES
Darnes de salmon au riesling à la ciboulette

Salmon is preferred in Alsace for preparing this quick, easy entrée, but sometimes trout or pike are used instead. A favorite accompaniment in the region for creamy fish dishes like this one is fresh
pasta, either lightly buttered or tossed with sautéed wild mushrooms.

MAKES 4 SERVINGS

2 shallots, chopped
2 tablespoons thinly sliced chives
4 small salmon steaks, about 1
  inch thick (approximately 1 1/2
  pounds total)

Salt and freshly ground pepper
3/4 cup Riesling wine
1 cup heavy cream
A few drops of lemon juice

Preheat oven to 425°F. Butter a gratin dish or other shallow baking
dish large enough to contain salmon steaks in one layer. Sprinkle
shallots and 1 teaspoon chives in dish. Set salmon steaks on top, season
with salt and pepper, and pour wine over them. Cover with buttered
parchment paper or foil and bake about 15 minutes, or until just
tender and flesh near bone has changed color to light pink. Carefully
transfer steaks to a platter and cover with paper or foil to keep warm.

Pour cooking liquid with shallots and chives into a medium,
heavy saucepan and bring to a boil. Boil until reduced to about 1/3
cup. Add cream and simmer over medium heat, whisking occasionally, until thick enough to coat a spoon. Add remaining chives and a
few drops lemon juice, and taste and adjust seasoning.

Drain any liquid from platter of fish. Carefully pull off skin from
each salmon steak, spoon sauce over fish, and serve.

NOTE: If using 1 1/2- or 2-inch salmon steaks, increase baking time
to 20 minutes.

🌿 SEA BASS WITH PISTOU SAUCE
Loup au pistou

In this aromatic summer entrée, the fish is marinated with basil and olive oil, cooked lightly in its marinade, and served at room temperature with pearl onions and cherry tomatoes. Pistou, the French version of pesto, has the brightest hue when a light-colored olive oil is used. Here, the pistou is made into a creamy sauce. Halibut or salmon steaks can be used instead of sea bass.

MAKES 4 SERVINGS

1 1/2 pounds sea bass fillet, about 1 inch thick, cut in 4 pieces
1 cup dry white wine
2 tablespoons olive oil

1 tablespoon coarsely chopped fresh basil leaves
Salt and freshly ground pepper
12 pearl onions (about 1/2 pound)

PISTOU SAUCE
2 medium-size garlic cloves, peeled
1 cup lightly packed fresh basil leaves (about 1 1/2 ounces), rinsed and thoroughly dried
1/2 cup mild olive oil

1 large egg, room temperature
2 teaspoons strained fresh lemon juice
Salt and freshly ground pepper
1/4 cup vegetable oil

12 cherry tomatoes

4 small sprigs basil for garnish

Put sea bass in shallow bowl. Combine wine, olive oil, chopped basil, and salt and pepper, and pour mixture over fish. Let stand to marinate 1 hour, turning twice.

Put onions in saucepan of water and bring to a boil. Drain and rinse under cold water, then peel onions with a paring knife. Return onions to saucepan and cover with water. Bring to a boil, cover, and simmer over medium heat until just tender, about 10 minutes. Rinse under cold water and drain thoroughly.

Transfer fish and its marinade to large skillet and bring to a simmer, basting occasionally. Reduce heat to low, cover, and cook until skewer inserted into fish comes out hot, about 8 minutes. Remove carefully to a platter with a slotted spoon and let cool to room temperature. Remove any pieces of basil stuck to fish and discard any liquid from plate.

PISTOU SAUCE

With blade of food processor turning, drop garlic through feed tube and chop finely. Add basil and ¼ cup olive oil and process by on/off turns until basil is coarsely chopped; scrape down sides often. Transfer to bowl; mixture will not be uniform.

Add egg to processor, pour in 1 teaspoon lemon juice, 1 tablespoon olive oil, and a little salt and pepper, and process until thoroughly blended. With machine running, add remaining olive oil and vegetable oil in slow, steady stream, blending until sauce is smooth and thick. Add about half the basil mixture and process until blended. Add remaining basil mixture and process. Add remaining teaspoon lemon juice and process until blended. Taste and adjust seasoning.

(Fish and sauce can be kept in separate dishes, covered, about 8 hours in refrigerator. Bring to room temperature before serving.)

Coat fish with sauce, surround with onions and tomatoes, alternating them, and garnish fish with basil sprigs. Serve any remaining sauce separately.

BRAISED HALIBUT WITH MUSSELS, GINGER, AND CREAM
Flétan braisé aux moules et au gingembre

Mussels are often used as a pretty garnish for braised fish in classic French cuisine, on their own or combined with other small shellfish. Their natural juices, like those of clams, make a tasty addition to the sauce. This recipe can also be prepared with sea bass steaks or fillets, ling cod fillets, or slices of skinned monkfish.   MAKES 4 SERVINGS

*1 pound mussels, scrubbed,
    debearded, and rinsed (see
    page 298)*
*⅓ cup plus 1 tablespoon dry white
    wine*
*2 tablespoons minced peeled fresh
    ginger*
*1 tablespoon plus 2 teaspoons
    butter, room temperature*
2 teaspoons all-purpose flour

1 medium-size shallot, minced
*4 halibut steaks (each about 6 or 7
    ounces)*
Salt and freshly ground pepper
*½ cup Fish Stock (see recipe), or
    ¼ cup bottled clam juice
    mixed with ¼ cup water*
½ cup heavy cream
1 tablespoon minced fresh parsley

Discard any mussels that do not close when tapped. Combine mussels, ⅓ cup wine, and 1 teaspoon ginger in a medium, heavy saucepan. Cover tightly and cook over high heat, shaking occasionally, until mussels open, about 4 minutes. Remove mussels with a slotted spoon; discard any that do not open. Reserve cooking liquid in small bowl. Let liquid stand 10 minutes so sand falls to bottom. Shell mussels, reserving any additional liquid in the small bowl. Pull off rubbery ring around each mussel. Ladle reserved mussel liquid through strainer lined with several layers of dampened cheesecloth.

Preheat oven to 425°F. Mash 2 teaspoons soft butter in small dish. Add flour and mix to form paste. Reserve at room temperature.

Generously butter a 10-cup oval gratin dish or other heavy shallow baking dish with some soft butter; sprinkle with minced shallot. Cut oval piece of parchment paper the size of the dish, and butter paper.

Remove any scales from fish steaks. Measure thickness of steaks at thickest point and calculate 9 minutes cooking time per inch.

Arrange fish pieces in baking dish in one layer. Sprinkle with 1 tablespoon wine, then with salt and pepper. Bring fish stock to a simmer in very small saucepan, and pour over fish. Set buttered paper directly on top of fish.

Bake until fish is opaque, as calculated above. After this time has elapsed, check fish: insert cake tester or thin skewer into thickest part of fish for about 5 seconds and touch tester to underside of your wrist; it should be hot to the touch. If fish is not quite done, bake another 1 or 2 minutes and test again.

Remove fish carefully to a platter with 2 wide slotted spatulas, reserving cooking liquid. Remove any skin with a paring knife. Remove any large pieces of shallot stuck to fish. Cover fish with its buttered paper and keep warm on top of stove.

Strain braising liquid, then combine with mussel liquid.

Melt remaining 1 tablespoon butter in small heavy saucepan over low heat. Add remaining ginger and sauté 1 minute. Add strained liquid and bring to a boil. Reduce heat to medium-low so liquid simmers. Add butter-flour mixture to simmering sauce in 2 portions, whisking constantly. Bring to a boil, whisking.

Whisk in cream and return to a boil. Simmer, whisking often, until sauce is thick enough to coat a spoon. Remove from heat and add mussels and parsley. Taste and adjust seasoning.

Discard any liquid that escaped from fish onto platter. Pour sauce with mussels over fish and serve.

SOLE WITH WHITE WINE BUTTER SAUCE AND DICED VEGETABLES
Sole à la brunoise de légumes

The first time I tasted the white wine butter sauce in this dish, I was amazed by how delicious it was. I learned it from my mentor, the great Chef Fernand Chambrette, when he was head chef of La Varenne Cooking School in Paris. MAKES 4 SERVINGS

WHITE WINE BUTTER SAUCE

3 cups Fish Stock (see recipe)
1 cup unsalted butter, cut in 16
   pieces
1 shallot, finely minced

1/3 cup dry white wine
2 tablespoons heavy cream
Salt and white pepper

2 medium-size carrots, peeled
1 large leek, white and light green
   parts only, thoroughly cleaned
1 celery stalk
Salt and freshly ground pepper
2 tablespoons butter

1 shallot, finely minced
1 1/2 pounds sole or flounder fillets
1/4 cup Fish Stock (see recipe)
1/2 teaspoon strained fresh lemon
   juice, or to taste

WHITE WINE BUTTER SAUCE

Boil fish stock in a large skillet over high heat until reduced to about 3/4 cup. Melt 1 piece of butter in a small heavy saucepan, add shallot, and cook, stirring occasionally, until soft but not browned. (Keep remaining butter in refrigerator.) Add wine to shallot mixture and bring to a boil, then add reduced fish stock and return to a boil, stirring occasionally. Boil until reduced to 2 or 3 tablespoons. Add cream. Simmer over medium heat, whisking occasionally, until mixture is reduced to 3 tablespoons. Season lightly with salt and white pepper. Cover and set aside. (Sauce can be prepared ahead to this point and kept, covered tightly, 1 day in refrigerator.)

Cut carrots in thin slices lengthwise. Cut each slice in thin strips, and the strips in tiny dice. Cut leek in tiny dice also. Peel celery to remove strings, then cut celery in tiny dice. Put vegetable dice in a shallow tray, sprinkle with salt and pepper, and mix well.

Preheat oven to 400°F. Spread 1 tablespoon butter on base and sides of a small ovenproof saucepan. Put vegetables in pan. Cut a round of parchment paper or aluminum foil and butter it. Put remaining tablespoon butter in the pan with vegetables and cover with paper round and then pan lid. Bake vegetables, stirring often, about 15 minutes, or until softened. Taste and adjust seasoning. (Vegetables can be kept, covered, 1 day in refrigerator. Reheat in covered pan over low heat.)

Butter a shallow baking dish and sprinkle minced shallot in it. Arrange sole fillets in dish, season with salt and pepper, and pour fish stock over fish. Cover with another piece of buttered parchment paper or foil. Bake about 10 minutes, or until tender when pierced with a skewer.

Meanwhile, finish sauce. Bring sauce mixture to a simmer, reduce heat to low, and add 1 piece of cold butter, whisking constantly. When butter piece is nearly blended into liquid, add another piece, still whisking. Continue adding butter pieces, 1 at a time, whisking constantly; the sauce should be pleasantly warm to the touch. (If at any time sauce becomes too hot and drops of melted butter appear, remove pan immediately from heat and whisk well; add next butter pieces off heat, whisking constantly. When temperature of sauce drops again to warm, return to low heat to continue adding remaining butter pieces.) Remove from heat as soon as last butter piece is incorporated. Add lemon juice, and taste and adjust seasoning. Serve as soon as possible. Sauce can be kept warm briefly on a rack above a pan of hot water, in double boiler, or in thermos.

To serve, carefully transfer fish to a platter or plates and drain off any liquid that has accumulated. If vegetables have given off liquid, drain them. Stir 2 or 3 tablespoons vegetables into sauce. Coat fish with sauce, and spoon remaining vegetable dice around fish. Serve any remaining sauce separately.

MONKFISH WITH LEEKS, TOMATOES, AND OLIVES
Lotte aux poireaux, aux tomates, et aux olives

In this Provençal-style entrée, the monkfish is gently braised in tomato sauce with garlic and aromatic vegetables, then garnished with black and green olives. Monkfish has a pleasant, firm, almost meaty, texture. Some people feel it resembles lobster and, in fact, some restaurateurs have been known to "stretch" lobster dishes by adding pieces of the less-expensive monkfish. MAKES 4 SERVINGS

1 1/2 pounds monkfish fillet, cut in 2 or 3 pieces crosswise

2 medium-size leeks, white and light green parts only, cut in half lengthwise and rinsed well

3 tablespoons all-purpose flour

2 tablespoons butter

4 tablespoons olive oil

1 small onion, chopped

1 small carrot, peeled and finely diced

1 medium-size celery stalk, diced

4 medium-size garlic cloves, coarsely chopped

4 ripe medium-size tomatoes (about 1 1/2 pounds), cut in eighths, or one 28-ounce can and one 14-ounce can whole plum tomatoes, drained and quartered

2/3 cup Fish Stock (see recipe) or 1/2 cup bottled clam juice

Salt and freshly ground pepper

1 bay leaf

1 large sprig fresh thyme, or 1/4 teaspoon dried leaf thyme, crumbled

1 teaspoon tomato paste

1/2 cup pitted green olives, drained well

3/4 cup pitted black olives, drained well

Skin monkfish by lifting one portion of skin and carefully freeing it by pulling and separating it from flesh with point of sharp knife. Continue with remaining skin, until white flesh is exposed. Cut leeks in 3-by-⅛-inch strips.

Dredge monkfish in flour, shaking off excess. Heat butter and 2 tablespoons oil in large deep skillet over medium-high heat. Add monkfish and brown lightly on all sides, then remove to a plate. Stir in onion, carrot, celery, and garlic, scraping up any browned bits from bottom of pan. Cook over low heat until vegetables soften, about 3 minutes; do not let them brown.

Return monkfish to skillet. Add tomatoes, fish stock, and salt and pepper. Add bay leaf and thyme, making sure to immerse them in liquid. Bring to a boil, reduce heat to low, cover, and cook 7 minutes. Turn monkfish over and cook until a skewer can pierce fish easily and comes out hot to the touch, about 8 minutes. Transfer fish to platter, cover, and keep warm.

Crush tomato pieces in skillet lightly with spoon. Simmer sauce over medium heat, stirring often, until tomatoes are very soft, about 10 minutes. Strain sauce, pressing firmly on vegetables in strainer to extract as much juice as possible; do not purée vegetables.

Heat remaining 2 tablespoons olive oil in large skillet over low heat. Add leeks and mix well. Cover and cook, stirring often, until tender, about 7 minutes.

Return sauce to skillet used to cook fish. Boil, stirring, until thick enough to coat a spoon, about 5 minutes. Stir in tomato paste until well blended. Stir in leeks and olives and simmer 1 minute. Remove from heat and taste and adjust seasoning.

Discard any vegetable dice attached to fish. Cut fish in thick slices. (Fish and sauce can be kept, covered, 8 hours in refrigerator.) If serving fish hot, return slices to skillet with a few tablespoons of sauce, cover, and reheat briefly. Transfer fish to a platter. Spoon sauce, olives, and leeks around fish, and garnish with a few black olives. Serve hot or cold.

🌿 BRAISED SALMON WITH ASPARAGUS AND LEMON-LIME SAUCE
Saumon braisé aux asperges et au citron vert

Perfect for spring, this colorful entrée features a light and tangy sauce made from the fish braising juices and a touch of lemon and lime. This recipe can also be prepared with whole trout, small whole bass, sea bass fillets, halibut steaks, or salmon steaks.

MAKES 4 SERVINGS

FISH VELOUTÉ SAUCE

1 tablespoon butter
1 tablespoon all-purpose flour
1 cup Fish Stock (see recipe), or 1/2 cup bottled clam juice mixed with 1/2 cup water

Salt and white pepper
1/3 cup heavy cream

1 small bunch thin asparagus (about 3/4 pound)
1 salmon chunk (2 1/2 pounds)
Salt and freshly ground pepper
1 medium-size shallot, minced
1 tablespoon dry white wine
1/2 cup Fish Stock (see recipe) or clam juice
1/2 teaspoon fresh strained lemon juice

2 to 2 1/2 teaspoons fresh strained lime juice
3 tablespoons butter, cut in 3 pieces, room temperature
3/4 teaspoon finely grated lemon peel
3/4 teaspoon finely grated lime peel
Fluted lemon and lime slices for garnish (optional)

FISH VELOUTÉ SAUCE

Melt butter in medium, heavy saucepan over low heat. Whisk in flour and cook over low heat, whisking constantly, until mixture turns light beige, about 2 minutes. Remove from heat and gradually whisk in fish stock. Set over medium-high heat and whisk until sauce thickens and comes to a boil. Reduce heat to low and simmer 5 minutes, whisking frequently. Add a pinch of salt and white pepper, then add cream and bring to boil, whisking. Reduce heat to low and simmer, whisking often, until thick enough to coat a spoon, about 5 minutes.

(Sauce can be kept, covered, 1 day in refrigerator. Reheat in medium, heavy saucepan, whisking, before continuing.)

Cut 2½-inch-long asparagus tips from stems. Reserve remaining stems for other uses.

Preheat oven to 425°F. Generously butter 10-cup oval gratin dish or other heavy shallow baking dish with soft butter. Cut oval piece of parchment paper to size of dish and butter paper.

Snip salmon fins and trim tail straight, using sturdy scissors. Rinse fish inside and outside, removing any scales, and pat dry. Measure thickness of fish at thickest point when it is lying flat, and calculate 9 minutes cooking time per inch. Season fish inside and outside with salt and pepper.

Sprinkle base of dish with minced shallot. Set fish in dish and pour wine over it. Bring fish stock to a simmer in very small saucepan, and pour over fish. Set buttered paper directly on top of fish.

Bake until fish is opaque, as calculated above. After the time has elapsed, check fish: insert cake tester or thin skewer into thickest part of fish for about 5 seconds and touch tester to underside of your wrist; it should be hot to the touch. If fish is not quite done, bake another 1 or 2 minutes and test again.

Remove fish carefully to platter with 2 wide slotted spatulas, reserving cooking liquid. Remove skin by scraping gently with a paring knife. Remove any large shallot pieces stuck to fish. Cover fish with its buttered paper. Set platter on top of stove to keep warm. Strain braising liquid into small saucepan.

Boil liquid over medium-high heat until reduced to 2 table-spoons. Meanwhile, cook asparagus tips, uncovered, in medium sauce-pan of boiling salted water over high heat until crisp-tender, about 2 minutes. Drain and keep warm.

Whisk fish-braising liquid into velouté sauce, bring to boil, and simmer until thick enough to coat a spoon. Remove from heat. Whisk in lemon juice and ½ teaspoon lime juice. Whisk in butter pieces, 1 at a time. Whisk in grated lemon and lime peels and an additional 1½ teaspoons lime juice. Taste and adjust seasoning; add ½ teaspoon more lime juice, if desired.

Discard any liquid that escaped from fish onto platter. Serve fish with asparagus tips and with fluted slices of lemon and lime, if desired. Serve sauce separately.

MARINATED TROUT WITH CHAMPAGNE HOLLANDAISE SAUCE AND SHRIMP
Truite marinée au champagne et aux crevettes

In the Champagne region of France people naturally cook with their local wine, which happens to be—champagne! Often they use "still" champagne, which has the flavor but not the bubbles, because these dissipate when the wine is heated anyway.

The label terminology of champagne can be confusing but is of crucial importance when choosing a bottle for cooking. The driest champagne is called "brut" and is the best choice for most purposes. "Extra dry" is slightly sweeter and "dry" is actually quite sweet and should be used only for making desserts. This sweetness might not be apparent when the wine is being sipped because the bubbles tend to counteract it, but if "dry" champagne is used in a sauce for fish like this one, the sauce ends up tasting amazingly like syrup!

MAKES 4 SERVINGS

4 small trout (9 to 12 ounces each)
Salt and freshly ground pepper
1 1/2 cups brut champagne or fine-quality dry white wine

1 onion, chopped
Pinch of thyme

CHAMPAGNE HOLLANDAISE SAUCE WITH SHRIMP
3/4 cup unsalted butter
1/4 pound small uncooked shrimp, shelled
4 egg yolks
1/4 cup brut champagne or fine-quality dry white wine

Pinch of salt
Pinch of white pepper or cayenne pepper
1/4 teaspoon lemon juice, or more to taste

Trim fins and tail of trout with sturdy scissors. If any dark material remains attached to backbone, scrape it off. Rinse trout and pat dry inside and outside. Put trout in a gratin dish and season with salt and pepper inside and outside. Add champagne and marinate in refrigerator 1 to 4 hours.

Preheat oven to 400°F. Add onion and thyme to dish of trout and bake about 15 minutes, basting occasionally, or until a skewer inserted in thickest part of flesh for 10 seconds comes out hot when touched to your inner wrist. Carefully remove trout, transfer to a platter, cover, and keep warm.

CHAMPAGNE HOLLANDAISE SAUCE WITH SHRIMP

Meanwhile, clarify butter for sauce: Melt butter in a small heavy saucepan over low heat. Skim off white foam from surface. Pour remaining clear butter into a bowl, leaving white sediment behind in saucepan. Let cool to lukewarm.

Strain trout cooking liquid into a sauté pan. Add shrimp and poach about 30 seconds on each side. Remove to a bowl with a slotted spoon and keep warm. Boil trout cooking liquid until reduced to ¼ cup.

In a medium, heavy nonaluminum saucepan, combine egg yolks, ¼ cup champagne, salt, and white pepper or cayenne and whisk briefly. Set pan over low heat and cook, whisking vigorously and constantly, until mixture is creamy and thick enough so whisk leaves a trail on base of pan. Remove pan occasionally from heat; it should not become so hot that you can't touch sides of pan with your hands. If the mixture does become too hot the yolks will curdle. When mixture is thick enough, remove it immediately from heat. Continue to whisk for about 30 seconds.

Gradually whisk in clarified butter, drop by drop. After sauce has absorbed 2 or 3 tablespoons butter, add remaining butter in a very thin stream, whisking vigorously and constantly. Stir in lemon juice. Gradually stir in some of the reduced trout cooking liquid, adding it to taste; do not thin out sauce too much. Taste and adjust seasoning. Set sauce uncovered on a rack above a pan of hot water or in double boiler.

Carefully remove trout skin with a small knife. Spoon a little sauce over each trout and garnish with shrimp. Serve remaining sauce separately.

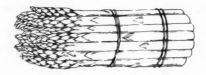

❧ SEA BASS WITH AVOCADO SAUCE
Bar aux avocats

When I worked briefly at La Ciboulette restaurant in Paris, we prepared a lovely sole with avocado sauce, which was the inspiration for this dish. I liked the chef's principle of preparing a sauce from a fruit or vegetable, then garnishing the plate with slices of the same fruit or vegetable. This recipe can also be prepared with salmon steaks and garnished with dill sprigs. MAKES 4 SERVINGS

*1 3/4 pounds sea bass steaks, about
   1 inch thick (2 or 4 pieces),
   rinsed, any scales removed,
   and patted dry*
1 tablespoon minced shallot
1/4 cup dry white wine
*1/4 cup bottled clam juice or Fish
   Stock (see recipe)*
Salt and freshly ground pepper

*1 ripe medium-size California
   avocado (about 1/2 pound),
   preferably Haas, room
   temperature*
*1/4 cup heavy cream, or a few
   teaspoons more, if needed*
Cayenne pepper to taste
A few drops of fresh lemon juice

Preheat oven to 425°F. Generously butter a shallow baking dish in which fish pieces can fit without overlapping. Cut a piece of parchment paper to size of dish and butter paper. Sprinkle minced shallot in dish. Arrange fish pieces in dish in one layer. In a cup, combine wine and clam juice, then pour mixture into dish. Season fish lightly with salt and freshly ground pepper. Set buttered paper directly on top of fish.

Bake fish 15 minutes, or until opaque. To check, insert a cake tester or a thin skewer into thickest part of fish for 5 seconds and touch tester to underside of your wrist; tester should feel hot. If fish is not quite done, bake another 1 or 2 minutes and check it again.

Carefully transfer fish to a platter with 2 wide slotted spatulas, reserving cooking liquid. Remove fish skin, if necessary, with a paring knife, and remove any large shallot pieces that are stuck to it. If there are 2 pieces of fish, cut each in half and, if desired, remove the central bone. Cover fish with its buttered paper and keep warm. Strain cooking liquid into a saucepan.

Peel avocado and cut half of it in lengthwise slices toward the pit.

Remove pit. Purée other half in a food processor until fairly smooth. Bring fish cooking liquid to a boil, then gradually add it to avocado purée in food processor, with motor running, continuing to process until smooth. Return mixture to saucepan.

Drain liquid that escaped from fish and whisk it into sauce. Heat sauce until it is just hot but not simmering. Whisk in cream and heat through. If sauce is too thick, gradually whisk in more cream, 1 teaspoon at a time. Season sauce to taste with salt, cayenne, and lemon juice; it should be well seasoned, not bland.

Spoon some sauce onto 4 plates and set fish pieces on top. Arrange avocado slices crosswise on fish, and serve any remaining sauce separately.

SEE PHOTOGRAPH (SALMON VARIATION).

 ## BRAISED SCROD WITH FRESH TOMATO SAUCE AND LEMON GRASS
Églefin braisé, sauce tomato à la citronnelle

This light main course is an ideal choice for summer. Complete the meal with fine-quality French bread, a cool green salad, and fresh fruit or sorbet. This recipe can also be prepared with fillets of haddock, ling cod, snapper, or halibut. MAKES 4 SERVINGS

TOMATO SAUCE.

1 tablespoon vegetable oil

2 pounds ripe tomatoes, peeled, seeded, and finely chopped, or two 28-ounce cans whole plum tomatoes, drained and chopped

Salt and freshly ground pepper

1/4 teaspoon dried leaf thyme, crumbled

2 small zucchini (1/2 pound total), quartered lengthwise and cut in 1 1/2-inch pieces

1 medium-size shallot, minced

1 1/2 pounds fillets of scrod or cod

1 tablespoon dry white wine

Salt and freshly ground pepper

1/3 cup Fish Stock (see recipe), or 1/4 cup bottled clam juice mixed with 1 tablespoon water

3 large garlic cloves, minced

1 tablespoon minced fresh lemon grass (see note)

TOMATO SAUCE

Heat oil in large saucepan over medium heat. Stir in tomatoes, salt, pepper, and thyme. Bring to a boil, reduce heat to low, and cook, uncovered, stirring occasionally, until tomatoes are very soft and sauce is thick, about 35 minutes. Sauce will be chunky. (Sauce can be kept, covered, 1 day in refrigerator. Reheat before continuing.)

Trim each zucchini piece to an oval shape, using paring knife to round out any sharp angles and cutting off most of part with seeds; leave on as much peel as possible.

Preheat oven to 425°F. Generously butter 10-cup oval gratin dish or other heavy shallow baking dish with some soft butter; sprinkle with minced shallot. Cut oval piece of parchment paper to size of dish and butter paper.

Run your fingers over fish fillets and carefully pull out any bones with tweezers, a pastry crimper, or sharp paring knife. Measure thickness of fillets at thickest point and calculate 9 minutes per inch cooking time.

Arrange fish pieces in baking dish in one layer. Sprinkle fish with wine and salt and pepper. Bring fish stock to a simmer in very small saucepan, then pour over fish. Set buttered paper directly on top of fish.

Bake until fish is opaque, as calculated above. After the time has elapsed, check fillets: For thin fillets, simply look at surface of fish to see whether it has lost its raw color. For fillets thicker than 3/4 inch, insert cake tester or thin skewer into thickest part of fish for about 5 seconds and touch tester to underside of your wrist; it should be hot to the touch. If fish is not quite done, bake another 1 or 2 minutes and test again.

Remove fish carefully to a platter with 2 wide slotted spatulas, reserving cooking liquid. Remove any large shallot pieces stuck to fish. Cover fish with its buttered paper. Set platter on top of stove to keep warm. Strain braising liquid and add to tomato sauce. Add garlic and lemon grass and boil, stirring often, until thickened, about 2 minutes. Taste and adjust seasoning.

Meanwhile, boil zucchini in large pan of boiling salted water, uncovered, over high heat until just tender, about 3 minutes. Drain thoroughly and keep warm.

Discard any liquid from fish platter. Coat fish with sauce, spoon zucchini around it, and serve remaining sauce separately.

NOTE: Lemon grass is available in Thai markets, specialty produce markets, and some supermarkets. To mince lemon grass: Peel off tough outer layers and cut off tough thin tops. Chop more tender inner part of thick stalk. You will need about a 1½-inch section to obtain 1 tablespoon minced lemon grass. If it is not available, substitute ¼ teaspoon grated lemon peel.

SEAFOOD BLANQUETTE WITH GREEN VEGETABLES
Blanquette de fruits de mer aux légumes verts

Originally a term reserved for veal or lamb, *blanquette* now also refers to a creamy seafood stew like this one. Other cooked vegetables can be substituted according to their seasons, and sautéed wild mushrooms can be added, too. Cooked lobster or crabmeat are also marvelous additions.   MAKES 4 SERVINGS

2 cups Fish Stock (see recipe) or
    packaged fish stock
½ cup dry white wine
8 jumbo shrimp (about 9 ounces),
    shelled and deveined, shells
    reserved
1 large lemon, cut in half
    (optional)
2 medium-size artichokes, or 8
    frozen artichoke heart pieces
    (optional)
Salt

½ pound Swiss chard, leaves only,
    rinsed thoroughly
6 ounces snow peas (also called
    Chinese peas), ends and
    strings removed
¼ pound small sea scallops
¾ pound salmon fillet, skinned
1 cup heavy cream
Freshly ground pepper
1 tablespoon minced fresh tarragon
1 tablespoon snipped fresh chives
1 tablespoon minced fresh parsley

Bring stock, wine, and shrimp shells to a boil in medium saucepan. Reduce heat to low and simmer, uncovered, 15 minutes. Strain stock.

Squeeze juice of ½ lemon into medium bowl of cold water. Prepare artichoke hearts from fresh artichokes (page 311), if desired. Put each in bowl of lemon water.

Squeeze juice from remaining lemon half into medium saucepan of boiling salted water. Add artichoke hearts, cover, and simmer over low heat until tender when pierced with knife, about 15 minutes for fresh artichokes, about 7 minutes for frozen. Cool to lukewarm in liquid. Using a teaspoon, scoop out hairlike choke from center of each fresh artichoke heart. Return artichokes to liquid until ready to use. Cut each fresh artichoke in 4 pieces.

Pile chard leaves, cut them in half lengthwise, then cut them crosswise in ½-inch-wide strips. Cook chard, uncovered, in large saucepan of boiling salted water over high heat until just tender, about 3 minutes. Rinse under cold water, drain well, and press gently to remove excess liquid.

Cook snow peas, uncovered, in large saucepan of boiling salted water over high heat 1 minute; they should remain crisp. Rinse under cold water and drain well.

Remove small white muscle from sides of scallops. Rinse scallops and pat dry. Run your fingers over salmon to check for bones and remove any you find with tweezers, a pastry crimper, or small sharp knife. Pat salmon dry, and cut in 1-inch cubes. (Ingredients can be prepared up to 4 hours ahead to this point and refrigerated.)

Bring stock to a boil in large deep skillet. Stir in ½ cup cream and bring to a simmer, stirring. Add a pinch of salt and pepper, then add shrimp and cook over low heat 1 minute. Turn shrimp over. Add salmon and scallops and cook until seafood is just tender, about 4 minutes more, shaking pan occasionally. Remove seafood with a slotted spoon and divide among shallow bowls. Cover and keep warm.

Boil sauce until reduced to about 1 cup. Whisk in remaining ½ cup cream and boil, whisking often, until sauce is thick enough to coat a spoon, about 10 minutes. Stir in vegetables and reheat briefly. Remove from heat and add tarragon, chives, and parsley. Taste and adjust seasoning. Drain any liquid that has escaped from seafood. Add vegetables to each bowl with a slotted spoon, pour sauce over fish, and serve immediately.

NOTE: If shrimp with heads are available, they will produce an even richer stock.

FISH QUENELLES WITH SHRIMP SAUCE
Quenelles de poisson, sauce aux crevettes

Quenelles are a delightful specialty of Lyon, and are found there even in small unknown restaurants. They make a wonderful party dish that everyone will enjoy, even people who think they don't like fish.

MAKES 8 FIRST-COURSE
OR 4 MAIN-COURSE SERVINGS

CHOUX PASTRY

1/2 cup plus 1 tablespoon all-purpose flour

1/2 cup water

1/4 teaspoon salt

1/4 cup (1/2 stick) butter, cut in pieces

2 eggs

1 1/2 pounds halibut or sole fillets

3 egg whites

1/2 teaspoon salt

1/4 teaspoon pepper

Freshly grated nutmeg

1 cup heavy cream

SHRIMP SAUCE

3/4 pound medium-size shrimp

5 tablespoons butter

1/2 onion, chopped

2 garlic cloves, finely chopped

2 2/3 cups Fish Stock (see recipe) or packaged fish stock

4 tablespoons all-purpose flour

1 1/2 tablespoons Cognac or brandy

Salt and freshly ground pepper

2/3 cup heavy cream

1 teaspoon tomato paste

Pinch of cayenne pepper

CHOUX PASTRY

Sift flour onto a piece of wax paper. Heat water, salt, and butter in a small saucepan until butter melts. Bring to a boil, remove from heat. Add flour immediately, and stir quickly with a wooden spoon until mixture is smooth. Set pan over low heat and beat mixture about 30 seconds. Remove and let cool for a few minutes. Add 1 egg and beat it thoroughly into mixture. Beat in second egg until mixture is smooth. Rub surface with a small piece of butter and let dough cool completely.

Remove any skin or bones from fish, pat dry, and cut into pieces. Purée fish in a food processor until very smooth. Gradually add egg whites with machine running and purée again until very smooth. Chill in food processor for 30 minutes.

Add salt, pepper, and nutmeg to fish mixture. Add choux pastry and purée to blend. With machine running, gradually pour cream into mixture. Scrape down sides very well and process a few seconds more to be sure mixture is thoroughly blended. Taste and adjust seasoning. Cover and chill 15 minutes, or up to 4 hours.

SHRIMP SAUCE

Shell shrimp, reserving shells; rinse shells. Melt 2 tablespoons butter in a medium saucepan. Add onion and cook over low heat about 5 minutes, or until soft but not browned. Add garlic and sauté 1 minute. Add shrimp shells and fish stock, bring to a boil, cover, and simmer 10 minutes. Strain shrimp stock.

Melt remaining 3 tablespoons butter in a medium saucepan. Whisk in flour and cook 1 or 2 minutes, until foaming but not browned. Gradually whisk in shrimp stock, bring to a boil, add Cognac or brandy, and salt and pepper and simmer, uncovered, 10 minutes, whisking occasionally. Whisk in cream and tomato paste and return to a boil. Simmer sauce 2 to 3 minutes, or until thick enough to coat a spoon. (Sauce can be kept, covered, up to 1 day in refrigerator. Reheat in medium saucepan over medium heat, whisking.)

Add shrimp to sauce and poach over low heat about 1 minute. Add a pinch of cayenne pepper, and taste and adjust seasoning.

Preheat oven to 375°F. To poach quenelles, bring a large saucepan or casserole of water to a boil and add a large pinch of salt. Reduce heat so water simmers. Using 2 tablespoons, shape chilled mixture into quenelles that are compact ovals by transferring them from 1 spoon to the other. Dip a third tablespoon into simmering water and use it to transfer each quenelle into the water. After all quenelles are shaped, cover pan and poach them over low heat 10 to 15 minutes, or until firm. Remove very carefully with a slotted spoon and drain on paper towels.

Transfer quenelles to 1 large or 2 or 3 medium buttered gratin dishes or other shallow baking dishes. Coat them generously with sauce and shrimp. Just before serving, bake quenelles in preheated oven about 10 minutes, until sauce is bubbling. Serve immediately.

TROUT WITH CABBAGE STUFFING AND DILL BUTTER SAUCE
Truite farcie aux choux, beurre à l'aneth

Cabbage has long been a staple in French country cooking, and with the current wave of returning to the roots of regional cooking, it has gained prestige and become a chic vegetable. Top chefs now use it in elegant dishes. Parisian chef Joël Robuchon of Jamin, for example, prepares langoustine ravioli with cabbage, and squab with cabbage and foie gras. Blanching the cabbage briefly and sautéing it in butter softens its taste, so that it goes well with the trout and its delicate sauce.   MAKES 4 SERVINGS

CABBAGE-DILL STUFFING

1 medium-size head green cabbage (about 2 pounds), cored and rinsed
1/4 cup butter

Salt and freshly ground pepper
1/2 cup heavy cream
1/4 cup snipped fresh dill

4 trout (about 1/2 pound each), boned (at market, or see note)
Salt and freshly ground pepper

1/4 cup dry white wine
5 small sprigs fresh dill

DILL BUTTER SAUCE

2 tablespoons minced shallots
2 tablespoons white wine vinegar
3 tablespoons dry white wine
2 tablespoons water
2 tablespoons heavy cream

Salt and white pepper
1 cup cold unsalted butter, cut in small pieces
4 tablespoons snipped fresh dill

CABBAGE-DILL STUFFING

Chop cabbage as fine as possible, preferably in a food processor in batches. In a large pan of boiling salted water, boil cabbage 3 minutes. Drain in a fine strainer, rinse under cold running water, and drain thoroughly; squeeze out excess liquid. In a large skillet, melt butter. Add cabbage and salt and pepper, cover, and cook over low heat 5 minutes. Transfer cabbage to a bowl and cool to room temperature. Stir in cream and dill, then taste and adjust seasoning. (Stuffing can be kept, covered, 1 day in refrigerator. Bring to room temperature before using.)

If trout was boned at fish market, run your finger along flesh about ¾ inch from backbone line on both sides of it to locate a row of small bones running parallel to backbone. With a sharp knife, expose bones, then pull them out with a pastry crimper or tweezers.

Preheat oven to 400°F. Cut off trout fins and shorten tail. Season interior of trout with salt and pepper to taste. Spoon one-quarter of stuffing into each trout and pack it in so it is compact. Set stuffed trout in a lightly buttered large shallow baking dish on their sides. Season with salt and pepper to taste. Add wine, 2 tablespoons water, and 1 sprig dill. Cover trout with buttered parchment paper or foil and bake 15 minutes, or until filling is hot when tested with a skewer.

DILL BUTTER SAUCE

Meanwhile, prepare sauce. In a small heavy stainless-steel or enameled saucepan combine shallots, vinegar, wine, and 2 tablespoons water and bring to a simmer. Simmer shallots in liquid over medium heat until liquid is reduced to 2 tablespoons. Stir in cream and simmer over low heat, whisking occasionally, until mixture is again reduced to 2 tablespoons.

Season lightly with salt and white pepper. Add 1 piece of cold butter, whisking constantly. When butter piece is nearly blended into liquid, add another piece, still whisking. Continue adding butter pieces, 1 at a time, whisking constantly. The sauce should be pleasantly warm to the touch. (If at any time sauce becomes too hot and drops of melted butter appear, remove pan immediately from heat and whisk well; add next butter pieces off heat, whisking constantly. When temperature of sauce drops again to warm, return to low heat to continue adding remaining butter pieces.) Remove from heat as soon as last butter piece is incorporated. Stir in dill, taste sauce, and adjust seasoning. Serve as soon as possible. Sauce can be kept warm briefly on a rack above a pan of hot water or in a double boiler.

Carefully transfer trout to a serving platter or plates. Using a paring knife, carefully remove skin from side of trout facing up, beginning near the tail.

Spoon a little dill butter sauce on and around trout. Decorate platter or plate with remaining dill sprigs and serve remaining sauce separately.

NOTE: To bone trout, detach small rib bones on each side of trout's backbone from flesh with the blade of a thin sharp knife. Carefully slide point of knife under backbone, without piercing skin. Cut through bone at tail end and near head, and carefully pull out bone, with small rib bones attached.

HALIBUT SALAD WITH WATERCRESS AND HAZELNUT OIL
Salade de flétan au cresson et à l'huile de noisettes

In France, steaming is a preferred technique for cooking seafood for salads because it keeps in their delicate, natural taste, as in this recipe. If you like, garnish each portion of this salad with some steamed shrimp or a few cherry tomatoes.

MAKES 4 FIRST-COURSE OR 2 MAIN-COURSE SERVINGS

2 bunches watercress (5 ounces each)

¾ pound halibut or sea bass fillets, in 4 pieces

HAZELNUT OIL VINAIGRETTE
2 tablespoons white wine vinegar
Salt and freshly ground pepper

3 tablespoons hazelnut oil
3 tablespoons vegetable oil

Salt and freshly ground pepper
2 tablespoons chopped fresh cilantro (coriander) or Italian parsley (optional)

Use upper part of watercress—tiny sprigs and leaves only—and discard the large stems. Thoroughly rinse watercress and dry it.

Cut each halibut piece in half crosswise, so it won't be more than ½ inch thick.

HAZELNUT OIL VINAIGRETTE
Whisk vinegar with salt and pepper, then whisk in hazelnut oil and vegetable oil. Taste and adjust seasoning.

Bring water to a boil in base of a steamer. Season halibut pieces lightly with salt and pepper on both sides. Put them in one layer in top part of steamer above boiling water, cover, and steam about 4 minutes, or until just tender. Drain quickly on paper towels. If necessary, steam halibut in 2 batches. Keep the first batch warm while steaming second.

Whisk vinaigrette again. Add enough vinaigrette to watercress to moisten it. Taste and adjust seasoning. Divide watercress among 2 or 4 plates.

Set halibut on watercress. Whisk remaining vinaigrette and spoon about 1 tablespoon over each piece of halibut. Sprinkle with fresh coriander, if desired, and serve immediately.

SOLE FILLETS WITH FRENCH SESAME SAUCE
Filets de sole, hollandaise à l'huile de sésame

The rich sesame sauce is a hollandaise in which sesame oil replaces part of the butter, and it is an ideal partner for the braised lean fish fillets. Use whatever fillets are freshest at your market—sole, flounder, halibut, sea bass, haddock, or cod will all be good. This dish requires good organization but is quick to prepare. For a festive touch, serve the fish with hot white rice sprinkled with toasted sesame seeds.

MAKES 4 SERVINGS

1 medium-size shallot, minced   *1 1/2 pounds sole or flounder fillets*

HOLLANDAISE SAUCE
3/4 cup (6 ounces) unsalted butter   *3 tablespoons water*
3 egg yolks   *Salt and white pepper to taste*

1 pound broccoli, cut in   *1/3 cup Fish Stock (see recipe), or*
   medium-size florets   *1/4 cup bottled clam juice*
1 tablespoon dry white wine   *mixed with 1 tablespoon water*
Salt and freshly ground   *2 to 2 1/2 teaspoons Chinese or*
   pepper   *Japanese sesame oil*

Preheat oven to 425°F. Generously butter a 10-cup oval gratin dish or other heavy shallow baking dish with some soft butter; sprinkle with minced shallot. Cut oval piece of parchment paper to size of dish and butter paper. Prepare pan of warm water, double boiler, or thermos for keeping sauce warm.

Run your fingers over fish fillets and carefully pull out any bones you find with tweezers, a pastry crimper, or sharp paring knife. If fillets are under 1/2 inch thick, fold them in half, with their whiter side facing out. Measure thickness of fillets at thickest point (leaving thin fillets folded in half) and calculate 9 minutes per inch cooking time. Arrange fish in baking dish in one layer.

HOLLANDAISE SAUCE

Melt butter in small saucepan over very low heat. Skim off white foam from surface and let cool until lukewarm.

Combine egg yolks, water, salt, and white pepper in small heavy saucepan and whisk thoroughly. Set saucepan over low heat and cook, whisking vigorously and constantly, until mixture is creamy and thick enough so that trail of whisk can be seen on base of pan, about 4 minutes. Remove pan occasionally from heat; sides of pan should not become too hot to touch with your hands. If mixture becomes too hot egg yolks will curdle. When yolk mixture becomes thick enough, remove pan immediately from heat. Continue to whisk mixture off heat for about 30 seconds.

Gradually whisk melted butter, drop by drop, into yolk mixture. After about 2 tablespoons butter have been absorbed, add rest of butter in a very thin stream, whisking vigorously and constantly. Do not add white sediment from bottom of butter saucepan. Set pan of sauce in pan of warm water off heat or in a double boiler or pour into thermos to keep warm.

Cook broccoli, uncovered, in large saucepan of boiling salted water over high heat until barely tender, about 4 minutes. Remove from heat and keep uncovered.

Season fish with wine and salt and pepper. Bring fish stock to a simmer in a very small saucepan, then pour over fish. Set buttered paper directly on fish. Bake in preheated oven until fish is opaque and has lost its raw color, as calculated above. If fish is not quite done, bake another 1 or 2 minutes and test again.

Carefully remove fish to platter with 2 wide slotted spatulas, reserving cooking liquid. Remove any large shallot pieces stuck to fish. Cover fish with its buttered paper and set platter on top of stove to keep warm.

Strain braising liquid into small saucepan and boil over medium-high heat, stirring often, until it is reduced to 3 tablespoons. Whisk reduced liquid gradually into sauce, then slowly whisk in 2 teaspoons sesame oil. Taste, add remaining sesame oil if desired, and adjust seasoning.

Discard any liquid that has escaped from fish onto platter. Drain broccoli. Spoon some sauce over fish, garnish with broccoli, and serve remaining sauce separately.

Shrimp

In France, shrimp is often cooked live in seawater and served un-shelled with crusty bread and fresh sweet butter. Nobody considers shelling the delicious rosy-pink shrimp at the table hard work; it's part of the fun.

Of course, the French don't stop there. With such a versatile shellfish, they had to create many fabulous dishes.

Shrimp harmonizes in the French kitchen with delicate creamy sauces and stands up to aggressive seasonings such as curry powder and garlic. Like scallops, they are a boon to the busy cook who wants to prepare an elegant meal. Besides, French cooks take advantage of the lovely pink shrimp to decorate their seafood plates and platters and to garnish their lavishly sauced fish entrées, such as Marinated Trout with Champagne Hollandaise Sauce and Shrimp. Shrimp of all sizes also make wonderful salads, combined with greens or crisp-tender vegetables and a light vinaigrette dressing.

It's best to buy shrimp uncooked; reheating cooked shrimp makes them rubbery. Even if they are to be served cold, it is better to cook them a short time before serving, to ensure that their flavor will be as fresh as possible. If a certain type of shrimp, such as bay shrimp, is only available cooked, buying it at a fish market is definitely prefera-ble to using canned shrimp.

Tiny shrimp are best used as a garnish or in salads. Small shrimp are perfect for first courses and larger shrimp or prawns for main courses. To give a more precise indication of the size of shrimp, markets label them with a number, which tells how many shrimp of that size would make a pound; the lower the number, the larger the shrimp.

The purpose of the shrimp's shells is to protect them, not only in the ocean but also in the pot! If they are to be cooked in the simplest way, in boiling salted water, shrimp should be left in their shells. If cooked shelled, the shrimp loses too much taste to the water.

Sometimes the goal of a recipe is to promote a flavor exchange between the shrimp and the sauce. In this case, the shrimp are shelled before cooking. To intensify the taste of a shrimp sauce, a good French trick is to first simmer the shells to make stock, and then to use it as the base for the sauce, as in Seafood Blanquette with Green Vegeta-bles, or to utilize the shells to make a shrimp butter, as in Shrimp Ragoût with Mushrooms and Baby Onions.

As with other seafood, the primary rule in preparing shrimp is to avoid overcooking them; only a few minutes are required, even for cooking large shrimp. If the shrimp are to be served in sauce, they rarely need precooking; heating them in the sauce is usually enough to cook them. When cooked in their shell, small shrimp are ready when their shells turn bright pink and large ones a minute or two after that happens. Out of their shells, they cook even faster and are done when the outer surface of their flesh turns pink and the inside becomes white.

If you're pressed for time, you don't need to shell the shrimp at all. Just serve them in their shells, as the French frequently do. There is a definite pleasure in eating shrimp this way, for a change. Just be sure to provide finger bowls. You'll save time and everyone will enjoy having a relaxed dinner *à la française.*

Hints

• Large shrimp should be deveined primarily to make them more attractive. To devein them, slit raw shrimp down the back and, with the aid of the tip of a small sharp knife, pull out the black "vein" or line that runs down the back. Veins are not found in every shrimp, though.

• In some areas of the country, very large shrimp are called "prawns."

SHRIMP WITH DICED VEGETABLES AND HERBED WINE SAUCE
Crevettes à la bordelaise

In the Bordeaux area, this entrée is traditionally prepared with crayfish or lobster pieces, but it is easier to make and equally sumptuous with shrimp. Unlike many other French sauces in which the *mirepoix*—or flavoring mixture of diced onions or carrots—is removed from the sauce, here it remains and adds color to the dish.

MAKES 4 SERVINGS

VEGETABLE AND WINE SAUCE

5 tablespoons butter

2 medium-size carrots, peeled and
   very finely diced

1/2 celery stalk, peeled and diced

1 onion, chopped

2 shallots, chopped

1/4 teaspoon dried leaf thyme,
   crumbled

1 bay leaf

2 fresh tarragon stems (optional)

1/2 cup Fish Stock (see recipe) or
   bottled clam juice or water

Salt and freshly ground pepper

3/4 cup dry white wine

1 1/4 to 1 1/2 pounds large shrimp,
   shelled and deveined

Salt and freshly ground pepper

3 large egg yolks

2 ripe medium-size tomatoes, peeled,
   seeded, and diced

Cayenne pepper to taste

1 tablespoon chopped fresh parsley

1 tablespoon chopped fresh
   tarragon, or 1 teaspoon dried
   leaf tarragon, crumbled

VEGETABLE AND WINE SAUCE

In a large skillet, melt 3 tablespoons butter; leave remaining butter at room temperature. Add carrots, celery, onion, shallots, thyme, bay leaf, and tarragon stems (if desired) to skillet and cook over low heat, stirring often, about 10 minutes, or until soft but not browned. Add fish stock and salt and pepper and bring to a boil, stirring. Simmer, uncovered, until most of the liquid has evaporated. Add wine and simmer, uncovered, 5 minutes. (Sauce can be kept, covered, 1 day in refrigerator; reheat before continuing.)

Add shrimp to sauce and season with salt and pepper. Cover and cook over low heat 2 minutes. Turn shrimp over, cover, and cook for 1 to 2 minutes more, or until just tender. Remove shrimp to a bowl with a slotted spoon, cover, and keep warm. Discard bay leaf and tarragon stems.

Transfer sauce to a saucepan and bring to a simmer. Beat egg yolks in a bowl and gradually beat in about 1/3 cup sauce. Return yolks to saucepan and add tomatoes. Cook over low heat, stirring constantly, about 2 minutes, or until sauce is slightly thickened; do not let sauce come to a boil or cook too long or it will curdle. Remove from heat and stir in remaining 2 tablespoons butter. Add cayenne, parsley, and tarragon. Taste and adjust seasoning. Spoon sauce onto a platter, arrange shrimp on top, and serve.

❧ SAUTÉED SHRIMP IN GARLIC BUTTER
Crevettes sautées au beurre d'ail

This recipe from Provence combines the best of both worlds. The shrimp are quickly seared in oil in their shells, which protect the delicate flesh from the hot oil. Then they are shelled and heated in garlic butter, which retains its fresh flavor because it is heated for only a short time.   MAKES 2 SERVINGS

2 large garlic cloves, minced
1 tablespoon chopped fresh parsley
2 tablespoons butter, softened
3/4 pound medium-size or small
   shrimp

1 to 2 tablespoons vegetable oil
Salt and freshly ground pepper

Chop garlic and parsley again together so they are very fine. Beat butter until very soft, then thoroughly mix in garlic and parsley. If possible, leave mixture at room temperature for 1 hour so flavors blend. (Garlic butter can be kept, covered, 1 day in refrigerator.)

Dry shrimp on paper towels. Heat 1 tablespoon oil in a large skillet. Add enough shrimp to make one layer, 1 at a time, remembering approximate order in which they were put in pan. After adding last shrimp, turn first shrimp over and continue turning over rest, in order. After turning over last shrimp, leave them to fry in hot oil for 30 seconds, then remove from pan. If pan is dry, add another tablespoon oil and heat it. Repeat frying with remaining shrimp. Spread cooked shrimp out on a plate and leave until cool enough to handle, then shell them.

Just before serving, add garlic butter to skillet and heat over medium heat. Add shrimp and salt and pepper and heat through, turning them over often, until they are hot and coated with butter that has just begun to sizzle. Serve immediately.

CREAMY RICE PILAF WITH SHRIMP AND BROCCOLI
Riz pilaf aux crevettes et aux brocolis

Seafood is a delightful addition to rice pilaf, turning it into a main course. Here the rice cooks in a light shrimp stock, then is combined with sautéed shrimp, broccoli, and tarragon. No further accompaniment is needed. MAKES 2 TO 3 LIGHT MAIN-COURSE OR 4 TO 6 FIRST-COURSE SERVINGS

14 ounces medium-size shrimp

SHRIMP STOCK (OPTIONAL)
Reserved shrimp shells
1 tablespoon butter
1/2 cup minced onion
3 cups water

3 fresh tarragon stems (without leaves)
Salt

2 cups Fish Stock (see recipe) or packaged fish stock (if not using Shrimp Stock)

PILAF
5 parsley stems (without leaves)
1 sprig fresh thyme, or 1/4 teaspoon dried leaf thyme, crumbled
1 bay leaf
3 tablespoons butter or vegetable oil
1/2 cup minced onion

1 cup long-grain white rice
1/4 teaspoon salt
Freshly ground pepper to taste
1 to 2 tablespoons butter or olive oil (optional)

1/4 cup heavy cream, room temperature
2 pounds broccoli, divided in medium-size florets

1 tablespoon butter
2 tablespoons minced fresh tarragon leaves

Shell and devein shrimp, reserving shells for shrimp stock.

SHRIMP STOCK (OPTIONAL)

Rinse shrimp shells and drain well. Melt 1 tablespoon butter in medium saucepan over low heat. Add onion and cook, stirring often, until softened, about 7 minutes. Raise heat to medium, add shrimp shells, and sauté until they begin to turn pink, about 2 minutes. Add water and tarragon stems, raise heat to high, and bring to a boil. Reduce heat to low and cook, uncovered, regulating heat so stock just simmers, 20 minutes. Strain stock and return to a clean saucepan. (Stock can be kept, covered, 1 day in refrigerator, or it can be frozen.)

Add shrimp to shrimp stock or fish stock with a pinch of salt and bring to a simmer. Reduce heat to low, cover, and poach until shrimp turn pink, about 2 minutes. Remove shrimp with a slotted spoon. Measure liquid and add enough water to make 2 cups. Return liquid to saucepan, cover, and keep warm.

PILAF

Position rack in lower third of oven and preheat to 350°F. Place parsley stems, thyme, and bay leaf on piece of cheesecloth, fold to enclose, and tie tightly. Cut round of parchment paper the same diameter as pan to be used for cooking rice (8 to 9½ inches), and butter paper.

Heat butter or oil in 8- to 9½-inch ovenproof sauté pan or deep skillet over low heat. Add onion and cook, stirring, until soft but not brown, about 7 minutes. Raise heat to medium, add rice, and sauté, stirring, until grains begin to turn milky white, about 4 minutes.

Bring stock to a boil over high heat, pour over rice, and stir once. Add cheesecloth bag, submerging it in liquid. Add salt and pepper, raise heat to high, and bring mixture to a boil. Press round of buttered paper, buttered side down, onto rice, and cover with tight lid. Bake in preheated oven, without stirring, 18 minutes. Taste rice; if it is too chewy or if liquid is not absorbed, bake 2 minutes more. Discard cheesecloth bag. (Shrimp and pilaf can be kept in separate containers, covered, in refrigerator. Reheat pilaf with 1 or 2 additional tablespoons butter or olive oil in a large skillet over medium heat, stirring with a fork.)

When rice is cooked, pour cream quickly and evenly over it; do not stir. Cover rice with its buttered paper and lid and let stand 4 minutes, or just until cream is absorbed, for slightly chewy rice; for more tender rice, let stand up to 10 minutes.

Meanwhile, put broccoli in medium saucepan containing enough boiling salted water to cover it generously. Return to a boil and cook, uncovered, until broccoli is just tender when pierced with a small sharp knife, about 5 minutes. Drain, cover, and keep warm.

Melt 1 tablespoon butter in large skillet over medium heat. Add shrimp and sauté just until hot, about 1 minute. Reserve 8 to 12 shrimp for garnish.

Use fork to fluff rice and to gently stir in minced tarragon, half the broccoli, and remaining shrimp. Taste and adjust seasoning. Gently transfer pilaf to serving dish, arrange reserved shrimp and remaining broccoli around rice, and serve.

❧ SHRIMP POACHED IN SPICED TOMATO SAUCE
Crevettes en sauce tomate épicée

For this light easy dish, the shrimp cook directly in the fresh tomato sauce, which gains zip from a touch of curry. Serve it with crisp-tender cauliflower or sautéed green and yellow summer squash and buttered rice with fresh herbs.   MAKES 4 SERVINGS

2 to 4 tablespoons butter
1 onion, finely chopped
1 1/2 teaspoons curry powder
1/4 cup dry white wine
1 1/2 pounds ripe tomatoes, peeled, seeded, and chopped

Salt and freshly ground pepper
1 1/2 pounds large shrimp, shelled and deveined
1 tablespoon chopped fresh parsley (optional)

Melt 2 tablespoons butter in a large skillet. Add onion and cook over low heat, stirring, about 10 minutes, or until soft but not brown. Add curry powder and continue to cook, stirring, 30 seconds. Add wine and simmer until it evaporates.

Add tomatoes, salt, and a small pinch of pepper and cook over medium heat, stirring often, about 20 minutes, or until mixture is very thick and most of moisture has evaporated. (Sauce can be kept, covered, 2 days in refrigerator. Reheat in large skillet before continuing.)

If shrimp are very large, cut them in half crosswise.

When tomato sauce is thick, set shrimp on top and season lightly with salt and pepper. Cover and cook over low heat 2 minutes. Turn shrimp over and continue cooking 2 to 3 minutes more, or until just tender. Taste sauce and adjust seasoning.

Remove pan from heat, add an additional 2 tablespoons butter, if desired, and stir until absorbed. To serve, transfer shrimp in their sauce to a serving dish and sprinkle with parsley.

❧ SHRIMP RAGOÛT WITH MUSHROOMS AND BABY ONIONS
Ragoût de crevettes à la bretonne

In this old-fashioned recipe, the shrimp and vegetables are moistened by a golden velouté sauce enriched with shrimp butter, cream, and egg yolks. Rice or fine-quality pasta is a perfect complement for this elegant entrée. Crabmeat, lobster, and scallops can also be prepared this way.　　　　　　　　　　　MAKES 8 SERVINGS

2 1/2 pounds large shrimp
10 tablespoons butter
1/2 pound pearl onions
Salt and freshly ground pepper

1/2 pound mushrooms, cut in half
*　　or quarters, if large*
A few drops of fresh lemon juice

VELOUTÉ SAUCE
2 tablespoons butter
3 tablespoons all-purpose flour
1 3/4 cups Fish Stock (see recipe), or
*　　packaged fish stock, or 1 1/4*
*　　cups bottled clam juice mixed*
*　　with 1/2 cup water*

Salt and freshly ground pepper

3 egg yolks
1/3 cup heavy cream

3 tablespoons chopped fresh parsley

To make shrimp butter: Shell shrimp, and crush shells with a pestle or a rolling pin. Melt 6 tablespoons butter in a medium, heavy saucepan over low heat. Add shells and cook, stirring often, about 15 minutes. Remove from heat. Add 3 cups very cold water and let stand; shrimp-flavored butter will rise to top. Skim off butter and transfer it to a clean small saucepan. Simmer about 2 minutes so any water it absorbed will evaporate. Strain butter to remove any pieces of shell; cover and refrigerate 1 hour, or up to 2 days.

In a medium saucepan, cover onions with water and bring to a boil. Boil 1 minute, drain, rinse under cold water, and drain well. Peel with a paring knife. Return onions to saucepan, cover with water, and add salt and pepper. Cook over medium heat about 20 minutes, or until they are tender. Drain onions, reserving 2 tablespoons of their cooking liquid.

Put mushrooms in a saucepan with lemon juice, 1/3 cup water, and a pinch of salt and pepper. Bring to a boil, reduce heat to medium, cover, and cook about 5 minutes, or until tender. Drain mushrooms, reserving 2 tablespoons of their cooking liquid. Add mushrooms to onions and keep warm.

VELOUTÉ SAUCE

Melt 2 tablespoons butter in a heavy saucepan. Add flour and cook over low heat for a few minutes, whisking; do not let it brown. Gradually whisk in fish stock and bring to a boil. Add reserved onion and mushroom cooking liquid, season with a little salt and pepper, and cook over low heat, stirring often, 10 minutes, or until thick enough to coat a spoon.

(Vegetables and velouté sauce can be kept in separate containers, covered, 1 day in refrigerator.)

A short time before serving, heat remaining 4 tablespoons butter in 1 very large or 2 medium skillets. Add shrimp and salt and pepper and sauté over fairly high heat until they begin to turn pink. Reduce heat to low and continue cooking, turning them over from time to time, for a total of 3 minutes, or until tender.

Meanwhile, reheat sauce. Whisk together egg yolks and cream in a bowl. Remove sauce from heat and gradually whisk about 1/2 cup sauce into yolk mixture. Return this mixture to remaining sauce, whisking vigorously. Cook 1 to 2 minutes over low heat, whisking; do not boil. Remove from heat. Add shrimp butter, a little at a time, stirring constantly. Add shrimp, onions, mushrooms, and parsley. Taste and add more salt, pepper, and lemon juice, if necessary. Serve immediately in deep plates.

SHRIMP AND SOLE TERRINE
Terrine de crevettes et sole

A seafood terrine is so impressive that it appears complicated, but this version is easy to prepare. It is made of a mousseline mixture, similar to that used for Scallop Mousselines with Tarragon Butter Sauce, and is baked in a loaf pan. Instead of the herb beurre blanc, you can serve the hot terrine with Shrimp Butter Sauce (page 292), tarragon cream sauce, or fresh tomato sauce; or cold with herb mayonnaise or Pistou Sauce (page 240) and garnished with cherry tomatoes or sliced tomatoes. MAKES 5 OR 6 SERVINGS

1 1/2 pounds sole fillets
3/4 pound raw medium-size shrimp,
*   shelled and deveined*
3 egg whites

1 teaspoon salt
1/2 teaspoon white pepper
Freshly grated nutmeg to taste
1 to 1 1/2 cups heavy cream

FRESH HERB BUTTER SAUCE
2 large shallots, finely chopped
2 tablespoons tarragon vinegar,
*   herb vinegar, or white wine*
*   vinegar*
3 tablespoons dry white wine
2 tablespoons heavy cream

1 cup cold butter, cut in 16 pieces
Salt and white pepper to taste
2 tablespoons chopped fresh
*   tarragon, chives, parsley, or a*
*   mixture of all three*

Pat sole fillets dry and check to be sure there are no bones or skin. Cut fillets in 1-inch pieces. Divide shrimp in two groups: one-third for grinding with fish and two-thirds for slicing.

In a food processor, purée half the fish with half the shrimp set aside for grinding until very fine. Add 1 egg white and process until blended. Remove to a bowl. Repeat with remaining fish, second half of shrimp set aside for grinding, and a second egg white. Leave mixture in processor and return first batch to processor. Add third egg white, salt, pepper, and nutmeg, and process until thoroughly blended and very smooth. Transfer to a bowl, cover, and refrigerate 30 minutes. Refrigerate work bowl of processor also. Cut remaining shrimp in thick slices and refrigerate.

Preheat oven to 350°F. Butter a 6-cup terrine mold or loaf pan. Line base of pan with wax or parchment paper, and butter paper.

Return fish mixture to food processor. With machine running, gradually pour in 1 cup cream in a slow, steady stream. If mixture is very thick and firm, gradually beat in another ½ cup cream. Taste and adjust seasoning; if adding more seasoning, process until combined. Transfer mixture to a bowl and thoroughly mix in shrimp slices so that they are evenly distributed.

Spoon fish and shrimp mixture into mold, and pack well. Be sure to push it into corners. Smooth top to an even layer and tap mold on table to be sure mixture is packed down. Cover with buttered paper and with a lid, if possible. If pan doesn't have a lid, cover with several layers of aluminum foil and seal top around edge of pan. (Terrine mixture can be kept, covered, 4 hours in refrigerator.)

Set mold in a larger pan and fill pan with very hot water about halfway up sides of terrine or loaf pan. Bake about 35 minutes, or until set; a skewer inserted into mixture and left in for 10 to 15 seconds should come out hot to the touch. Remove mold from pan of water and let sit about 10 minutes before unmolding.

FRESH HERB BUTTER SAUCE

Begin preparing sauce while terrine is baking. In a small heavy-based saucepan simmer shallots in vinegar and wine over medium heat until liquid is reduced to about 2 tablespoons. Add cream and simmer over low heat, whisking occasionally, until mixture is reduced to about 3 tablespoons. Cover and set aside at room temperature. Keep butter in refrigerator until ready to use.

To finish sauce, set pan of shallot mixture over low heat and season lightly with salt and white pepper. Add 1 piece of cold butter, whisking constantly. When butter piece is nearly blended into liquid, add another piece, still whisking. Continue adding butter pieces, 1 at a time, whisking constantly. Sauce should be pleasantly warm to the touch. (If at any time sauce becomes too hot and drops of melted butter appear, remove pan immediately from heat and whisk well; add next butter pieces off heat, whisking constantly. When temperature of sauce drops again to warm, return to low heat to continue adding remaining butter pieces.) Remove from heat as soon as last butter piece is incorporated. Strain sauce, if desired. Stir in fresh herbs, and taste and adjust seasoning. Serve as soon as possible.

To serve, unmold terrine onto a platter or board; drain off any excess liquid. Cut carefully in ½-inch slices with a sharp knife. Set 1 or 2 slices on each plate, and spoon about 2 tablespoons sauce around them. Serve any remaining sauce separately.

NOTE: If serving cold, chill in mold and unmold a short time before serving. Serve a spoonful of homemade herb or tomato mayonnaise alongside each slice.

Scallops

An important destination for religious pilgrims during the Middle Ages was the shrine of Saint James in Compostela, Spain. Along the way the pilgrims ate scallops from the coastal waters and saved the shells. When they returned home, possession of a scallop shell was a status symbol, evidence of their pilgrimage. Scallops began to be called *coquilles Saint-Jacques* or Saint James shellfish, and the name is used in France to this day. One variety of scallop is even referred to as *pèlerines* or pilgrims.

Whatever their historical or religious significance, scallops seem to have received more than their share of blessings. They are the sea's gift of natural fast food. Busy cooks should consider them when planning special dinners, as they turn any meal into a feast. Their delicate flavor and creamy texture make them delightful companions for the best French sauces and enable them to stand on their own, without a sauce.

In France, scallops are often sold live in their beautiful shells, as fresh as possible, with their tasty bright-orange coral attached. Here they are sold "naked" and we are spared the work of prying the shells open. This way, unlike other types of seafood, there is no waste. Although scallops are expensive, the price is for pure meat.

Scallops cook quickly by almost any method. Poach, steam, sauté, deep-fry, bake, or broil them—they will cook in a matter of minutes.

But scallops must be treated with respect. Never overcook them or they become rubbery. When in doubt, cook for a shorter rather than a longer time. For this reason, it is best not to prepare them ahead and reheat them.

Wide availability is still another reason to make use of scallops to prepare a delicious meal at short notice. There is no need to travel far to find them; frozen scallops are sold at most supermarkets. When buying frozen scallops, choose those that do not appear to be falling apart. However, fresh scallops have more flavor than frozen and keep their shape better, especially during sautéing. The tiny, sweet bay scallops and the larger sea scallops can be used interchangeably in most recipes, although bay scallops have a slightly shorter cooking time.

Scallops are good partners for almost any vegetable. With the scallops, serve chilled white wine and provide plenty of crusty French bread. For a festive French presentation, the scallops may be served in scallop shells. To get the shells make a pilgrimage to a nearby gourmet cookware shop.

Hints

- Scallops exude moisture after they are cooked. If they are to be served with a separately prepared sauce, this liquid could dilute it. To avoid this, put the cooked scallops on paper towels to absorb their excess liquid before saucing. This is not necessary when scallops are cooked directly in the sauce.
- If scallops with bright orange roe are available, use them for more colorful entrées.

SURPRISE SCALLOP PACKAGES
Coquilles Saint-Jacques en papillote

As with steaming, baking scallops and vegetables in packages, called *en papillote,* locks in their natural flavors. The classic way to do this is to use parchment paper, but foil is easier to handle and works just as well.   MAKES 4 SERVINGS

1 1/2 *pounds sea or bay scallops*

2 *large ripe tomatoes, peeled and*
   seeded

16 *large fresh spinach leaves, with*
   stems, rinsed

12 *very white mushroom caps, cut*
   in thin slices

1/4 *cup butter, cut in 16 pieces*

Salt and freshly ground pepper

Preheat oven to 450°F. Rinse scallops and discard small white muscle at side of each, if using sea scallops. Dry scallops thoroughly on paper towels. Dice tomatoes and put them in a colander to drain.

Cut 4 large sheets of foil about 12 inches square. Butter their centers well. Holding spinach leaves together by their stems, dip them in boiling water for 2 seconds, then set them on paper towels and remove stems.

Put 4 spinach leaves with their attractive sides down on buttered center of each foil sheet, so that they form an **X**. Divide scallops evenly and set on top; season with salt and pepper. Cover with mushroom slices, then with tomato pieces, and season them also. Put 4 butter pieces on top of each "pile" of vegetables. Fold foil in half diagonally to form a rough triangle and roll corners that meet to close package. Then fold other 2 corners so they meet first 2. Roll edges to completely seal packages, and set them on a baking sheet.

Just before serving, bake packages in preheated oven 10 minutes. Set each package on a plate and serve; packages are opened at table. Or, if desired, open them in the kitchen and spoon scallops and vegetables onto individual plates.

STEAMED SCALLOPS WITH CURRY BEURRE BLANC
Coquilles Saint-Jacques à la vapeur, beurre blanc au curry

Steaming is a great way to cook scallops—it keeps them moist and very tender and highlights their pure, delicate taste. For a beautiful platter, arrange briefly cooked broccoli florets in a ring around the scallops, which have been coated with the rich curry sauce. Add fresh bread or rice to complete the fast, delectable meal.

MAKES 6 SERVINGS

2½ pounds sea or bay scallops   2 tablespoons heavy cream
2 large shallots, finely chopped   1 teaspoon curry powder
2 tablespoons white wine vinegar   Salt and freshly ground pepper
¼ cup dry white wine   1 cup cold butter, cut in 16 pieces

Rinse scallops and discard small white muscle at side of each, if using sea scallops. Refrigerate scallops until ready to cook.

In a small heavy-based saucepan simmer shallots in vinegar and wine over medium heat until liquid is reduced to about 2 tablespoons. Add cream and curry powder and simmer over low heat, whisking occasionally, until mixture is reduced to about 3 tablespoons. Season lightly with salt and pepper. Keep butter in refrigerator until ready to use. (Mixture can be kept, covered, about 3 hours at room temperature.)

To steam scallops, bring a large quantity of water to a boil in bottom of a steamer.

Finish sauce just before serving: Reheat shallot mixture over low heat. Add 1 piece of cold butter, whisking liquid constantly. When butter piece is nearly blended into liquid, add another piece, still whisking. Continue adding butter pieces, 1 at a time, whisking constantly. Sauce should be pleasantly warm to the touch. (If at any time sauce becomes too hot and drops of melted butter appear, remove pan immediately from heat and whisk well; add next butter pieces off heat, whisking constantly. When temperature of sauce drops again to warm, return to low heat to continue adding remaining butter pieces.) Remove from heat as soon as last butter piece is incorporated. Serve as soon as possible. (Sauce can be kept warm on a rack above hot water.)

Set scallops in top part of steamer and season with salt and pepper. Cover and steam 2 minutes, turn them over, and steam for 2 to 3 minutes more, or until tender. Drain quickly on paper towels.

Reheat sauce over medium heat, stirring. To serve, set scallops on a platter or plates and spoon a little sauce over them. Serve remaining sauce separately.

SCALLOPS WITH WHITE WINE AND TOMATOES
Coquilles Saint-Jacques au vin blanc et aux tomates

For this light and easy recipe, the scallops cook directly in the sauce. Summer squash or green beans, and white or brown rice or couscous make fine accompaniments.   MAKES 4 SERVINGS

2 tablespoons butter or olive oil
1 carrot, finely chopped
1 onion, finely chopped
1/2 celery stalk, finely chopped
1 1/2 teaspoons fresh thyme leaves,
    or 1/2 teaspoon dried leaf
    thyme
1 bay leaf
4 large ripe tomatoes, peeled, seeded,
    and chopped, or two 28-ounce
    cans whole plum tomatoes,
    drained and chopped

1/3 cup dry white wine
1/4 cup Fish Stock (see recipe) or
    bottled clam juice (optional)
Salt and freshly ground pepper
1 1/2 pounds sea or bay scallops
2 tablespoons chopped fresh Italian
    parsley, cilantro (fresh
    coriander), or regular parsley

In a large skillet, heat butter or oil. Add carrot, onion, celery, thyme, and bay leaf. Cook over low heat, stirring often, about 5 minutes, or until soft but not brown. Stir in tomatoes, wine, and stock, if desired, and add salt and pepper to taste. Bring to a boil, reduce heat to medium, and simmer, uncovered, stirring often, 15 to 20 minutes, or until mixture is thick. Discard bay leaf. Taste sauce and adjust seasoning. (Sauce can be kept, covered, 1 day in refrigerator. Reheat in large skillet before continuing.)

Meanwhile, rinse scallops and discard small white muscle at side, if using sea scallops. Refrigerate scallops until ready to cook.

Just before serving, put scallops on hot sauce mixture and season with salt and pepper. Cover and cook over low heat 2 minutes, turn the scallops over gently, and continue cooking, covered, for 2 to 3 minutes more, or until tender. Remove from heat. Serve scallops on top of sauce, and sprinkle with parsley.

❧ SAUTÉED SCALLOPS WITH ZUCCHINI
Coquilles Saint-Jacques aux courgettes

For a delectable dinner in a few minutes, prepare this easy entrée of sautéed scallops served on a bed of sautéed zucchini, and accompany it with a salad of grilled peppers or fresh tomatoes. Since scallops contain a large amount of moisture, they must be thoroughly dried before they are coated with flour for sautéing; otherwise their moisture will combine with the flour to make a pasty mess. The easiest way to dry them is to place them in a single layer on a paper towel–lined tray, then cover them with another paper towel and pat them dry. Do not crowd the scallops in the pan when sautéing; otherwise, they will stew.   MAKES 4 SERVINGS

1 ½ pounds sea scallops
4 small zucchini
3 tablespoons vegetable oil
8 tablespoons butter
Salt and freshly ground pepper

⅓ cup all-purpose flour
1 garlic clove, very finely minced
3 tablespoons chopped fresh parsley,
*   or 2 tablespoons chopped*
*   cilantro (fresh coriander)*

Rinse scallops and discard small white muscle at their sides; dry thoroughly on paper towels. Cut zucchini in sticks about 1 ½ inches long.

Heat 1 tablespoon oil and 2 tablespoons butter in a skillet. Add zucchini sticks and salt and pepper to taste and sauté about 2 minutes, tossing often.

Just before serving, season scallops with salt and pepper. Dredge them with flour, tapping to remove excess.

Heat another tablespoon oil and 3 tablespoons butter in a very large skillet until very hot. Add half the scallops and sauté over fairly high heat about 1 minute, to brown. Carefully turn them over and continue to sauté about another minute, or until they are light brown and tender. Transfer to a tray lined with paper towels and keep warm, uncovered, in a 300°F. oven. Add remaining tablespoon oil and 3 tablespoons butter to pan and sauté the remaining scallops. Transfer to lined tray.

Reheat zucchini, add garlic and parsley, and sauté together over medium heat for 1 to 2 minutes. Taste and adjust seasoning. Arrange zucchini on a platter and set scallops on top. Serve immediately.

SCALLOPS WITH SAFFRON, TOMATOES, AND VERMOUTH
Coquilles Saint-Jacques au safran, aux tomates, et au vermouth

I learned to prepare this superb entrée from Parisian chef Fernand Chambrette—with whom I co-authored *La Cuisine du Poisson*—who is famous for his fabulous fish dishes. The scallops cook directly in the creamy sauce so they remain very tender. In the chef's original version, the sauce was enriched even further with hollandaise sauce, but this recipe is simpler to prepare and lighter. Garnish the plate with fresh pear tomatoes, if you like. MAKES 4 SERVINGS

1 1/4 pounds sea scallops
2 tablespoons butter
3 shallots, minced
3/4 pound ripe tomatoes, peeled,
  seeded, and diced
Salt and freshly ground pepper

2/3 cup heavy cream
1/3 cup dry vermouth
Scant 1/4 teaspoon saffron threads,
  crushed
1 tablespoon minced fresh parsley
  (optional)

Rinse scallops and remove small white muscle at their sides. Drain and dry on paper towels. If any are very large, cut them in half horizontally.

Melt butter in a sauté pan or deep skillet. Add shallots and cook over low heat, stirring often, 3 to 4 minutes. Add tomatoes and a pinch of salt and pepper and cook over high heat, stirring often, about 5 minutes, or until mixture is dry.

Stir in cream, vermouth, and saffron and bring to a boil. Reduce heat to medium, add scallops, stir, and cook about 2 minutes, or until they are tender and white. Using a slotted spoon, remove them and transfer to a hot buttered platter; cover and keep warm. Boil cooking liquid, stirring occasionally, until thick enough to coat a spoon. Taste and adjust seasoning. Pour sauce over scallops and mix well. Sprinkle with parsley if desired and serve immediately.

SEE PHOTOGRAPH.

❧ SCALLOP SALAD WITH WALNUTS
Salade de coquilles Saint-Jacques aux noix

There is a reason why many people fancy warm seafood salads. Fish and shellfish served immediately after cooking taste best and provide an exciting contrast to crisp, cool greens. The salad is also good at room temperature, but loses flavor when refrigerated.

MAKES 4 FIRST-COURSE OR 2 MAIN-COURSE SERVINGS

12 leaves leaf lettuce
2 teaspoons French walnut oil
½ cup walnuts
Salt

2 carrots, peeled
¾ pound sea or bay scallops
Freshly ground pepper

WALNUT OIL VINAIGRETTE
2 tablespoons white wine vinegar
6 tablespoons French walnut oil

Salt and freshly ground pepper

Wash lettuce, dry thoroughly, and chill until ready to use.

Heat 2 teaspoons walnut oil in a small skillet over low heat. Add the walnuts and a pinch of salt and sauté lightly 2 minutes over low heat. Be careful not to let them burn. Transfer to a bowl and keep at room temperature until ready to use.

Cut carrots in thin lengthwise strips, put in a small saucepan, and cover generously with water. Add a pinch of salt, bring to a boil, and cook 1 minute. Drain thoroughly. Keep at room temperature until ready to use.

Remove small white muscle from side of each scallop, if using sea scallops. Rinse scallops and dry thoroughly. If sea scallops are large, cut them in half horizontally. Keep in refrigerator until ready to use.

WALNUT OIL VINAIGRETTE

In a small bowl, whisk vinegar with walnut oil and salt and pepper to taste.

Just before serving, tear lettuce leaves into 2 or 3 pieces and arrange them on plates or on a platter.

Put scallops in a steamer above boiling water, season lightly with salt and pepper, cover, and steam about 3 minutes, or until just tender. Drain quickly on paper towels.

Whisk dressing again, and spoon about one-third over lettuce. Arrange the scallops on top in a ring and spoon all but 1 tablespoon of remaining dressing over them. Put carrots in center of ring and spoon last tablespoon of dressing over them. Sprinkle walnuts around ring of scallops, and serve immediately.

SCALLOP MOUSSELINES WITH TARRAGON BUTTER SAUCE
Mousselines de coquilles Saint-Jacques, beurre blanc à l'estragon

Mousselines are creamy molded seafood mixtures that are smooth like pâtés and are usually served hot. Rich but light-textured, they are one of the most delicious seafood dishes. Making mousselines the old-fashioned way was hard work—the seafood was pounded in a mortar and then pushed through a sieve—but now it's easy because the scallops are simply ground in a food processor. The mousselines are baked in ramekins in a water bath, then unmolded and coated with the sauce. Crisp-tender vegetables and rice pilaf make pleasant complements. The mousselines are also marvelous with Shrimp Butter Sauce (page 292), garnished with a few shrimp.

MAKES 6 SERVINGS

1 1/2 pounds sea scallops
2 egg whites
1 teaspoon salt

Pinch of white pepper
Pinch of freshly grated nutmeg
1 3/4 cups heavy cream

TARRAGON BUTTER SAUCE
2 large shallots, finely chopped
2 tablespoons tarragon vinegar or white wine vinegar
3 tablespoons dry white wine
2 tablespoons heavy cream

1 cup cold butter, cut in 16 pieces
Salt and white pepper
2 tablespoons chopped fresh tarragon

Rinse scallops and dry thoroughly. Remove small white muscle on side of each scallop. Purée scallops in a food processor until very smooth. Add egg whites and purée again until very smooth. Refrigerate in food processor for 30 minutes.

Add salt, white pepper, and nutmeg to scallop mixture. With machine running, gradually pour in cream. Taste and adjust seasoning. Refrigerate 15 minutes, or up to 4 hours.

Preheat oven to 400°F. Heavily butter six ¾-cup ramekins, and fill them nearly to top with scallop mixture. Set them in a shallow pan and add enough hot water to come halfway up sides of ramekins. Cover with buttered paper and bake about 15 minutes, or until scallop mixture is firm; a skewer or cake tester inserted into mixture should come out clean. Remove from oven and keep warm.

TARRAGON BUTTER SAUCE

Begin preparing sauce while mousselines are baking. In a small heavy-based saucepan, simmer shallots in vinegar and wine over medium heat until liquid is reduced to about 2 tablespoons. Add cream and simmer over low heat, whisking occasionally, until mixture is reduced to about 3 tablespoons. Cover and set aside. Keep butter in refrigerator until ready to use.

Finish sauce just before serving. Set pan of shallot mixture over low heat and season lightly with salt and white pepper. Add 1 piece of cold butter, whisking liquid constantly. When butter piece is nearly blended into liquid, add another piece, still whisking. Continue adding butter pieces, 1 at a time, whisking constantly. Sauce should be pleasantly warm to the touch. (If at any time sauce becomes too hot and drops of melted butter appear, remove pan immediately from heat and whisk well; add next butter pieces off heat, whisking constantly. When temperature of sauce drops again to warm, return to low heat and continue adding remaining butter pieces.) Remove from heat as soon as last butter piece is incorporated. Strain sauce, if desired. Stir in tarragon and taste and adjust seasoning. Serve as soon as possible.

Unmold mousselines onto plates and coat them with sauce. Serve immediately.

Lobster and Crab

"Cardinal of the sea" is what the French call the lobster. The nickname draws attention not only to its exquisite meat, but also to the lobster's shell—its deep-red color when cooked is like that of a cardinal's hat. And the lobster essence this shell imparts to sauces is a great bonus to cooks. Many classic entrées containing lobster sauce are therefore referred to as *à la cardinal,* even when they contain no lobster pieces at all.

Lobster lovers tend to forget that the meaty tail of the lobster is not the only important part. When purchasing a lobster, it is best to choose a whole one, including head and claws. First of all, the meat of a live lobster is fresher, as is that of a live crab. In addition, the flavor of their shells makes for superb sauces, in the same way that fish bones add depth to sauces served with fish.

The shell of a lobster has the power to impart a lobster taste to a larger quantity of sauce than is needed to coat the meat of the shellfish. There always is plenty of sauce left over for use in other dishes, which makes it possible to have two lobster meals for the price of one.

This is why so many traditional fish, egg, and rice recipes call for lobster sauce. When lobster sauce is served with certain fish, such as the springy-textured monkfish, one even has the impression of eating lobster.

A unique cooking method is used to draw out the good taste from lobster shells. The lobsters are cut in pieces, sautéed, and cooked in liquid that later becomes the sauce. The shells are then separated from the meat, crushed, and returned to the liquid to simmer slowly, so that their essences enter the sauce. A similar type of sauce can be made from small whole crabs.

Another method for cooking lobster, crab, and most other shellfish is to poach them whole in a special vegetable stock called a court bouillon, as in Lobster in Saffron Sauce. The court bouillon can also be used to make a sauce.

Whole lobsters and crabs can also be purchased cooked, as can lobster tails and crabmeat. When these are freshly cooked, they are a boon to the busy cook. Heated gently and paired with a rich sauce, such as Leek Cream (page 216) or Shrimp Butter Sauce (page 292), cooked lobster or crabmeat can be the basis of a wonderful dinner in minutes. They are also delicious served cold, with fresh tomato sauce, Pistou Sauce (page 240), or homemade herb mayonnaise.

The following recipes illustrate the two major styles of lobster and crab sauces: one creamy and white (Lobster with White Wine, Cream, and Herbs), the other tomato-based and red (Lobster à l'Americaine). Both can be varied by the addition of chopped fresh herbs, such as basil, tarragon, or chives, or a small amount of spices such as curry powder or paprika.

In France, the time-honored accompaniments for sauced lobster or crab are buttered white rice or steamed potatoes, but now many cooks prefer to serve fresh pasta and fresh green vegetables, such as briefly cooked zucchini strips, spinach leaves, or broccoli florets. Indeed, a lobster or crab in a luscious sauce on a bed of fresh noodles, garnished with perfectly cooked fresh garden vegetables, seems like a culinary marriage made in heaven.

Hints

• The importance of freshness cannot be emphasized enough. Buy lobster or crab not more than 1 day before cooking it. Even the most talented chef cannot prepare a delicious dish from seafood that has lost its freshness.

• To make use of the special cooking technique for preparing an intense lobster-flavored sauce, you need to use fresh lobsters and sauté the pieces raw. It is possible to have the lobster killed and even cut at the fish market. Only the head, but not the tail, should be split in half. The liquid that escapes from the lobster when it is pierced should be saved, because it too contributes flavor to the sauce. The lobster should be cooked as soon as possible because it keeps better once cooked.

• Cooked crabmeat is very perishable; use it within 1 day of purchase.

❧ LOBSTER WITH WHITE WINE, CREAM, AND HERBS
Homard à la crème d'herbes

Lobster with a creamy sauce is so synonymous in France for glorious food that it inspired a Parisian restaurateur to name his restaurant Homard à la Crème, or "lobster in cream." Serve this dish as they did at the restaurant, if you like, with a colorful mixture of fresh peas, carrots, green beans, and turnips.

MAKES 4 FIRST-COURSE OR 2 TO 3 MAIN-COURSE SERVINGS

2 lobsters (1 1/2 pounds each)
3 tablespoons butter
1 large onion, chopped
2 small carrots, chopped
2 tablespoons vegetable oil
1 cup dry white wine, such as
  Chablis
1 cup Fish Stock (see recipe) or
  packaged fish stock or bottled
  clam juice
Salt and freshly ground pepper

1 bay leaf
1 sprig fresh thyme, or a pinch of
  dried leaf thyme
5 parsley stems
1 tablespoon all-purpose flour
1 cup heavy cream
Pinch of cayenne pepper
2 tablespoons chopped fresh herbs,
  such as tarragon, chives, or a
  mixture of both

To cut lobsters: Put a lobster on a board, hard shell up, with its head to your right. Cover tail with a cloth and hold lobster firmly behind head with your left hand. With the point of a sharp heavy knife, pierce through cross mark on center of head, down to board; lobster is killed at once. Continue splitting lobster body lengthwise as far as tail. Cut tail in 3 or 4 slices. Cut claws from body and crack them with the heel of the knife. Save liquid from lobster. Discard head sac. Repeat with other lobster.

In a large deep skillet or sauté pan, melt 2 tablespoons butter. Add onion and carrots and cook over low heat, stirring often, about 10 minutes, or until soft but not brown. In another large heavy skillet, heat 1 tablespoon oil until very hot. Add half the lobster pieces and sauté over high heat, turning pieces over occasionally, for about 2 minutes, or until they begin to turn red. With a slotted spoon, transfer pieces to pan of onions and carrots. Heat remaining tablespoon oil in skillet from lobster, add remaining lobster pieces, and sauté them over high heat in same way as first ones. Transfer them to pan containing other lobster pieces.

Pour wine into pan used to sauté lobster and bring to a boil, stirring. Pour it over lobster pieces in second pan and add fish stock or clam juice, reserved lobster juices (if available), a small pinch of salt and pepper, the bay leaf, thyme, and parsley stems. Bring to a boil, reduce heat to medium, cover, and simmer for 10 minutes.

Remove lobster pieces with a slotted spoon. Carefully remove lobster meat from tail pieces. Remove meat from claws. Put lobster heads and all shells in a heavy bowl and crush them with a pestle, rolling pin, or other heavy object. Return crushed shells to sauce and simmer, uncovered, over medium heat 10 minutes.

Soften remaining tablespoon butter. Using a fork, mash it in a small bowl with flour until smooth.

Strain sauce into a saucepan, pressing hard on lobster shells to extract the juices. Bring to a boil. Whisk in cream and return to a boil. Gradually whisk in butter-flour mixture in 2 additions. Add a pinch of cayenne, and taste and adjust seasoning. Cut lobster meat in cubes and add to sauce. (Lobster in sauce can be kept, covered, 1 day in refrigerator.) Heat lobster over low heat, stirring gently. Sprinkle with chopped herbs, and serve.

LOBSTER WITH SAFFRON SAUCE
Homard à la sauce au safran

This is an easy way to cook lobster—it is poached in court bouillon, a quick vegetable stock accented with wine. Court bouillon can also be used to cook other seafood, especially crabs, shrimp, and crayfish, and fish of all sizes. Here the court bouillon, after gaining flavor from the lobster, is also used as the basis for the creamy saffron sauce.   MAKES 2 SERVINGS

COURT BOUILLON

3 quarts water	*2 bay leaves*
2 medium-size carrots, quartered lengthwise, and cut in thin slices	*2 sprigs fresh thyme, or ¹/₂ teaspoon dried leaf thyme*
1 leek, white and light green parts only, cleaned, quartered lengthwise, and cut in thin slices	*5 stems from Italian or regular parsley (without leaves)*
	2 medium-size garlic cloves, peeled
	6 black peppercorns
1 teaspoon salt	*1¹/₂ cups dry white wine*

2 lobsters (1¹/₄ to 1¹/₂ pounds each)	*2 tablespoons chopped fresh Italian or regular parsley*
¹/₄ teaspoon crumbled saffron threads	*Salt and white pepper*
	Hot cooked rice or pasta
³/₄ cup heavy cream	
1 medium-size ripe tomato, peeled, seeded, and diced	

COURT BOUILLON

Combine water, carrots, leek, and salt in a large saucepan or stockpot. Wrap bay leaves, thyme sprigs, parsley stems, garlic, and peppercorns in a piece of cheesecloth and tie tightly. Add to pot. Cover and bring to a boil, then reduce heat to low and simmer 20 minutes. Remove ³/₄ cup of vegetables with a slotted spoon, drain thoroughly, and reserve. Add wine to mixture in stockpot.

Bring court bouillon (without reserved vegetables) to a boil in a large saucepan or stockpot. Put 1 lobster head-first into court bouillon. Bring to a boil, cover, and cook over medium-high heat 10 minutes.

Remove lobster with tongs and put in a large bowl of cold water. Repeat cooking with second lobster. Reserve ³/₄ cup court bouillon for sauce. Leave lobsters until cool enough to handle.

Pull off each lobster tail with a twisting motion. Press on sides of tail with both hands to break bars on underside of shell. Slip tail meat from shell. Pull off lobster claws and crack them with a lobster cracker, nutcracker, or heel of a heavy knife; remove meat, discarding piece of cartilage inside. Little meat is found in head and legs, but head can be split in half and meat picked at; meat can be removed from legs with lobster forks or thin skewers. Cut tail piece in 4 or 5 slices, and claw meat in 2 or 3 pieces each.

Strain reserved ¾ cup court bouillon into a medium, heavy saucepan. Add saffron and boil until liquid is reduced to 2 tablespoons. Stir in cream and bring to a boil. Boil, stirring often, until sauce is thick enough to coat a spoon, about 5 minutes.

Just before serving, add reserved ¾ cup vegetables from court bouillon to sauce. Add tomato dice and lobster meat and warm over low heat until just hot. Stir in parsley. Taste, and add salt and white pepper, if needed. Serve with rice or pasta.

LOBSTER À L'AMÉRICAINE
Homard à l'américaine

This classic is also known as Lobster à la Provençale because the sauce contains the region's characteristic flavorings of garlic, olive oil, and tomatoes. It is one of the most important master recipes of French cooking and is often used as the basis for other dishes. When my husband and I dined at La Réserve restaurant on the outskirts of Bordeaux, we enjoyed this dish served in the form of a pasta gratin— the lobster was set on a bed of macaroni, topped with a sprinkling of Gruyère, and lightly browned in the oven; the pasta absorbed the flavor of the sauce and the effect was fabulous. The chef of the restaurant of a grand hotel in Paris even used the sauce in a veal fricassee and garnished it with several slices of the lobster. Cooks also follow the same principle to make the sauce from spiny lobsters, small crabs, and crayfish. This recipe makes a generous amount of sauce, enough to moisten a side dish of pasta or to use another day to accompany grilled or sautéed fish fillets.

MAKES 4 FIRST-COURSE OR 2 TO 3 MAIN-COURSE SERVINGS

2 lobsters (1½ pounds each)
¼ cup olive oil
2 shallots, or 1 small onion,
  chopped
1 large garlic clove, chopped

¼ cup Cognac or brandy
1½ cups dry white wine
1 cup Fish Stock (see recipe) or
  packaged fish stock, bottled
  clam juice, or water

1 1/2 *pounds ripe tomatoes, chopped,*
  or one 28-ounce can and one
  14-ounce can whole plum
  tomatoes, drained and chopped
Salt and freshly ground pepper
1 bay leaf
Pinch of fresh thyme or dried leaf
  thyme
5 parsley stems

2 to 4 tablespoons butter
2 tablespoons all-purpose flour
1 tablespoon tomato paste
2 tablespoons water
Cayenne pepper
2 tablespoons chopped fresh
  tarragon or fresh Italian or
  regular parsley

Cut lobsters in pieces as on page 287.

In a large heavy skillet, heat half the oil until very hot. Add half the lobster pieces and sauté over high heat, turning pieces over occasionally, about 2 minutes, or until they begin to turn red. Remove pieces with a slotted spoon. Heat remaining oil in pan, add remaining lobster pieces, and sauté them in the same way as first ones. Remove them with a slotted spoon.

Add shallots or onion to pan and cook over low heat, stirring, until soft but not brown. Add garlic and cook a few seconds. Return lobster pieces to pan, pour in Cognac or brandy, and bring to a boil, stirring. Add wine, stock, tomatoes, reserved lobster juices (if available), a small pinch of salt and pepper, bay leaf, thyme, and parsley stems. Bring to a boil, reduce heat to medium, cover, and simmer 10 minutes.

Remove lobster pieces with a slotted spoon. Carefully remove lobster meat from tail pieces. Crack claws gently with lobster cracker, nutcracker, or heel of a heavy knife and remove the meat from them. Put lobster heads and all shells in a heavy bowl and crush them with a pestle, rolling pin, or other heavy object. Return crushed shells to the sauce and simmer, uncovered, over medium heat for 10 minutes.

Soften 2 tablespoons butter. Using a fork, mash it in a small bowl with flour until smooth.

Strain sauce into a saucepan, pressing hard on lobster shells to extract the juices. Bring to a boil. In a small bowl, whisk tomato paste and 2 tablespoons water until smooth, then whisk mixture into lobster sauce. Bring to a simmer. Gradually whisk in the butter-flour mixture, in 4 or 5 additions. Add a pinch of cayenne. Taste and adjust seasoning. Pour half the sauce into a dish and reserve.

Cut lobster meat in cubes and add to sauce. (Lobster in sauce can be kept, covered, 1 day in refrigerator.) Heat over low heat, stirring gently. Remove from heat, stir in an additional 2 tablespoons butter, if desired, and half the chopped herbs. Taste and adjust seasoning. Sprinkle with remaining herbs and serve. Serve remaining sauce separately, or reserve for another meal.

CRAB WITH SHRIMP BUTTER SAUCE ON A BED OF FRESH PASTA
Crabe au beurre de crevettes sur lit de pâtes fraîches

The crab in its luscious shrimp sauce is one of my favorite seafood creations. It is also good with flavored pasta, such as lemon or herb fettuccine, with mixed white and green noodles, or inside a ring of rice pilaf. At the lovely Pré Catelan restaurant in the Bois de Boulogne, the "woods" near Paris, I feasted on a crayfish with a similar sauce, served with chanterelle mushrooms.

MAKES 5 FIRST-COURSE OR 3 MAIN-COURSE SERVINGS

SHRIMP STOCK

1 tablespoon vegetable oil
1 tablespoon butter
1/2 onion, chopped
3/4 pound medium-size shrimp, unshelled
3 ripe medium-size tomatoes, peeled, seeded, and chopped, or 6 canned plum tomatoes, drained and chopped

1/2 cup dry white wine
1/2 cup Fish Stock (see recipe) or bottled clam juice or water
5 sprigs parsley
1 sprig fresh thyme, or 1/2 teaspoon dried leaf thyme, crumbled
1 bay leaf

SHRIMP BUTTER SAUCE

1/3 cup dry white wine
2 tablespoons white wine vinegar
2 tablespoons very finely minced shallots
Shrimp Stock

1/2 cup heavy cream
Salt and cayenne pepper
1/2 cup cold unsalted butter, cut in 8 pieces

3/4 pound fresh crabmeat

1 teaspoon strained fresh lemon
    juice

8 to 9 ounces fresh fettuccine or
    linguine, or 6 to 8 ounces
    dried

1 tablespoon vegetable oil

1 tablespoon butter

Salt and freshly ground pepper to
    taste

1 tablespoon dry white wine

2 tablespoons chopped fresh parsley

SHRIMP STOCK

Heat oil and butter in large heavy saucepan over low heat. Stir
in onion and cook until translucent, about 10 minutes. Add shrimp,
increase heat to high, and sauté until pink, about 2 minutes. Remove
shrimp from pan with a slotted spoon.

Stir in tomatoes, wine, stock or water, parsley sprigs, thyme, and
bay leaf and bring to a boil. Reduce heat to low. Crush or chop half
the shrimp and return to simmering stock. Shell remaining shrimp and
reserve for garnish. Crush or chop shells and add to stock. Cover and
simmer stock gently 40 minutes. (Stock can be kept, covered, 1 day
in refrigerator.)

SHRIMP BUTTER SAUCE

Combine wine with vinegar and shallots in a small heavy saucepan over medium-high heat and boil until reduced to about 2 tablespoons. Remove from heat. Strain shrimp stock into shallot mixture,
pressing on ingredients with back of spoon to extract all of liquid.
Place over high heat and cook, stirring frequently and skimming
occasionally, until mixture thickens and is reduced to about 1/3 cup,
about 10 minutes. Add cream and small pinch of salt and cayenne and
simmer until thick enough to lightly coat a spoon. (Sauce can be kept,
covered, several hours in refrigerator; keep butter pieces refrigerated.)

Pick over crabmeat, discarding any bits of shell or cartilage.

To finish sauce: Bring cream mixture to a simmer, reduce heat
to low, and add 1 piece cold butter, whisking liquid constantly. When
butter piece is nearly blended into liquid, add another piece, still
whisking. Continue adding butter pieces, 1 at a time, whisking constantly. Sauce should be pleasantly warm to the touch. If at any time
sauce becomes too hot and drops of melted butter appear, remove pan
immediately from heat and whisk well; add next butter piece off heat,
whisking constantly. Return to low heat and continue adding remain-

ing butter pieces. Remove from heat as soon as last butter piece is incorporated. Add lemon juice. Taste and adjust seasoning. Keep sauce warm on rack above hot water or in a double boiler.

Cook pasta in a large pot of boiling salted water about 2 to 4 minutes for fresh, about 4 to 7 minutes for dried, or until al dente. Drain thoroughly, transfer to a bowl, and toss with about 1/3 cup sauce.

Meanwhile, heat 1 tablespoon oil and 1 tablespoon butter in a medium skillet over medium heat. Stir in crab and cooked shrimp. Add salt, pepper, and 1 tablespoon wine and cook until heated through. Add parsley, and taste and adjust seasoning.

To serve, divide pasta among 3 or 5 plates and ladle a little sauce over it. Top pasta with crab and shrimp, and spoon more sauce over it. Serve remaining sauce separately.

SEE PHOTOGRAPH.

 SEAFOOD AND MOREL CRÊPES
Crêpes aux fruits de mer et aux morilles

The most wonderful of ingredients—crab, shrimp, morel mushrooms, and a velvety sauce—are enclosed in these buttery crêpes, so it is not surprising that the result is superb!   MAKES 4 SERVINGS

CRÊPES
2 large eggs
*3/4 cup plus 1 tablespoon milk, or
    a little more if needed*

1/2 cup all-purpose flour
1/2 teaspoon salt
4 tablespoons unsalted butter

SEAFOOD AND MOREL FILLING
*3/4 pound medium-size shrimp,
    shelled and deveined*
*1 1/2 cups Fish Stock, (see recipe) or
    packaged (frozen) fish stock*
Salt
*1/2 ounce dried morels, soaked in
    hot water to cover for 30
    minutes*
3 tablespoons Madeira

3 tablespoons butter
3 tablespoons all-purpose flour
3/4 cup heavy cream
*1 cup fresh crabmeat (about 4 1/4
    ounces), picked over*
4 teaspoons snipped chives
Freshly ground pepper
1 tablespoon melted butter

CRÊPES

Prepare batter in food processor (see following note if food processor is not available). Combine eggs, ¼ cup milk, flour, and salt in work bowl and mix using several on/off turns; batter will be lumpy. Scrape down sides and bottom of work bowl. With machine running, pour ½ cup milk through feed tube and process about 15 seconds. Scrape down sides and bottom of work bowl thoroughly. Blend batter another 15 seconds.

Strain batter if lumpy. Cover and let stand at room temperature about 1 hour. (Batter can be refrigerated, covered, up to 1 day. Bring to room temperature before continuing.)

Melt butter in small saucepan over low heat. Remove from heat and gradually whisk 2 tablespoons melted butter into crêpe batter. Pour remaining butter into small cup. Skim off foam to clarify. (Batter should have consistency of heavy cream. If it is too thick, gradually whisk in more milk, about 1 teaspoon at a time.)

Heat crêpe pan or skillet with 6- to 6½-inch base over medium-high heat. Sprinkle with few drops of water; if water immediately sizzles, pan is hot enough. Brush pan lightly with some clarified butter; if using nonstick crêpe pan, no butter is needed. Remove pan from heat and hold it near bowl of batter. Working quickly, fill a quarter-cup measure half full of batter (to easily measure 2 tablespoons) and add batter to one edge of pan, tilting and swirling pan until its base is covered with a thin layer of batter. Immediately pour any excess batter back into bowl.

Return pan to medium-high heat. Loosen edges of crêpe with metal spatula, discarding any pieces of crêpe clinging to sides of pan. Cook crêpe until its bottom browns lightly. Turn crêpe over carefully by sliding spatula under it. Cook until second side browns lightly in spots. Slide crêpe out onto plate. Top with sheet of wax paper or foil, if desired. Reheat pan a few seconds, then continue making crêpes with remaining batter, stirring it occasionally with whisk. Adjust heat and add more clarified butter to pan, if necessary. If batter thickens on standing, very gradually whisk in a little more milk, about 1 teaspoon at a time. Pile crêpes on plate as they are done. This makes about 12 crêpes. A few may tear, so it is wise to make extra.

SEAFOOD AND MOREL FILLING

Preheat oven to 425°F. if planning to serve crêpes as soon as they are ready. Cut shrimp in half crosswise. Bring fish stock to a simmer in a medium saucepan. Add salt and shrimp, cover, and poach over low heat until shrimp turn pink, about 2 minutes. Transfer shrimp to bowl with slotted spoon, reserving liquid.

Rinse soaked morels and drain well. Cut large morels in 2 or 3 pieces. Add morels and 1 tablespoon Madeira to shrimp cooking liquid, cover, and cook over low heat 10 minutes. Remove morels with a slotted spoon, reserving liquid.

Melt butter in medium, heavy saucepan over low heat. Whisk in flour and cook over low heat, whisking constantly, until mixture turns light beige, about 2 minutes. Remove from heat. Gradually whisk in morel cooking liquid. Increase heat to medium-high and bring sauce to a boil, whisking constantly. Whisk in 1 tablespoon Madeira, then whisk in cream and return to a boil, whisking. Reduce heat to low, return morels to sauce, and simmer, uncovered, stirring occasionally, until sauce heavily coats a spoon, about 7 minutes. Remove from heat. Leave morels in sauce. Set aside 1 cup sauce for serving separately and stir in 16 shrimp pieces.

Discard any liquid at bottom of bowl of remaining shrimp. Stir shrimp into remaining sauce, which will be used for filling. Dice any large pieces of crabmeat and add all of crabmeat to filling mixture. Stir in 2 teaspoons chives. Add pepper, and taste and adjust seasoning.

Butter 14-by-8-inch baking dish or other shallow baking dish. Spoon 3 tablespoons filling onto lower third of less attractive side of crêpe. Beginning at edge with filling, roll up each crêpe, and arrange them in a single layer in dish. Brush crêpe with melted butter. (Crêpes can be prepared to this point and kept, covered, up to 1 day in refrigerator; sauce should be reserved, covered, in separate bowl. Bring to room temperature and preheat oven before continuing.)

Bake crêpes in preheated oven until hot, about 10 minutes. Bring sauce just to a boil in a small saucepan. Remove from heat and stir in remaining tablespoon Madeira and remaining 2 teaspoons chives. Add pepper, and taste and adjust seasoning. To serve, transfer crêpes to plates, and spoon a little sauce with shrimp and morels over each crêpe.

NOTE: To prepare crêpe batter in a blender, combine eggs, ¾ cup plus 1 tablespoon milk, flour, and salt in blender. Mix on high speed until batter is smooth, about 1 minute.

To prepare batter in a bowl, sift flour into medium bowl. Push flour to sides of bowl, leaving large well in center of flour. Add eggs, salt, and 3 tablespoons milk to well and whisk ingredients in well briefly until blended. Using whisk, stir flour gently and gradually into egg mixture until mixture is smooth. Gradually whisk in remaining milk.

Mussels

It is difficult to understand why clams are used much more often than mussels in the United States, while mussels are preferred in France. Both types of mollusk are equally available to Americans and Frenchmen. This situation is reflected also in culinary literature. Our cookbooks contain a wealth of clam recipes but few for mussels. French cookbooks concentrate on mussels and, when they mention clams at all, they usually just instruct the reader to "cook them like mussels."

Mussels do have a slight advantage in their beautiful color. Their shiny blue-black shells and bright orange or yellow flesh make them perfect for garnishing otherwise pale fish dishes.

Yet clams and mussels are similar in many ways. Both are delicious steamed and added to creamy pasta sauces, or baked with garlic butter. If you are used to preparing clams, there is no reason not to use mussels.

Mussels are easy to cook and relatively inexpensive. A treat to enjoy, even in France's simplest restaurants, is a deep plate piled high with *moules marinière,* plump, freshly steamed mussels with shallots and white wine. It is as common there as clam chowder is here.

Actually, both clams and mussels should not really be *cooked,* but simply heated just until they open. Once open, they should be removed from the heat because further cooking toughens them and makes them rubbery. Very fresh mussels and small clams are so tender that they are sometimes served raw in France, just like oysters.

Some mussel recipes might seem perplexing because they require cooking the mussels dry, then using the liquid for the sauce, although no liquid has been added. The reason is that mussels hold seawater inside them and when heat forces them open, this liquid comes out.

The cooking liquid of both clams and mussels is prized in the kitchen because of the good flavor it adds to seafood sauces and soups. In fact, clam juice is even sold here in bottles so it can be used in sauces when clams are not available or not needed for the recipe. Clam juice is usually an acceptable substitute for fish stock, although it is more salty and sometimes should be diluted with water.

Saltiness is characteristic of clams and mussels, especially of their cooking liquid. For this reason, a little of this liquid goes a long way and should be added gradually to a sauce. Salt should never be added to clams or mussels as they cook.

For both types of mollusks, generally smaller is better. Large clams tend to be tough, so try to choose littleneck, Ipswich, or similar small clams. In France, small mussels from Normandy and Brittany are considered best.

The strong flavor of mussels and clams can be balanced by combining them with other ingredients that have plenty of character, such as garlic and mustard, or with acidic ingredients, such as dry white wine and tomatoes. The freshness of herbs also complements their taste, particularly robust herbs such as thyme, oregano, and basil. Adding rich ingredients such as cream, butter, or mayonnaise, or using the mollusks in a sauce for pasta or rice are also effective techniques for taming their vigorous flavor.

Switching clams and mussels in recipes can be fun. They can also be paired in the same dish, to give an interesting combination of colors, tastes, and textures; together they impart the wonderful natural aroma of the sea.

Hints

• Mussels must be cooked live in order to be good. If any are already open, tap them gently against the sink or other surface; they will close again if still alive. If a mussel remains open, discard it. After cooking a batch of mussels, discard those that do not open.

• To clean mussels: Rinse the mussels in a colander several times under cold running water; do not let them soak in the water. Use a knife to scrape them clean of particles stuck to their shells and to pull out pieces of the beard that joins them together. After mussels are cleaned, their shells should look bright and shiny.

- Live mussels can be kept in the refrigerator 2 or 3 days, but not in a closed plastic bag. It is best to transfer them to a bowl and cover them loosely with a paper towel.

BAKED MUSSELS WITH ESCARGOT BUTTER
Moules au beurre d'escargots

These mussels are heated in the same garlic butter used for baking snails. Small clams can be prepared the same way. The dish is inspired by the *moules farcies* (stuffed mussels) that I enjoyed at La Coquille restaurant in Cannes. Provide crusty French bread for dipping in the delicious butter.

MAKES 4 FIRST-COURSE OR 2 MAIN-COURSE SERVINGS

6 to 8 tablespoons unsalted butter, softened
4 large garlic cloves, finely minced
1/4 cup chopped fresh parsley

Freshly ground pepper and salt
2 pounds mussels
Kosher salt (optional)

Thoroughly beat butter, garlic, and parsley together with a wooden spoon or mash them with a fork until blended. Add freshly ground pepper and only a small pinch of salt. (Seasoned butter can be kept, covered, 1 day in refrigerator.)

Preheat oven to 425°F.

Clean mussels as described on pages 298–99. Discard any open mussels that do not close when tapped. Put in a large saucepan, cover, and heat over high heat, shaking pan often, about 5 minutes, or until mussels open. Discard any that do not open. Remove mussels from cooking liquid.

When mussels are cool enough to handle, remove top shell of each. Transfer mussels in their bottom shells to a baking dish, setting them on a bed of coarse (kosher) salt or on crumpled foil, if necessary, to prevent them from rolling.

Divide garlic butter among mussels, then bake in preheated oven about 7 minutes, or until butter melts and mussels are very hot. Serve immediately.

❧ MUSSELS IN PROVENÇAL TOMATO SAUCE
Moules en sauce tomate à la provençale

For this dish, the tender, plump mussels can be served either in or out of their shells. Instead of mussels, clams can be used, or a mixture of both, although they should be cooked in separate sauce-pans because their cooking times are different. Accompany this ragoût with rice or toasted sourdough or French bread.

MAKES 4 FIRST-COURSE OR 2 MAIN-COURSE SERVINGS

2 tablespoons olive oil
1 small onion, or ½ large, chopped
2 garlic cloves, chopped
1½ pounds ripe tomatoes, peeled, seeded, and chopped, or one 28-ounce can and one 14-ounce can whole plum tomatoes, drained and chopped
½ cup dry white wine

¾ teaspoon fresh thyme leaves, or ¼ teaspoon dried leaf thyme, crumbled
1 bay leaf
Salt and freshly ground pepper
2 pounds mussels
1 to 2 tablespoons thin strips of fresh basil or chopped fresh Italian parsley or regular parsley

Heat olive oil in a heavy skillet. Add onion and cook over low heat, stirring often, until soft but not brown. Stir in garlic and cook 30 seconds. Add tomatoes and stir 2 minutes over medium-high heat. Pour in wine and add thyme, bay leaf, a small pinch of salt, and pepper. Cook, stirring often, 12 to 15 minutes, or until thick. Discard bay leaf. (Sauce can be kept, covered, 2 days in refrigerator.)

Meanwhile, clean mussels as described on pages 298–99. Discard any open mussels that do not close when tapped. Put mussels in a large saucepan, cover, and heat over high heat, shaking pan often, about 5 minutes, or until mussels open. Remove mussels with a slotted spoon; discard any that do not open. Cover the mussels to keep them warm. Carefully pour mussel liquid into a bowl without adding any of sand remaining on bottom of saucepan. If cooking liquid in bowl is still sandy, leave liquid undisturbed for 10 minutes; then carefully pour into another bowl, leaving sand behind.

Reheat tomato sauce, if necessary. Gradually add half the mussel liquid and taste; if a saltier taste is desired, add more mussel liquid. Heat mixture again until slightly thickened but not dry. If serving hot, add mussels in their shells, cover, and heat briefly. Taste and adjust seasoning. Serve hot, cold, or at cool room temperature in bowls, and sprinkle each serving with basil or parsley.

MUSSELS WITH RICE AND PEAS
Moules au riz aux petits pois

When prepared with olive oil, this colorful dish can also be served as a salad. Simply season the finished dish with a few squeezes of lemon juice and serve at room temperature or briefly chilled.

MAKES 4 FIRST-COURSE OR 2 TO 3 MAIN-COURSE SERVINGS

2 to 2 1/2 pounds small mussels
Salt
1 1/4 cups long-grain white rice
1 pound fresh peas (about 1 cup
*   shelled), or 1 cup frozen peas*
4 tablespoons olive oil or butter
3 tablespoons chopped green onion
*   (white and green parts)*

Freshly ground pepper
1 ripe medium-size tomato, peeled,
*   seeded, and diced*
2 tablespoons chopped fresh Italian
*   parsley or regular parsley*

Clean mussels as described on pages 298–99. Discard any open mussels that do not close when tapped. Put in a large saucepan, cover, and heat over high heat, shaking pan often, about 5 minutes, or until mussels open. Discard any that do not open. Remove mussels from cooking liquid. Shell mussels, pulling off rubbery ring around each.

In a large saucepan, bring 2 quarts water to a boil and add a pinch of salt. Add rice, stir once, and boil, uncovered, about 12 to 14 minutes, or until just tender; check by tasting. Drain, rinse with cold water, and leave to drain in colander for about 5 minutes.

In a medium saucepan, boil enough water to generously cover

peas and add a pinch of salt. Add peas and boil, uncovered, until just tender, about 7 minutes for fresh peas, about 3 minutes for frozen. Drain thoroughly.

(Ingredients can be prepared several hours ahead to this point and refrigerated, but in this case peas should be rinsed with cold water.)

Heat 2 tablespoons oil or butter in a large skillet or sauté pan over low heat. Stir in green onion and cook about 30 seconds. Add peas, rice, salt, and pepper and heat mixture over low heat, tossing lightly, until hot. Add remaining oil or butter, mussels, and tomato and heat another 1 or 2 minutes. Cover pan and let rice stand about 2 minutes. Add parsley and toss. Taste and adjust seasoning. Serve hot or at room temperature.

Stocks and Techniques

Stocks

Homemade stock can make the difference between a satisfactory dish and a fabulous one. Fortunately, stock requires almost no attention on the part of the cook as it simmers. Stocks freeze well, and so do the ingredients required to make them.

In France, as in our country, people are busy and many do not make stock often. In many families, the weekly custom of preparing *pot au feu,* poached meat and vegetables in a rich broth, has become much less common, and thus people do not have a meat broth at hand all the time.

Many fine cooks make use of canned or commercial frozen stock or broth at least once in a while. Meat, chicken, and even fish stocks are now available. These make possible quick sauces that can be very good. I find that unsalted broths usually make better sauces than salted ones, especially in the case of sauces that must be reduced. Canned broth of regular concentration usually tastes better than the type that must be diluted with water.

Hints

• It is convenient and wise to make enough stock for several uses and to freeze it in small batches.

• To defrost stock quickly, set the container in a pan of hot water for a few minutes. Transfer frozen liquid to a saucepan, cover, and warm over low heat until defrosted.

✿ FISH STOCK
Fumet de poisson

Fish stock gives a wonderful flavor to sauces that accompany fish. It requires only 20 minutes of simmering.

MAKES ABOUT 1 QUART

1 1/2 pounds fish bones, tails, and heads of non-oily fish, gills removed, or 1 pound fish pieces for chowder (see note)
1 tablespoon butter
1 onion, sliced

About 5 cups water
5 parsley stems
1 sprig fresh thyme, or 1/4 teaspoon dried leaf thyme, crumbled
1 bay leaf

Rinse fish bones under cold running water 5 minutes; drain.

Melt butter in large heavy saucepan over low heat. Add onion and cook, stirring often, until soft but not brown, about 10 minutes. Add fish bones or fish pieces, enough water just to cover, parsley stems, thyme, and bay leaf. Bring to a boil, skimming surface occasionally. Reduce heat to low and simmer, uncovered, skimming occasionally, 20 minutes. Strain through a fine sieve; do not press on solid ingredients. (Stock can be kept, covered, 1 day in refrigerator, or it can be frozen 2 months.)

NOTES: Salmon bones can be used for fish stock for a sauce to be served with salmon. If you are using mushroom caps, you can add the stems to fish stock for flavor, provided they are not dark.

CHICKEN STOCK
Fond de volaille

Chicken stock is a useful, all-purpose light stock that adds a good flavor to a great variety of French soups and sauces. With just a little salt, pepper, chopped fresh herbs, and perhaps a few cooked vegetables, homemade chicken stock is a very good soup on its own.

MAKES ABOUT 2 1/2 QUARTS

3 pounds chicken wings, chicken backs, or a mixture of wings, backs, necks, and giblets (except livers)
2 onions, quartered
Green part of 1 leek, cleaned (optional)
2 medium-size carrots, quartered

2 bay leaves
10 parsley stems
About 4 quarts water
2 sprigs fresh thyme, or 1/2 teaspoon dried leaf thyme, crumbled
1/2 teaspoon black peppercorns

Combine chicken pieces, onions, leek, carrots, bay leaves, and parsley stems in a stockpot or other large pot. Add enough water to cover ingredients and bring to a boil, skimming foam that collects on top. Add thyme and peppercorns.

Reduce heat to very low so that stock bubbles very gently, partially cover, and cook, skimming foam and fat occasionally, for at least 2 or up to 3 hours.

Strain stock into large bowls; discard mixture in strainer. If not using immediately, cool to lukewarm. Refrigerate until cold and remove solidified fat from the top. (Stock can be kept 3 days in refrigerator; or it can be frozen for several months.)

❧ BEEF STOCK
Fond de boeuf

Beef stock greatly enhances pan sauces and other sauces for beef because it gives a rich meaty flavor. Brown veal stock is an all-purpose stock that is good with any meat and is a favorite of restaurant chefs. White veal stock is used in delicate dishes of veal and other meats.

MAKES ABOUT 5 OR 6 CUPS

5 pounds meaty beef soup bones, preferably knucklebones, chopped in pieces by butcher

2 onions, rinsed but not peeled, root end cut off

2 medium-size carrots, scrubbed but not peeled, cut in half crosswise

2 celery stalks, cut in 3-inch pieces

2 bay leaves

10 parsley stems

4 large garlic cloves, unpeeled

1/2 pound ripe tomatoes, quartered, or one 14-ounce can whole plum tomatoes, drained and quartered (optional)

About 4 quarts water

10 black peppercorns

2 sprigs fresh thyme, or 1/2 teaspoon dried leaf thyme, crumbled

Preheat oven to 450°F. Roast bones in roasting pan in oven, turning them over occasionally, until they begin to brown, about 30 minutes. Add onions and carrots and roast until browned, about 30 minutes.

With a slotted metal spatula, transfer bones and vegetables to stockpot or other large pot and add celery, bay leaves, parsley stems, garlic, tomatoes, and enough water to cover ingredients. Bring to a boil, skimming foam from top. Add peppercorns and thyme, partially cover, and cook over very low heat so that stock bubbles very gently, 6 to 8 hours, skimming foam and fat occasionally. During first 2 hours of cooking, add hot water occasionally, if necessary, to keep ingredients covered. Strain stock. Skim off fat if using immediately; or cool, refrigerate until cold, and remove solidified fat from the top. (Stock can be kept in refrigerator 2 days, or it can be frozen several months.)

BROWN VEAL STOCK
Substitute meaty veal bones, preferably knucklebones, for beef bones.

WHITE VEAL STOCK

Substitute meaty veal bones, preferably knucklebones, for beef bones. Omit step of browning bones and vegetables. Omit tomatoes.

Put bones in a large pot. Add enough cold water to cover and bring to a boil. Simmer 2 minutes, then drain, rinse with cold water, and drain well. Return to pot, and add remaining ingredients and 1 rinsed leek (either whole leek or only green part), if available. Follow recipe, simmering stock 4 to 6 hours.

RICH DUCK STOCK
Fond de canard

This stock is made from the giblets of a duck you are cooking whole, plus the bones of an extra duck from which you remove the meat for another use; or save the carcass the next time you cut the meat pieces from a duck (for example, when making Duck Ragoût with Tomatoes, White Wine, and Peas or Duck Breast with Mango Sauce). MAKES ABOUT 3 CUPS

Giblets (except liver) and 1 reserved carcass from 1 duck (4½ to 5 pounds)
Wishbone, neck, wing tips, gizzard, and heart of another duck to be cooked whole, patted dry
2 onions, quartered
2 medium-size carrots, cut in quarters crosswise

About 10 cups water
2 medium-size celery stalks, cut in half
2 bay leaves
4 sprigs fresh thyme, or 1 teaspoon dried leaf thyme, crumbled

Preheat oven to 400°F. To remove wishbone from duck: Set duck on its back and lift neck skin. First bone above neck is V-shaped wishbone. Outline it carefully with boning knife and pull out wishbone; add it to giblets for stock.

Set duck on its side and carve off leg and thigh at thigh joint. Repeat on other side.

To remove breast meat: Using boning knife, slit breast meat along 1 side of breastbone. Remove breast half from bone in 1 piece by scraping carefully with knife, keeping its point against bone, and at same time pulling meat gently. When meat is released from bone, cut skin to free breast half. Repeat with other side. (Reserve duck breasts, leg pieces, and liver for another use; if duck is fresh, pieces can be frozen.)

Chop duck carcass in 6 or 7 pieces and put in medium, heavy roasting pan. Add other bones and giblets. Roast until lightly browned, about 30 minutes. Add onions and carrots and continue roasting until vegetables begin to brown, about 30 minutes.

Transfer mixture to large saucepan (about 5 quarts) with a slotted spoon. Pour off fat from roasting pan. Place roasting pan over medium-high heat. Stir in 1 cup water. Bring to a boil, scraping up any browned bits. Pour these pan juices into saucepan containing duck bones and vegetables. Add celery, bay leaves, thyme, and enough water to cover. Bring to a boil, skimming occasionally. Reduce heat to low, cover partially, and simmer gently 6 hours, skimming occasionally. Strain stock into large heavy saucepan, pressing on bones and vegetables. Skim off fat thoroughly. Boil until stock is reduced to about 3 cups. (Stock can be kept, covered, 2 days in refrigerator, or it can be frozen several months.) Skim fat from surface of stock before using.

❧ SIMPLE DUCK STOCK
Fond de canard simple

This duck stock cooks more quickly than Rich Duck Stock. It makes use of the giblets of the duck to be cooked, and its flavor is intensified by the addition of chicken stock. It can be substituted for Rich Duck Stock in recipes.   MAKES 1 2/3 TO 2 CUPS

Wishbone (optional), neck, wing
    tips, gizzard, and heart of 1
    duck, patted dry
2 tablespoons vegetable oil
1 onion, finely diced
1 medium-size carrot, finely diced
1 medium-size celery stalk, finely
    diced (optional)

3 cups Chicken Stock (see recipe) or
    prepared broth
2 sprigs fresh thyme, or 1/2
    teaspoon dried leaf thyme,
    crumbled
1 bay leaf

To remove wishbone from duck, set duck on its back and lift neck skin. First bone above neck is **V**-shaped wishbone. Outline it carefully with boning knife and pull out wishbone. Chop duck neck and wing tips in several pieces, using heel of heavy knife.

Heat oil in medium, heavy saucepan over medium-high heat. Add wishbone, neck, wing tips, gizzard, and heart and sauté, stirring often to prevent sticking, until browned, about 7 minutes. Remove to plate with a slotted spoon.

Add onion and carrot to saucepan, reduce heat to medium, and sauté, stirring and scraping often, until vegetables begin to brown, about 10 minutes. Return sautéed duck pieces to pan along with any juices on plate. Add celery, chicken stock, thyme, and bay leaf and bring to a boil, scraping in browned juices. Reduce heat to low, cover, and simmer 30 minutes. Set cover partially askew and simmer another 30 minutes to 1 hour; check occasionally and regulate heat to be sure stock simmers. Strain stock, pressing on bones and vegetables. (Stock can be kept, covered, 2 days in refrigerator; or it can be frozen several months.) Skim fat from surface of stock before using.

SIMPLE GOOSE STOCK
Substitute neck, wing tips, gizzard, and heart of 1 goose for those of the duck.

QUICK BROWN SAUCE
Fond de veau lié

This is a popular alternative to traditional brown sauce, which requires hours of simmering. It is delicious when made with home-made stock, but it can be made with packaged stock or broth as well. If you like, prepare a double or triple quantity and keep it on hand in the freezer. All that is needed to turn it quickly into a tasty sauce is a splash of Madeira or Port and a little salt and pepper.

MAKES ABOUT 1 CUP

2 teaspoons vegetable oil
1/2 onion, diced
1/2 carrot, diced
1 1/2 cups Brown Veal Stock or
    Beef Stock (see recipe)
1 sprig thyme, or 1/4 teaspoon dried
    leaf thyme, crumbled

1 bay leaf
2 tablespoons cold water
1 teaspoon cornstarch, potato
    starch, or arrowroot

In medium, heavy saucepan, heat oil over medium-high heat. Add onion and carrot and sauté, stirring often, until well browned. Do not let mixture burn. Add stock, thyme, and bay leaf and bring to a boil, stirring. Simmer, uncovered, over very low heat for about 20 minutes.

Strain into another saucepan, pressing on vegetables. Skim as much fat as possible from surface. Simmer over medium heat until reduced to 1 cup. In small bowl, whisk cold water and cornstarch or potato starch or arrowroot to form a smooth paste, then gradually pour into simmering sauce, whisking constantly. Return to a boil, whisking constantly. Simmer 1 or 2 minutes, if necessary, until thickened. (If not using immediately, dab surface of warm sauce with small piece of butter to prevent skin from forming. Sauce can be kept 2 days in refrigerator, or it can be frozen several months.)

TOMATO-FLAVORED BROWN SAUCE
Coarsely chop 2 ripe medium-size fresh tomatoes or 4 canned plum tomatoes and add to stock with herbs. Whisk 1 teaspoon tomato paste with starch mixture before adding to stock.

CHICKEN-FLAVORED BROWN SAUCE
For chicken recipes, if chicken wing tips and neck are available, sauté them together with onion and carrot, and substitute chicken stock for veal or beef stock.

Techniques

To Shape Artichoke Bottoms or Hearts

Squeeze juice of ½ lemon into medium bowl of cold water.

Break off stem of 1 fresh artichoke. Break off largest leaves at bottom and put artichoke on its side on board. Holding a very sharp knife or small serrated knife against side of artichoke (parallel to leaves), cut off lower circle of leaves, up to edge of artichoke heart. Turn artichoke slightly after each cut. Rub exposed edges of artichoke heart with cut lemon.

Cut off central cone of leaves just above artichoke heart. Cut off leaves under base and trim base so it is round, removing all dark green areas.

Rub again with lemon. Put artichoke in bowl of lemon water. Repeat with remaining artichokes.

To Peel and Seed Tomatoes

Using a paring knife, cut the cores from the tomatoes. Turn the tomatoes over and slit the skin in an X-shaped cut. Prepare a large bowl of cold water.

Put the tomatoes in a pan of enough boiling water to generously cover and boil about 10 to 15 seconds, or until the skin begins to pull away from the flesh along the cut. Remove the tomatoes with a slotted spoon and put them in the bowl of cold water. Leave for a few seconds.

Remove and pull off the skins with a paring knife.

To seed tomatoes, cut them in half horizontally with a large knife. Hold each half over a bowl, cut side down, and squeeze to remove the seeds.

To Clean Leeks

Cut off the root ends of the leeks; remove and discard the coarse outer leaves and about 1 inch of the leek tops.

Split each leek twice lengthwise, beginning about 1 inch from the root end and cutting toward the green end.

Holding each leek by its root end, dip it several times in cold water. If dirt remains, soak the leeks in cold water for several minutes. Then separate the leaves under running water to rinse away any clinging dirt, and drain.

To Taste and Adjust Seasoning

Professional cooks taste often when they cook, and theirs is a good example to follow. The amounts of salt and pepper to add to a sauce depend on the ingredients in the dish and on your taste. Most dishes should be seasoned at the beginning of or during cooking, and the seasoning should be adjusted just before the dish is served. To adjust the seasoning, taste the sauce and decide whether a little more salt or pepper (or cayenne pepper, nutmeg, or lemon juice, if included in the recipe) would improve the flavor. Add a little and taste again. Usually several tastings are needed before the dish seems just right.

To Check Whether a Sauce Is Thick Enough to Coat a Spoon

Dip a metal spoon into the sauce. Run your finger across the back of the spoon. If your finger leaves a distinct line in the sauce that adheres lightly to the spoon, it is thick enough.

To Truss Poultry

Trussing chicken or other poultry before roasting keeps the bird in a neat, attractive shape and holds the neck skin over the breast to protect this meat. However, the cook in a hurry can omit this step.

If you are going to truss poultry, thread a trussing needle with string and tie a knot at the eye. With the chicken on its back, hold legs so ends point up. Insert needle between thigh and drumstick of one leg and push it through sides of chicken below breastbone and then out through other leg. Turn chicken over. Push needle through closer wing, then under backbone, then through other wing, securing wings to back. Turn chicken on its back and tie ends of string tightly.

Using a second piece of string, insert needle through lower part of drumstick, then through skin of chicken near tail, through end of other drumstick, and back through skin of chicken. Tie ends of string tightly.

To Carve Roast Poultry

Poultry can be easily carved in two steps:

1. Remove the drumstick and thigh piece from each side by cutting through the joint that joins the thigh to the body. The piece can then be divided into 2 sections or the meat carved from it, according to its size.

2. For chickens, cut off the breast section from the back section with a heavy knife or poultry shears. Cut the breast section in half.

—For ducks and geese, cut down the center of the breast section with a boning knife or other sharp knife, dividing the breast meat in 2. Cut under each breast half to separate it from the breast bone and remove the meat. The breast meat can then be cut in slices.

—For turkey, cut the breast meat in thin lengthwise slices while it is still on the bird.

To Cut Chicken in Pieces

This method of cutting chicken produces 8 small pieces or 4 servings, each of which includes both light and dark meat, plus 2 back pieces that are used to flavor the sauce.

Pull out and discard fat from chicken. Using a large knife, cut off wing tips. Reserve wing tips and neck for adding flavor to sauce, or save for chicken stock.

Using a boning knife or other medium-size sharp knife, cut skin between leg and body. Outline the small round piece of meat (the "oyster") in center of back behind each leg, so this piece will remain attached to leg meat. Pull leg back until joint attaching it to body is visible. Remove leg by cutting through joint, then along body to separate rest of leg meat. Repeat with other leg. Move drumstick in order to feel joint between it and thigh. Separate each leg piece in 2 by cutting through this joint.

Holding chicken, neck side down, divide back half from breast half by cutting along edge of rib cage with knife, so that rib bones remain attached to back section. Use a heavy knife or poultry shears to separate back from breast section at neck end.

Move wing to feel joint attaching it to body. With a boning knife, cut through joint and cut off a lengthwise strip from the edge of the breast meat along with wing, so this strip remains attached to wing. Repeat with other wing.

Use heavy knife or poultry shears to cut breast section in half crosswise. If any small sharp bones protrude from breast meat, cut them off with poultry shears and discard them.

Crack back section in half with your hands or with a heavy knife.

Index

ABOUT THE AUTHOR

Prior to writing her cookbook series, Fresh from France, international cooking columnist Faye Levy developed creative recipes and wrote innovative articles on French cuisine for America's foremost cooking magazines, including cover stories for both *Gourmet* and *Bon Appétit*. Faye has lived in three continents and during this decade has written ten outstanding cookbooks in three languages.

Faye Levy is the only American to have written a book on French cooking for the French. *La Cuisine du Poisson,* the cookbook she co-authored with Fernand Chambrette, was published by Flammarion. Faye is also the first woman to be included in Flammarion's cookbook series, *"les grands chefs,"* that includes Escoffier, Bocuse, and Lenôtre. She holds the Grand Diplôme of the first graduating class of the famous Parisian cooking school La Varenne, where she spent over five years. Faye is the author of the school's first cookbook, *The La Varenne Tour Book.* As La Varenne's editor, she planned the school's curriculum and developed and drafted the recipes for the award-winning cookbooks, *Basic French Cookery, French Regional Cooking,* and *The La Varenne Cooking Course.*

Faye Levy scored a culinary coup in 1986 when two of her books won Tastemaker Awards. *Faye Levy's Chocolate Sensations* was voted the Best Dessert and Baking Book of the year by the International Association of Cooking Professionals/Seagram Awards; and *Classic Cooking Techniques* won as the best Basic/General Cookbook. A year later, her *Fresh from France: Vegetable Creations* also won an IACP/Seagram award and was chosen by *Publishers Weekly* for their honor list of "The Best Books of the Year."

Praised by the food editor of *Gourmet* magazine as "one of the finest cooks in the country" and by *The New York Times* as "an expert chef," Faye devotes her talents to teaching the art of cooking through her classes and writings. Her *Bon Appétit* magazine column, "The Basics," which she wrote for six years, is a comprehensive and concise cooking course. A frequent contributor to major newspapers, Faye has published articles in the *Boston Globe, The Washington Post,* the *Chicago Tribune,* the *New York Post,* the *Philadelphia Inquirer,* the *Detroit News,* the *Portland Oregonian,* the *Milwaukee Sentinel,* the *San Francisco Chronicle,* the *Los Angeles Herald Examiner,* and numerous other newspapers across the country.

Faye Levy is the only person whose recipes have appeared in the prestigious collections of America's top two food magazines, The Best of Gourmet
and The Best of Bon Appétit series. She is one of the principal contributors
to the just-published *La Varenne Pratique.* Her recipes were featured in
Time-Life's Good Cook and Healthy Home Cooking series and in many
other celebrated volumes of culinary work.

Faye Levy lived in Israel seven years and is an honor graduate of Tel
Aviv University. She is currently the monthly cooking columnist of Israel's
foremost women's magazine, *At.*